THE EMBATTLED LYRIC

Verbal Art STUDIES IN POETICS

Lazar Fleishman and Haun Saussy, Editors

THE EMBATTLED LYRIC

Essays and Conversations

in Poetics and Anthropology

NATHANIEL TARN

Stanford University Press · Stanford, California 2007

Stanford University Press
Stanford, California

Library of Congress Cataloging-in-Publication Data
Tarn, Nathaniel
    The embattled lyric: essays and conversations in
poetics and anthropology / Nathaniel Tarn.
       p. cm.
    Includes bibliographical references and index.
    ISBN-13: 978-0-8047-5053-0 (cloth : acid-free paper)
    ISBN-13: 978-0-8047-5054-7 (pbk. : acid-free paper)
       1. Poetry, Modern—20th century—History and criticism.
2. Literature and anthropology.   I. Title.

PN1271.T37 2007
809.1'9355—dc22   2006028410

Typeset by Westchester Book Group in 10/13.5 Garamond and
Cochin display

Contents

Preface

This book is a very substantially altered new edition of *Views from the Weaving Mountain* published by Lee Bartlett in his *American Poetry Book* Series at the University of New Mexico in Albuquerque in 1991.

The following pieces have been taken out. From Section One: "Poetry & Communication," "The World Wide Open," and "Open Letter for an Order of Silence." The whole of Section Two except for "Initiation and the Paradox of Power" and "The Choral Voice," which have been retained in Section Three in order to show something of the relations between my anthropological and poetic thinking. Pieces on Antonin Artaud, on Octavio Paz, and on Translation theory, have been added to Section Two and one, "On Refining a Model of Poetic Production," has been added to Section Three. Finally, a very substantial interview addressing issues in this book, preceded by a critical study, the work of Dr. Shamoon Zamir, Director of American Studies, King's College, London, has been placed as a coda to the volume. The original Preface in the *Views* volume is still worthy of perusal as a statement of intent concerning my overall project.

I would like to thank again a number of writers, poets, critics, and artists who have helped me to clarify my thoughts and given direct or indirect but always valuable support over the years: Robert Adamson, Charles Alexander, Charles

Altieri, Jane Augustine, Jean Paul Auxéméry, Jennifer Bartlett, Georges Bataille, Lucien Biton, Paul Blackburn, Daniel Bouchard, Hayden Carruth, Henri Cartier-Bresson, Isac Chiva, Paul Christensen, Clark Coolidge, Stanley Corngold, Beverley Dahlen, Christopher Daniels, Michel Deguy, Richard Deming, John Digby, Joseph Donahue, Edward and Jennifer Dorn, Marcel Duchamp, Robert Duncan, Theodore Enslin, Margot Fonteyn, Philip Foss, Tony Frazer, Gene Frumkin, Forrest Gander, Albert Gelpi, Alberto Giacometti, Allen Ginsberg, Fedora Giordano, Marcel Griaule, Richard Grossinger, Lyn Hejiniau, Michael Heller, Lindsay Hill, Brenda Hillman, Susan Howe, Ivor Indyk, Kenneth Irby, Pierre Joris, George Kearns, John Kinsella, Nancy Kuhl, David Lenfest, Nathaniel Mackey, Hector Manjarrez, John Matthias, Cleo McNelly, Sarah Menefee, Christopher Merrill, Christopher Middleton, Bradford Morrow, Eric Mottram, Mark Nowak, Geoffrey O'Brien, Peter O'Leary, Charles Olson, John Olson, Toby Olson, Michael Palmer, Kenneth Patchen, Sherman Paul, Octavio and Marie-Jo Paz, Marjorie Perloff, Dennis Phillips, Peter Quartermain, George Quasha, Kenneth Rexroth, Ian Robinson, Jerome and Diane Rothenberg, Anthony Rudolf, Andrew Schelling, Gershon Scholem, Henri and Nô Seigle, Richard Sieburth, Nina Subin, John Taggart, Dennis Tedlock, Roberto Tejada, Hans Ten Berge, John Tranter, Paul Vangelisti, Anne Waldman, Eliot Weinberger, David Wevill, C. D.Wright, and Shamoon Zamir. A great many other names and gratitudes will be found in this volume. My family, many personal friends, and many students have added to the mix. I apologize profoundly to anyone my aging brain has mislaid.

I would like to thank my dear friend Lee Bartlett as the original initiator of this part of my project as well as Professors Albert Gelpi, John Felstiner, and William McPheron of Stanford University and Norris Pope and my editors at Stanford University Press and Westchester Book Services for their kind help and treatment of this new edition.

My fellow-poet and wife, Janet Rodney, has provided unbounded support as well as insights and modifications too numerous to list.

Section One
Toward Any America Whatsoever

Toward Any Geography/
Toward Any America Whatsoever

*America has not been discovered; America will have no peace
until it is discovered.*

—Richard Grossinger

In the matter of removal here, of change: as of all changes of name, persona, career, uniform, et al.—the world is infinitely more reluctant to let go of you than
you are of it, pursues you with labels long after you have eaten, consumed, di-
gested, and excreted the product, forgotten its very existence. You could write
books on the nomenclatures and cartographies hung around your neck for the
whole duration of your *c.v.*, as you could of those you painfully acquire, by yourself, like a new set of teeth, or a new spine. And books about those who won't
open their fists. And others about those who won't open their hands.

Longitude: The Litvak assembly line is an earthshrinker with one major snag.
The snag is an island, rotten since Atlantis, neither East nor West—as such reefs,
now sea, now land, are apt to be—where the line coughs, hiccups, stops a while,
only to go on a little later to its manifest destinies. Who knows the languages
there? Everyone sounds like an actor. Who knows his name? They change it. But
it is the carry thru of the line I'm into: the reason it stopped and started again
when it did—carrying parts beyond the snag and leaving others behind. So many
times the line could have slid over the snag, so many times nearly did. Way back
surely, a could-have, as my lineage broke onto Manchester from the emergence,
and as a brother lineage went on West. Then, while the boots began their march

and my singing canary died of earthquake—on the beaches of Dover, who knew what ship, what nation, was to come? And while the bombs fell and the lions roared in a zoo nearby, hurried whispers each morning sent some away: they were not seen again the day after. Moving West within the snag: so far as we could see, two days before the rest of the world, a fleet sail to crush those boots meantime. Newspaper map of the Republic, its states and capitals learned off by rote, the flag rising and setting in nearby hills. Dying early. Wanting to die. And saved by names like Mystic, Providence, Nantucket. To wit (when Cambridge had lain down, trailing its phoney accents on ever-green lawns) gone back into France for a last divorce in re this language / the divorce failing, the once and for all remarriage—and out to the Windy City, via New Haven, Conn.

The younger lineage, after the emergence, beyond the snag, breaks open Broadway and eats that avenue. Family portraits in many a theater still. My father's early joys: Sydney, Stanwick, Jolson—say Sylvia, Barbara, Al: American-style. These were old stars to me, praktikly muthers. And my toys? Oh, one Crashing Thunder, for instance, of the same lineage, from the same first village, with my grandfather's face: bookbinder among horsethieves. Used to say "Damn these Americans" and come to have his meat cooked by two Europeans every evening (carried his cutlets and chops under his arm in a paper bag) and used to spin the Winnebago for another thousand miles. We couldn't work whatsoever.

Fifty-One: pepperoni stews near the Red Door bookstore and a bedroom on 63rd from which I could reach out to touch a Black couple's sheets on a bed next door. Jazz clubs where I knew Jazz at last in context. Store-front churches so far into the night world we never thought we'd make it back. Newspapers gliding in vacant lots seen from the El at 2 A.M.; Tarn's only song in a whole night of guitars. Duchamp on 14th Street in NYC: chess and frugal teas; shades of Breton at Larré's and the great griefs of Kwakiutl and Haida on Central Park West. And Havana old-style, the day of all days the last boss took the throne.

Lately I've brought the burial sheet to America—with its black clouds against a woollen sky. Who are the cantors of this world? Mad singers all, to bell, or guitar. As the exiles went East, cursing the Jews out of it, who took over their voices in these States? With Ishmael we came out of Med., into Atlantic, into Pacific. O.K. But before that / way before: try to remember. Spain's might against Lost Tribes and the Lost Tribes of what exactly? Fallen Jerusalem . . . into these conclusions.

Fifty-Two: out of the Windy City and South. To inform the spine. *R'muxux kaaj, r'muxux ulew:* navel of sky, navel of earth. Months on my knees behind *this* Don Juan, learning a language he thought I already knew. Penelope in the night, calling back to the island. Bloom: as I write I remember: yes, enthroned between two candles.

"There are some in this *pueblo, señor,* there are some in this *pueblo,* mother-father, think you a god." Like that—sitting on the corner of the desk. There had been a bringing back, a resurrection from the pig-pound of a figure who ran like filigree thru 1525. Great walker this figure, traitor to Xrist: man-woman and hot seducer of this world. Judas Iscariot, Michael Archangel, Peter of the Stone, Simon Magus, Pedro de Alvarado Conquistador, Angel of Hills and Rains, Old man of the dying year and of its resurrection. And Ahasuerus, I see, among volcanos. We made the rain / we made the sun—depending on the time of year it was and where the cardinals were at and who carried the burdens. And then, there were many years in the very far East.

Sixty-Seven: New York City, Ann Arbor, Denver, Mesa Verde, Acoma Sky-City, Walpi and its snakes in dust of all the days of the year, Grand Canyon of the Colorado, Arches and Tetons, Cody, Billings, Montana, and back to Montreal. Toronto, Calgary, Canadian Pacific, Vancouver, Nanaimo, Seattle, San Francisco, and the three archangels singing on Tamalpais.

Sixty-Nine: Niagara Frontier. Out of the White City and back to the navel. The old white shirt, gone out of date: a museum piece: exclamations. The crimson scarf of priesthood: exclamations. I light two candles at the feet of Santiago and sleep seventeen years. Waking, I find Don Juan bending over me and we go back to his compound: his twenty-eight grandchildren dance for joy. We talk to the old god, we talk to the new. One night I go back to see if they still shut doors against the whirlwind. We dance in the melodious night, the fathers and I; I recite the salutations. I drink myself into stupor and vomit and am laid to rest. Huge scorpions dance in the small space: home is the party going on while you are resting. Joyous Lake emerges in Shining Heaven, signifying breakthru. The spine is confirmed.

Just before that: a Nowhere southward. Chakra of the ass, I guess, could fall no further down. We had begun in Cuzco: to the Lord of Earthquakes. Vallejo out of prison at last, stars over the White City and royal feasts in the night. The betrothal at Intihuatana; the meaning of height made clear. Seventy: the journey North. As I bow to the Virgen de los Conquistadores in the Holy Faith, I have brought the spine North out of South and thru Center; I realize South into North and North into West. Seventy-One: the Hierogamy.

Out of the Holy Faith, Mescalito had been: three fat men of Nambe wagging ass and dancing on their heels. Old printer friend saying: "If you'd put it in a movie, they wouldn't believe it." Quietly, like that, as they went round a rock.

Further Northwest, thru Wind River, suckle at Tetons again to the night of the bride. Oh Western Star, how I'd never thought to write ballads again! Endless fuck among flies, armored sunlight, the mother-father in joy, and each of us giving birth to the other. There had been crucifixion in the southern spine, there had been counter-crucifixion in the Holy Faith, and, here, at last, the pair of us: standing at the western door. Mescalito preceding this time: a turquoise bird. Bearded man out of Cody, proud on horse among peers, the flags of the States waving in their unimaginable colors—opening the door to the ultimate State, beyond which the West could not move. Eden in Wyo., clothed in but one silver necklace, silver water from Stetson to mouth humping the fast Shoshone, and coming back among old men's beards, in hills of light, to dissolution. I came to see yr. mother's wedding—I pray thee, do not mock me, fellow-student, I think it was to see my father's funeral—Indeed, my Lord, it follow'd hard upon—Thrift, thrift, Horatio! the marriage baked-meats did coldly furnish forth the funeral tables.

For, because she had climbed from her long sleep to peak several times, and in so doing very precisely had remained attached to these bones, they had possibly tried the western door too soon and so she fled back, poor wretch, murdered by the America she was fleeing. While he had never peaked, sailing merely among the mountain-walkers, orgasm a curious selfishness were it to be perpetrated by him, when Love in its eternal form could not allow of anything less than cosmic enjoyment: uninterrupted congress in the semblance of heaven. Thus they remained among flies and fallen (the bodies left behind among the flies for the rest of their days) and the sage did not burn in a great fire without consumption and its perfumes faded back among snows. The Flame burns upward; the Lake seeps downward: signifying opposition. What race was it then had been founded, what dream-children, sex of each other's sex? For he HAD talked to the spirits of the place, and, as a brother had foretold, the spirits had listened and blessed.

(Whom shall I take as the Muse of this West: Mrs. Henry James or D. W.? D. W.'s genius in our day is to give voice to woman's sense of betrayal at man's hand and to raise betrayal to beauty. By virtue of sexual history, man's elegiac mode has been with us very much longer. Biologically: I cannot but affirm my sense of man's pain as partaking of this selfsame age-old terror which is the burden of all song. Woman's song comes to us with more immediate voice ["bleeding from the cunt," as it were] than man's is able to: man's elegy has had an older history on *paper*. Adam and Eve walking out of Eden: she thinking of what he has done toward this; he thinking of her part in it. And both of them unable to see that they were moving from Eden to Eden—that, hence-forward, with the one proviso of ignorance, Eden would not be in one place, but everywhere about them.)

And would you believe it, unknown to the myth, belting back thru South Dakota, thru Minnesota—past these very same Sioux, these very same Winnebago—in the sick car which would hardly carry me away, and back over sea to Erin, and thence to Arran, where land collapses into sea. The silence. Fields of shuddering stone. White angel birds and butterflies on the edge of disaster. The evening air crazy with rabbits and wrens. Labyrinth of walls, crushed flat by sky: eye getting used to seeing light thru stone, in order to know where to pass. Grand Canyon of the Atlantic, cyclopean dream of stone: a Machu Picchu in the sea. Sheerness of cliffs, tables laid for the sea gods, crushed flat by their huge feet— from which they dive into the sea's last rage with their terrible laws. Availed himself of a great fish, passing like table to the sea, to celebrate his coming to the Faroes, and to America, offering his god among the water spirits of old and new— met in a knot of waters.

Perhaps it all begins from "Jacataqua": this time round, at least. At least, some starting point must be endured. The Indian girl: Fiedler et al.: what does it really come to? There is still perhaps in the *Grail* too much of the romance of the Indian? (And I must learn why he talks of Poe at the end, and not Thoreau or Emerson, Whitman or Ishmael.) The Indian, for him, was what the East had been to the exiles: hence the exiles no doubt ransomed the greater day. Columbus, remember, was looking for India. But, *pace* all those who sink into the Indian in this land, WHAT true link is there between this aborigine and ourselves? True they were migrants also, the earliest migrants too, the earliest migrants into the land of nails-in-the-feet: and where did they come from indeed? Old world Asia. Turn, world, turn: the circle will never cease to turn.

There was this carpenter: last Jew / first Christian. I am late in the East, early in the West: this clan is mine. Bringing the white scarf to America, out of the island, carrying East into West: meeting those who had brought the crimson scarf from East to West in our sense, though continuing eastward in theirs—what is this but the wandering assumption of all the priesthoods of the world, gathering them into the body, gathering them into the life, and then taking the life into the poem? The world has voice in us, we are the crust of its imaginations. Persecuted, flying, ultimate tribes/tribes seeming forever lost, now found again at the western gate. The Xristians will never open us again to look for the heart and bowels within our bodies. He last appeared threefold in the garden of the Carribees; he was last seen in Lexington, Tennessee, in St. George, Utah, and also at Harts Corner in the State of New York. And he had come from Siberia to America via the Bering Straits, like they said, down thru Alaska and across the Continent. The river runs back; the clocks return and we are all one man.

("The Land! don't you feel it? Does it make you want to go out and lift dead Indians tenderly from their graves, to steal from them—as if it must be clinging even to their corpses—some authenticity, that which—Here not there." But are we, repeat are we, ever *truly adopted*?)

While many say that they will not answer, these dead Indians. Or that they will answer beyond our time, so much beyond our time, we ourselves may be looking in vain. If we have NOT BEEN Indians—in previous incarnations, or in this one: what then? We build Long Houses, hoping some come to meet us. There is nothing but hope.

I talk to some friends about America and Europe, and about that precision we had seemed to require in the idea before the form, and their notion—born of all the holy singers in this land—that the price we pay is in the borning of form as it first breathes. "Unrealized language of the present" / my "language not yet born." Perhaps it is all one: and perhaps that is why one is here in Poetry, why one has been here since before childhood. But think not always of those who have gone from here East. Spare a thought for those who have come West.

I cannot, in motion, accept that America was built at all, ever. I accept that it is being built now, out of the sense of "our day." It is not we who killed instead of loving the Red Man: the night has white linings in some of these souls. Galileo? Science was never as dangerous to society as Poetry is about to be dangerous now.

Guild of the Iron Age. Poets are falling from the trees in the bitter autumn of this economy. Who shall protect? There is so much to be done in common, so much in the very method of our gifting here, could we but transcend irritabilities. Oh race of irritable men, soften your selfhoods! Eurydice of ashes, resume our needs!

Toward any geography. Toward any America whatsoever.

1972

Child as Father to Man in the American Uni-Verse OR Dr. Jekyll, the Anthropologist, Emerges and Marches into the Notebook of Mr. Hyde, the Poet

I

Last year, Mr. Hyde, the poet, received a letter from a member of the English Department at a university in Philadelphia. She informed him that she had been asked to write an article on his work for a prominent dictionary of literary biography. She had been working all summer and had been most impressed by his poetry. She asked if they could meet for detailed discussions. Mr. Hyde called, and they had a pleasant talk. After a while, answering his suspicions, she revealed that he was to be included in the volume on post-war *British* poetry. Mr. Hyde said that he had now been in the United States for twelve years, was a citizen, and had been a champion of American poetry, even in England, for ten years or more before that. She was very sorry. She had even been preparing a conference paper as well. Her editor called later that day: would Mr. Hyde not reconsider this "foolish casting away of a chance at an academic reputation?" Mr. Hyde talked about the virtues of consistency. The editor put down the phone with a marked, sorrowful finality. A terminal case. Mr. Hyde has never heard another word about the matter.

There had been other occasions on which Mr. Hyde had found himself to be a "job" to do. Yet, over the years, he had begun to wonder whether, once past the

Statue of Liberty, the tired, poor, huddled, and yearning poet stood a chance in hell of ever really being accepted in America. A curious business. You read that a kind judge has finally given an illiterate old Russian his citizenship without a word of English to his credit. But the poet? *No Señor!* Citizenship, maybe; status of American poet, *nyet*. And this is the last country on earth you are supposed to be able to *choose!* Picking up from William Carlos Williams on the Americans and the British, Mr. Hyde would have a great deal to say about this in future years.

~

Mr. Hyde, the poet, was born aged five with a poem his mother still preserves. Britain was kind to him and, indirectly, saved his life. Despite persistent rumors of his Britannicity, this had always been a marginal quality in him: he was indisputably French, born in Paris of a French–Rumanian mother and a Lithuanian–British father. He was there seven years and then a further four in a French-speaking *lycée* in Belgium. He arrived in England a week before World War II. He was an alien and moved into his first English classrooms with something like terror. He was called "Frog" major; his brother, "Frog" minor. Of course, he was marked by public school (British: private) and later by Cambridge.

During the Blitz in England (Cumberland Hotel, London, right next to the AA batteries in *Hyde* Park), the only book he had managed to imbibe was a child's life of Abraham Lincoln. The Blitz took away his Latin and his violin, but it left him Lincoln. Just before the Blitz: why had everyone in his dorm in Bristol been whispered at one evening or another—and disappeared the next morning . . . to America!? Mr. Hyde was dying to go too. After the Blitz: Cornwall and an evacuated school-life like a military camp's. The surrealists he had devoured with a passion he imagined to be all dead in a time as old as Mycenae. They had not saved him from constant depression. What had, unlikely as it may sound, was the history of the Pilgrims in, of all things, Nevins and Commager. There had been a U.S. flag at a base some twenty minutes from the school: he would go to watch it as often as he could in the evenings when it was ceremonially lowered. On his dorm wall, he had pinned a *Daily Telegraph* map of the U.S. and had learned the capitals of the forty-eight by heart. An understanding biology teacher had lent him some American literature: James Thurber is all he can remember of that; Fitzgerald, O'Hara, Steinbeck may have been in there too. On the English side, a passion for Virginia Woolf had caused him to be accused of neglecting Shakespeare!

Mr. Hyde had always read French for happiness and had returned to France to reassume his language after Cambridge in 1948. He had thus begun a long, painful, and losing battle with bilingualism. He had written French for some three years but had only produced twenty-fifth-rate echoes of his idol Apollinaire. In these circumstances he had wandered into a flea-pit which was showing a film called *Rendez-vous de Juillet*. It was the first movie about the generation of St. Germain des Prés. The hero triumphed as an explorer to the dismay and contempt of the small elite in anthropology, known in France as *ethnographes*. In the course of the movie, the hero happened to visit the Musée de l'Homme. Mr. Hyde, realizing that he had never seen that museum, had taken himself there the next day, had marveled at what he saw and had returned to his "garret," there to tremble for three days. He had then returned to the museum and enrolled as a student. He had told no one, and his grandmother, with whom he roomed, thought, like all good French grandmothers, that he went someplace every day to misbehave himself. He had worked with Marcel Griaule, Germaine Dieterlen, Pierre Métais, André Leroi-Gourhan, Paul Lévy, above all with Claude Lévi-Strauss. And he would have taken his first exams in total incognito had his parents not happened along for a visit. He had reassured them (those "savages"!) that the disreputable and good-for-nothing Mr. Hyde was about to be replaced by an eminently respectable and presentable academic careerist ("Oh Professors!")—while sure, naturally, that anthropology and poetry were identical twins. Dr. Jekyll had emerged out of the flea-pit movie house and taken over Mr. Hyde with a vengeance.

Dr. Jekyll and Mr. Hyde then shared a body for many years, for many more years in fact than most such people have shared a body. But, as Dr. Jekyll accumulated more degrees than he knew what to do with, Mr. Hyde found that *he* could not live at peace with him and constantly strove to regain his liberty. For many years, in effect, Mr. Hyde went about with a glazed look on his face, a famished appearance contrasting with Dr. Jekyll's shining complacencies. For, in fact, anthropology and poetry were *not* identical twins. The recording angel and the creative angel had begun their interminable war.

In Paris, Mr. Hyde had walked the city deep into the night, imagining that he would die if he were ever sundered from it. Anthropology, most of which is written in English, sundered him. It seemed that, after two years of anthropology in Paris, you had to go abroad. By this time, Mr. Hyde had adopted the fashionable stance of suspicion vis-à-vis all matters American held by the overwhelming majority of European students. Yet it was to Chicago—after an inane orientation to the "mysteries" of American democracy at Yale (or democracy *tout court*: Europe, after all, still had "problems")—that a Smith-Mundt-Fulbright scholarship in anthropology finally led him. He crashed George Murdoch at Yale, as well as Ralph Linton (full of tales about Ruth Benedict's witchcraft); he crashed Abraham Kardiner in New

York, lunched with Julian Steward and Alfred Kroeber at Columbia; was treated to a Chinese meal at the Smithsonian by Matthew Stirling and William Fenton, with a visit on the side to the Bureau of Indian Affairs. At Chicago, there were Robert Redfield, Fred Eggan, Sol Tax, and Sal Washburn. He had sent back to Paris reports on the new American physical anthropology and been the first to report on Lévi-Straussian kinship theory in one of his classes. Over at Northwestern University, where he would go to see a "real American campus, with real girls and ice-cream," he followed Melville Herskovits and William Bascom. The latter suggested a working vacation in Havana: he arrived, coincidentally, on the day Batista took over for the last time, met the great painter Wilfredo Lam and the musicologist Fernando Ortiz, and studied *Santería*.

On the Chicago campus, there seemed to be no way of contacting anyone literary: finishing a Ph.D. requirement in one year flat kept him busy eighteen hours a day. He endured the grey Gothic, learned to say, "I love you," to the U of C girls, and the peripatetic Paul Radin (very possibly a kinsman of his) virtually lived in his apartment. There is a movie—*The Last Picture Show*—which has the sound track of precisely that year in Chicago: he wishes he could see it, say, every three years.[1]

Somewhere, like a needle in several dozen haystacks, lay the information that could conceivably have led Mr. Hyde to Black Mountain College. Instead, in June 1952, he went for a year's fieldwork to Guatemala. By the time he returned, he was writing in English again and France now seemed to be out of the question. *Larvatus Prodeo:* he assumed a sea change. Back in Britain, anthropology was in its virulent social anthropology–*only* phase and he was told by more than one practitioner that he had better bury all thoughts of poetry if he wanted a serious career in the field. For many years, nothing further was said: he found it hard to get a word in edgewise into the notebooks entirely taken over by his skinmate, Dr. Jekyll. Life revolved around Raymond Firth, Isaac Schapera, S. F. Nadel, Edmund Leach, Maurice Freedman, and Christoph von Führer-Haimendorf at the London School of Economics and the School of Oriental and African Studies. An occasional tea with Arthur Waley provided a welcome change.

Then, Burma. He had wanted Nepal or Japan, but it had been pointed out to him that job openings lay with Burma. When back from an exhausting eighteen months' fieldwork there, a young Canadian poet, David Wevill, met with in Mandalay, took him to the Friday evening sessions of a group called "The

1   On this period, see Nathaniel Tarn, "The Literate and the Literary: Notes on the Anthropological Discourse of Robert Redfield," in Nathaniel Tarn, *Views from the Weaving Mountain* (Albuquerque: University of New Mexico Press, 1991).

Group." This was in 1961 or 1962. It met in the house of Edward Lucie-Smith, who later left poetry for art criticism. Over tea and cookies, the likes of Philip Hobsbaum, Peter Redgrove, George MacBeth, John Digby, Fleur Adcock, and Peter Porter (Ted Hughes had left recently) politely tore the guts out of each other's poems, the custom being for one poet per evening to have a batch mimeographed for discussion. Sensing little in all this beyond a neo-"Movement" social faction (with the likes of Philip Larkin putting him to sleep back there), Mr. Hyde stayed on a while for the sake of the literary companionship, missing as he did the amenities of the Parisian café. The Group was kind to him, however. Through MacBeth's contacts at the BBC, he was eventually chosen to be the Group poet presented on the Third Program, with the poems appearing in *The Listener*.

Little by little a British "career" had occurred. The First Guinness Prize for Poetry at Cheltenham—the first and last prize he has ever received—led to his first book with Jonathan Cape and, a year later, with Random House in New York. Friendships with John Fowles, George Steiner, and Arnold Wesker had contributed to this debut. This in turn, when he had left anthropology in 1967, led to two very productive years with Cape as founding director of the Cape–Goliard Press (it had been his idea to marry the creativity of Barry Hall and Tom Raworth's Goliard Press with the distributive powers of Cape) and general editor of Cape Editions. Some forty books—starting off with Lévi-Strauss, Barthes, and Charles Olson—in Cape Editions; some twenty-five in Cape–Goliard; and a substantial number of authors in the general list were the result. Mr. Hyde was fired in 1969 on the ostensible grounds that the books were not earning money, and Cape retreated back into a gentility from which it has never moved since. During this time, he had made himself unpopular in Britain as part of a small team publishing Objectivists, Black Mountaineers, and their kin when these were in the wilderness of their own wilderness. As a young poet-critic recently put it, "[T]he fate of American poetry was for these years virtually in the hands of British publishers."[2]

When had the American shift begun? Eliot, Pound, Cummings, Crane, Melville, Whitman, James went back to his college days. In 1961, as convener of a seminar in the sociology of Theravāda Buddhist institutions at the Tenth Pacific

---

2   See Nathaniel Tarn, "The Work Laid Out before Us in This Disunited Kingdom," in Tarn, *Views from the Weaving Mountain*. Stuart Montgomery's Fulcrum Press, of course, deserves first place in a history of the New American Poetry in England. For this period, see also the Tarn supplement, *Boundary 2* 4, no. 1 (1975); and the Tarn entry in Rosalie Murphy, ed., *Contemporary Poets* (Chicago: St. James Press, 1970), 1077–79.

Sciences Conference, he had been to Hawaii—and on to Japan—via San Francisco. One night, at the City Lights Bookstore, he had bought himself blind: many things he hardly knew about, seized up more or less by instinct. Was this when he had picked up Olson, probably *The Distances* rather than the *Maximus* poems? Or *Maximus to Dogtown*? Something of Duncan's? of Whalen's? McClure's *Dark Brown*? In any event, by 1963 or so, Jonathan Williams had been in Hampstead with Ron Johnson, urging the faithful on into unknown fields, sending them to buy up neglected titles at Peter Russell's ailing bookstore. The American Embassy still believed in readings for Brits in those days and had an excellent library for poetry and records. Patchen's readings to jazz were one discovery among many.

By 1967, on officially joining Cape, he had been hot to compete with Stuart Montgomery's Fulcrum Press, a major achievement of the time, for everyone he could attract: Olson, Duncan, Zukofsky were those he had called his "three pillars," but there were also Ginsberg, Snyder, Blackburn, McClure, Levertov, Jonathan Williams, the Objectivists—among others. Some, like W. C. Williams, Creeley, Dorn, and Oppen, already had their British publishers. This had also been the time of the great Festival Hall poetry scenes where Olson read with such giants as Neruda and Ungaretti, though also, given British proclivities (Alvarez's *The New Poetry* with Penguin), with Robert Lowell and John Berryman. The years of many meetings: Zukofsky, Burroughs, Ginsberg in their dealings with Cape; Olson in London and, his first contract to hand, at Bled in Yugoslavia after the Spoleto Festival, circa 1968; Ed Dorn at Essex; Duncan at readings in London, with an interview at the BBC; McClure when producing *The Beard* at the Royal Court. . . . On a trip twice across the U.S. and Canada and back to say goodbye to anthropology and hello to editing (in 1967): Paul Blackburn, Toby Olson, and Robert Vas Dias at Aspen; Duncan, Rexroth, and William Everson reading *together* on Tamalpais; and Kenneth Patchen (whose English *Selected Poems* he had suggested doing for Cape) one midnight in Palo Alto immediately after Tamalpais! And it was Robin Blaser who had given him his first reading on the American continent at Simon Fraser in Vancouver, B.C. Rich years indeed!

~

Mr. Hyde, having symbolically murdered Dr. Jekyll in 1967 by resigning from the world's best job in Southeast Asian anthropology and having lost his employment at Cape, could only put his ass where his words had gone and moved to the

United States. Something of the mood of the time can be caught in a British-Australian critic's review of Mr. Hyde's book on Vallejo in Peru, in the course of which, ignoring Vallejo completely, the critic found no less than three occasions to blast the author for moving "to the profitable pastures of the American poetry reading circuits." As for the receiving end: well, we Americans are very good at roasting a new arrival during his first year and ignoring him ever after until it is time to write his obituary. Or, to put it in the words of a young poet-critic correspondent, "Perhaps it looked then as if American poetry was more of a team you could join than it appears to be at present." Had any one of us realized that those war-ridden sixties and early seventies were actually a goddamn poetry BOOM TIME for heaven's sake? And that we had all loved each other then like brothers and sisters?

Now you cannot move around like Mr. Hyde without a modicum of permanent culture shock. Which is why, no doubt, Dr. Jekyll had invaded Mr. Hyde in the first place, all those years ago. Which is also why all the anthropologists now swarming out of closets and howling to be *poets* seem awfully *young* to Mr. Hyde at this stage of the game. Why, even our "Ethnopoetics" here seem very young! Wasn't Paris swarming with "Ethnopoetics" in the late forties? Wasn't Griaule's Dogon material, fresh off the press, the finest poetry in the world? Ogotemmeli the greatest sage? Hadn't Artaud of the Tarahumara just died? Weren't André Breton and Benjamin Péret still going at the "magic of the marvelous," which had been around, to the point of tedium, for so many years in Dada and Surrealism? Weren't large stretches of Maurice Leenhardt's Oceanic material as good ethnophilosophy as the African? Couldn't you sit around in the cafés with Octavio Paz discussing the Aztec and the Maya? Hadn't Lévi-Strauss in his war-time days had a good deal of truck with the surrealists? Weren't Aimé Césaire and Malcom de Chazal responding from the French Antilles, not to mention the whole of *Négritude?*

And, coming to these shores twenty years later, could one not get Ginsberg to admit that *Kaddish,* arguably his finest poem, would never have sounded quite the same without the litanies of Breton? Weren't some prominent members of the New York school working hard on further adaptations (soon to become dilutions in less able hands) of Surrealism? England, perhaps, bypassed all this—but France and the U.S. did not. Come to think of it, Eliot and Pound had probably remained American (*pace* Eliot) precisely because they could incorporate *the other* while the British could not. Perhaps this was the price of *that* kind of empire: you couldn't have it that large, that specific *and* incorporate. But—it is hardly for

Hyde to speak of this. Jerome Rothenberg himself has amply documented his sources, and, if he hadn't, a historian of James Clifford's caliber would undoubtedly do it for him.[3]

Thus, trailing these European mists, glorious or otherwise, Mr. Hyde had begun moving here by teaching a summer course at SUNY Buffalo in 1969, with fellow teachers Anselm Hollo and James Wright, in the Department of English. Rothenberg had been around, working with the nearby Seneca. Early in 1970, after a time in Guatemala, Mr. Hyde had immigrated as a research fellow and visiting professor in Romance languages at Princeton. By 1971, he was at Rutgers and became professor of comparative literature there, commuting from the Delaware River at New Hope, Pennsylvania, to New Brunswick, New Jersey. He was present with Rothenberg and Dennis Tedlock at the birth of *Alcheringa* in Santa Fe. A friendship was initiated with George Quasha at Stony Brook; Richard Grossinger (whom Hyde encouraged to start a publishing firm) and *Io* were encountered in Vermont; Snyder, on a visit to Princeton where he was interviewed for *Alcheringa,* after an initial meeting at Notre Dame.[4] Dr. Generosity's was a reading place in New York City, later Bard College up the Hudson, president Robert Kelly. The list is long, but a context was forming: those listed in my preface as well as George Economou, Jackson Mac Low, Armand Schwerner, Ted Enslin, Keith Wilson, David Antin, Jim Harrison, Allen Planz, Michael Anania, John Matthias, Jack Shoemaker, Michael Davidson, Lindy Hough, Barbara Einzig, Rachel Blau Du Plessis, Clayton Eshleman, Peter Michelson, Jack Collom, Larry Goodell, Pierre Joris, Rochelle Ratner, Leslie Scalapino, Laura Chester, John Taggart, Margaret Randall, Geoffrey Young, David Meltzer, Simon Ortiz, Diane Wakoski, Rochelle Owens, Charles Stein, and John Peck were among early friends. Between then and the time of this writing, Mr. Hyde visited every state in the Union, including three consecutive summers in Alaska and many seasons in New Mexico. The land itself remained the greatest love. And

3 A Hydean pleasure at this late date is to see this history coming into print in the work of James Clifford, *Person and Myth: M. Leenhardt in the Melanesian World* (Berkeley: University of California Press, 1982); James Clifford, "On Ethnographic Surrealism," *Comparative Studies in Society & History* 23, no. 4 (1981): 539–64; James Clifford, "Power and Dialogue in Ethnography: Marcel Griaule's Initiation," *History of Anthropology* 1, no. 1 (1983): 121–56; and James Clifford and George E. Marcus, eds., *Writing Culture: The Poetics and Politics of Ethnography* (Berkeley: University of California Press, 1986).

4 Nathaniel Tarn, "From Anthropologist to Informant: A Field Record of Gary Snyder," *Alcheringa* 4 (Fall 1972): 104–13.

the dream of a "Young America" of the poets which took such a hard beating after the end of the Vietnam War. . . .

~

"Symbolical murder?" By this is meant that Mr. Hyde extricated himself from
Dr. Jekyll circa 1967 and, while they have been seeing something of each other from
time to time, they have lived apart ever since. What had Hyde's problems with Jekyll
amounted to? Two. First, anthropology appeared to be getting more and more trivial,
and, second, the language it was written in appeared to be fading into unreadability.

When it had begun, anthropology seemed to have some sort of message,
echoes of which were still heard at the time of Dr. Jekyll's emergence. Hence the
illusion that this discipline and poetry were twins. Anthropology had been part of
a grandiose campaign to kill off God, mainly by toppling his knight: the Victorian
gentleman. It was the science which would finally justify and extend to the whole
world the cry of Liberty, Equality, Fraternity. At least, many hoped so: it was hard
at the time to realize that nineteenth-century man could patronize his subjects by
studying them as easily as by cramming them into black holes. Black Holes of Cal-
cutta and not phenomena in outer space.

It helped that many founders of anthropology were Jews. Anthropology was to
be a light to the Gentiles. It was to ferret out the last Jew in every one of us from
every corner of the still huge globe, from every refuge in which the lost tribes
might have hidden themselves, and exorcise him by exposure to the common day.
A sister science, psychoanalysis, did much the same for the Jew inside every Gen-
tile: we were all to be equal at last. And, by the by, is it by chance that so many of
our leading writers today are Jews?

As a result, the first anthropologists were respectable liberal scholars and more-or-
less gentlemen—a few were ladies—and they were generally listened to by large and
faithful publics. The information they had to impart was a facet of that news without
which people fancied they could not live or breathe. Those who adhered to a readable
style—the common currency of the educated reader of liberal journals down to our
own era of near total illiteracy—were as newsworthy as television is today. In some
sectors, this has been the case until recently: a good example is Margaret Mead.

It is difficult to fix in time the moment of change. To be sure, there had always
been individuals whose style could be commended in passing, as if it were a bonus
added to any scientific validity they were credited with: think of Robert Redfield in
the U.S. or Evans-Pritchard in the UK. By and large, however, the picture faced today is one of a catastrophic decline into jargon. It is worth differentiating between

technical language as scientific language expressing itself in an unavoidable new way because the old way is no longer adequate and *jargon* as a pseudo-technical language, evolved mainly, when all is said and done, to protect entrance into and performance within an academic discipline. Part of this protection involved mimicry on the part of the so-called social sciences aping the exactitude of their senior siblings, the exact sciences. The search for "social laws" has been a major cause of jargonization— although, ironically, some of those most responsible—Radcliffe-Brown in England, Lévi-Strauss in France—have not, in their own work, overstrained the common tongue. Without any imputation of a shadow over his objectivity, it is made clear by a work such as *Tristes Tropiques* that the latter could have been a very considerable "creative" writer had he chosen that path of expression.

The fate of anthropological discourse has also, of course, been linked to that of all elite discourse in our time. At best, among the scholars and teachers, academic books and articles have become an almost completely closed field, serving only colleagues and the students of colleagues, incestuous in their preoccupations, playing interminable little games with internal quarrels and differences of view, posing, strutting, trotting out new "strategies" as if they were about to transform the world: even when they contain new information, such works are painful to read, to sift, to utilize. At worst—to remain with the discipline in question—the average anthropologist today writes in a jargon so atrocious and so bland that not even his colleagues can hack it any more: witness a recent claim that the profession's cardinal organ, the *American Anthropologist,* had become virtually unreadable. Only the most dramatic information can now get past the universal somnolence and out into the world: to compound matters, because it is not written by professionals, it is usually falsified *en route.*

Among undergraduates, we experience a deterioration so major that educators are still ferreting out its causes, whether it be in our deliquescent schools, our delinquent bookstores—the average academic bookstore in this country is almost a criminal undertaking—or the profound recesses of the fatal tube. Is it any wonder that Mr. Hyde still grins on recalling remarks made to Dr. Jekyll by British social anthropologists at the time of his doctorization: not only "Forget all French and American stuff, you will never amount to anything until you have been trained here," but also the stuff about "plowing poetry back into yourself to let it come up as social science"? If the latest generation writes well it may be due to mass alienation from the academic side of the discipline (with all its dangers) and to such phenomena as "Ethnopoetics" as well as the realization that anthropology is, after all, text.

If Jekyll and Hyde were ever to be re-united, what would a viable anthropology have to be like for them? First, it would have to give up most of its pretensions at the elucidation of "social laws" insofar as the whole or the larger units of human society are concerned. Little of this has carried us forward one jot in the art of living together. Second, it would stress the study of history, especially in the form of ethnohistory where we try to bridge the gap between the archeological past and the ethnographic present of most peoples. It would delight above all in ethnography: the faithful record of our most attentive responses to the material and spiritual cultures of such peoples. It would pay the greatest attention to the way in which such ethnography was written, striving to go beyond *belles lettres* toward a language with scientific and literary properties both, but governed primarily by literature, so that its results could be available to all culturally literate readers. It would be modest in its philosophy, recognizing that the knowledge gathered is first and foremost the property of the people studied and only secondarily everyone's property within what Robert Duncan has called the "Symposium of the Whole." In cases where the ability of a people to record its life was outmatched by the powers menacing or set to destroy that people, the anthropologist would merely be a bridge between the past s/he could record and the future s/he could place back in the hands of the younger generations of that people. If the anthropologist wished to exercise his/her mind in intellectual games—Jekyll has a predilection for symbolic systems—s/he would do it on the clear understanding that these are and should remain games, not to be used for oppressive purposes or any pretence at superior knowledge.

Much of this, it should be acknowledged, has already been claimed by various forms of radical anthropology: that anthropology which sees the discipline as a handmaiden to an era of European and American imperialism. It is in the sphere of writing—the vehicle or vehicles in which the information is expressed—that Mr. Hyde may have views which go beyond what most anthropologists would desire for themselves.

II

Mr. Hyde still speaking:

In the course of my six-year-long English literary life, I determined that (a) English poetry had been virtually dead since Hopkins at best, or since Blake at worst; (b) British, as opposed to English, poetry was Celtic if it was anything, with men like Yeats, MacDiarmid, David Jones, and Dylan Thomas as the only ones I cared for deeply (in very varied ways), or was marginal to mainstream English as in the case of the remarkable Basil Bunting; (c) an international wandering *mestizo,* additionally Jewish, could be neither English nor Celt; (d) the English language (all spoken versions of which since my first arrival in 1939 had struck me as arbitrary, almost theatrical) could therefore live for me only in a new country, a *chosen* country; (e) the new country in which energy was being rammed into the language was the U.S. of A.; (f) this country was available by its very charter and definition and seemed, on the surface, to be most welcoming; and (g) everyone had made a terrible mistake in not sending me there during the Blitz.

I know that here I am being unjust to a number of fine poets who learned from the Pound–Williams tradition and, under cruel neglect for the most part, persisted over the years in creating an English version of that tradition. Roy Fisher, Gael Turnbull, and some of their associates would be among them. Somehow, none excited me as much as their American counterparts, except perhaps J. H. Prynne.

Just as, in most religions, there seems to be a main, orthodox church and a shadow, heterodox church complementing it, so there seemed to be an America in England and an England in America. England in America (Anglophilia) seemed to me to be covered by the term "academic" (against which the "New American Poetry," as defined by the Don Allen anthology, constantly battled): its strongholds located in the Ivy League schools, their reading circuits and antiquated magazines, as well as in the *New York Times Book Review* and the *New York Review of Books:* the last of Her Majesty's possessions in these our States. One distressing aspect of these publications—*The Nation* is another prime example—is that, while their political leanings range from liberal to radical, their attitudes to poetry are anti-modernist/pomo, i.e., in the jargon, postmodern. America in England was composed of the sacred trio I called the "suicide club" (Lowell, Berryman, Plath) as the overwhelmingly model-poets of the "Movement" and its immediate successors. You could add what was known and frequently disliked of the Pound–Williams tradition and of the Beats. Charles Tomlinson, in the record of an Englishman who remained one, quotes my *bête noire* among the neo-Movement people, Ian Hamilton, on his Zukofsky symposium in Hamilton's magazine *the Review:* "The editorial motive of *the Review* in this project has been a documentary one. We believe that the movement ought at least to be known about."[5] The crass superciliousness of this, matched in a hundred treatments of Black Mountain, Objectivism, the San Francisco Renaissance, and other such American endeavors in papers like the *Times Literary Supplement* or magazines like *the Review,* could not

---

5   Quoted in Charles Tomlinson, *Some Americans: A Personal Record* (Berkeley: University of California Press, 1981), 67.

be overcome: it could only be flown. Even today, the pyramidal structure of the English poetry establishment, topped by the Poet Laureate, has not yet been broken despite years of courageous opposition by growing numbers.

I believe that the years 1967–69 were the decisive ones for me. Despite the Americaward title poem of the first book, *Old Savage/Young City,* and its successor *Where Babylon Ends,* these must probably be accounted, stylistically and structurally, as English books. The works I remember feeling close to at this time were those of Christopher Middleton, David Wevill; some of Ted Hughes, Peter Redgrove, George MacBeth, and Jon Silkin; the *Migrant* and *Grosseteste* poets; as well as younger writers, more American influenced, like Tom Raworth, Lee Harwood, and Eric Mottram, often associated with the Trigram and Fulcrum presses; and poet–artists like John Digby, my close friend. The break came with the third book *The Beautiful Contradictions* in 1969 and an article, "World Wide Open: The Work Laid before Us in This Disunited Kingdom."[6]

Despite opposition to "little-englandism," the early poems had remained tight, highly crafted ("wordsmithed"), and "closed." The content reached beyond England but the form did not. One liberating force may have been Neruda—but less than has been said or supposed as a result of my translation activities. More to the point: suddenly, one day, MacDiarmid was to read in London. I realized that I did not know his work. His *Collected Poems* (published in the States, of course, with a small Scottish edition!) had recently become available. Here was a man who seemed like a mountain so tall that the English sheep grazing on its sides could not even see it. Here was a long thin line, sanctioning the long breath-line which had already been noticed by some as characteristic of my work. Here, above all, was a man who seemed able to put almost anything into a long poem—without sacrificing lyric conciseness when he wanted it—and with a straightforwardness at that which appeared much more available than the esoteric reaches of Pound and Eliot. Here was someone whose politics were far more acceptable than theirs.

In the context of "little-englandism," it seemed almost impossible, for varied reasons, to go back to Pound and Eliot at that moment. It *did* seem possible, for varied reasons, to go forward to MacDiarmid—personally available as well as most engaging into the bargain—and I believe that it is under his impulse, among others, that *The Beautiful Contradictions* was written. Another "father-figure" was Charles Olson. Not so much, initially, the Olson of *Maximus* as the earlier poet of *The Distances,* to me, at the time, linguistically the most invigorating book of

---

6   In Tarn, *Views from the Weaving Mountain.* See also the Nathaniel Tarn supplement in *Boundary 2* 4, no. 1 (1975).

the post-Poundian era. Strangely, it was not until very much later that I came to Williams and I suffered from that. For lyricism, I believe I am indebted to a number of Europeans such as Rilke, Lorca, Apollinaire, Breton, Michaux, and Supervielle. Patchen and Dylan Thomas, *inter alia,* were undeniable influences on its Formative horizon.

The burden of "World Wide Open," then, was an attack on "little-englandism" (see also part 14 of *The Beautiful Contradictions*) from three main directions: the Pound–H.D.–Williams tradition and its associated movements in the "New American Poetry" (I came to know these more thoroughly after moving to the States); the Celtic Belt and Regional England; and the worlds of Latin America, Asia, and Europe. The guideline for me was stated in part 1 of *The Beautiful Contradictions:* "We have no alternative to taking the whole world as our mother" (continuing, "since no one can pretend to own anything of permanence / or to anchor his roots in any particular plot / or speak in anything but borrowed languages").

The rest of the story is, in a sense, the attempt to match such universalism with the belief that America is a family of nations rather than a single nation; that this family alone offers a newcomer roots, and that, since everyone in America "borrows languages," someone like myself could aspire to be an American poet. Hence the long *periplous* through the American continents in the wake of Olson's opening to *Call Me Ishmael.* This was to lead to such books as *Lyrics for the Bride of God, The House of Leaves, Alashka* (written jointly with Janet Rodney), *At the Western Gates, The Desert Mothers,* and *Seeing America First.* A prose piece, "Toward Any Geography / Toward Any America Whatsoever," states, rather cryptically, the myth of the continental spine (illustrated later on the cover of *Atitlán/Alashka*) and its role in focusing the major part of this phase of the work.[7] Letters received at this time, from major writers here in the traditions I respect, confirmed for me my belief in *The Beautiful Contradictions* as a turning point. Robert Duncan, for instance, wrote on April 23, 1970,

> *The Beautiful Contradictions* arrivèd yesterday from Random House and while
> I am still in the first high of the first reading (Cantos One and Two) I must write
> to express the steady excitement, exaltation and pleasure in your music (from the
> opening commanding my reading in sound) and in the study and life-learning
> that flows in that music. So much moves already that is of the very heart of the
> matter for me, come up from a sea too deep to freeze into the simplicity of this

---

7   As "Toward Any Geography / Toward Any America Whatsoever," in this volume. See also Doris Sommer, "America as Desire(d): Nathaniel Tarn's Poetry of the Outsider as Insider," *American Poetry* 2, no. 1 (Fall 1984): 309–23.

"humanity" we would create in ourselves. "to make an end of it" you propose, as once, when standing by the road hitch-hiking it came to me to "let it go free—"

You will know from lines of my working what a companionship I feel in reading these poems.

And now for a moment deserting this letter I return and find the first line of Three 'We shall make a very long poem of it all of us together'—it is disturbing (thrilling and forbidding) to read lines so close to *the heart of the matter*. . . .

I love the conversion to a poetry. And here, your special role as being the agent of my books' going to England and your studies and concerns in common with mine—now revealed and verified—verifies my own appointments. You have taken your individuality in your manhood and that is the deepest commitment of language—of its commonality. . . .

It takes an Englishman forever to welcome you, though when he does, it is frequently for life. An American welcomes you immediately but knows in his sinews that America is mobile and will soon move him or you on to someplace else. It is also true that, immigrating in 1970, you were coming, without realizing it, into a poetry boom time. With hindsight, opposition to the Vietnam War seems to have been immensely favorable to poetry: the revival of public readings launched by the "New Americans" of the fifties and sixties now reached its peak; bookstores flourished in the centers and in many regions; there seemed to be no end to literary festivals, circuits, little magazines, gatherings of the clans.

There *was* an end, abrupt, almost tangible: the end of that particular war. Since that time, I have never once wished to leave this land which I love with a passion as great as that of any compatriot. Yet I know extremes of solitude and abandonment, the likes of which were unthinkable at the time of arrival. Spread out over the immensity of this continent, we have each gone back, I guess, to our own solitudes. The history of our time in poetry is no doubt in the letters. Looking at the Olson–Creeley correspondence and many other such: it was like this, no doubt, as the "New Poetry" came to birth.[8]

A statement made circa 1969 sums up much of my biosphere at the time. It may bear repeating here:

Poetry for me is the discovery of a sound which arises out of unimpeded listening. The sound, once recognized, can assume a number of voices; my life-history happens to have given me no convincing English of my own. I have always been fascinated by the interplay between restricted and elaborated codes, between

8   The Charles Olson–Robert Creeley *Correspondence* is published by the Black Sparrow Press; George F. Butterick, ed., *Charles Olson and Robert Creeley: The Complete Correspondence*, 9 vols. (Santa Barbara, CA: Black Sparrow Press, 1980–90).

common parlances and formal rhetorics. Form is usually allowed to grow out of content, though I am aware of moving toward more and more open form as I discover that there is less and less that *cannot* be discussed in poetry. In the early work, my anthropological experience prompted me to speak out of various *personae* associated with *Old Savage;* an old, wise Amerindian or Melanesian, aware of what our culture has done to his, forgiving, sad at his own destruction principally because it mirrors the destruction of the whole natural earth. Dropping anthropology as a profession has enabled me to speak as an anthropologist and add the dialectic of observer and observed to the previous one-dimensional picture. As a result, politics have become a major factor in recent work such as *The Beautiful Contradictions.* This complex material is offset by simple lyrical-erotic sequences such as occur in *October.* The aim is to work toward more and more satisfactory resolutions of the tension between simplicity and complexity.

We may be living at a time when only the exasperation of contradictions is possible for the artist; synthesis is closed to her/him because of the intolerable weight of new information s/he must shoulder each day. In this situation, poetry is more than ever a discipline, the means whereby a poet not only discovers, but literally creates her/himself out of the total flux. It follows that poetry for poetry's sake, decoration *et al,* is intolerable.

Translation is i) a duty within the Republic of Letters; ii) a way of allowing various voices to speak; iii) a means of letting air into the beds of our own letters. Editorial activity is an extension of translation, not only from languages but from disciplines. *Transformation* is a key concept, linking early allegiances to Surrealism with present interests in Structuralism.[9]

III

If anthropology's mission has been lost or dispersed, what of literature's? One thing is clearly of relevance in our context: literature's raids on anthropology's preserve have been more and more insistent as well, in some respects, as more and more successful. Clearly, literature fancies it needs anthropology more than anthropology fancies it needs literature. The inspiration which anthropology has afforded poets—to go no further back than Pound and Eliot, or St. John Perse and Segalen, or Neruda, Vallejo, and Paz, in the age of Frazer, Harrison, or the author of *From Ritual to Romance*—to say nothing of Marx and Engels, Freud or Jung, Mauss, Durkheim, or Lévi-Strauss—can scarcely be said to have abated when we

---

9 Tarn entry, *Contemporary Poets.* In the same entry, Martin Seymour-Smith writes, "Tarn's poetry is . . . the most non-traditional and foreign-influenced of any British poet now writing." I might today write "*Transformaction.*"

now have a virtual school of "Ethnopoetics" devoted both to the accessing of "primitive and archaic poetries" into our culture through the best available techniques of *twentieth-century* translation *and* to the mutual effect upon each other of such poetries and our own—granted that Native poets very much continue to produce poetry all over this world.

In fact, the scenario is one of very considerable interaction. Seen positively, it can be regarded as one of commensality in which everyone profits. I fear, though, that, seen negatively, it is one of . . . cannibalization. What I'm not sure of is who is cannibalizing whom. Is Jekyll eating Hyde? Or Hyde eating Jekyll? Are both being eaten: by other Jekylls and Hydes, or by something else? Or are both Jekyll and Hyde eating something else?

When leaving the Old World for the New, the problem of who is being addressed in poetry becomes the main one of all, far more important than it has ever been before. In one, crucial, sense, we choose whether to address an elite of specialists (other poets or professional students of poetry) or a general reading public. My personal preference would go to both—if necessary to the extent of producing different works for each—but it rarely falls out that way.

And it is not, for me, a matter of the United States alone. It is, it has to be, a matter of ourselves as members of a polity and of those we choose to regard as aliens, sometimes *owned* by us, or as underprivileged *others,* both inside and outside our borders. This in turn is a paradigm of the way we look at and treat the *other* throughout the universe.

Ultimately, it is a matter of what we should mean by "nation"—the dream of Rimbaud's "nations in joy"—the real meaning of *nation:* local, regional, metropolitan, continental. And the meaning of universe. UNI-VERSE. A very few have begun on this: notably, and nobly, Gary Snyder (though I often disagree with him on many issues). But this is for the future.

I return to a narrower theme: the distinction between poetry addressed to an elite and poetry addressed to the people at large, or that section of it which has not been consumerized out of existence as a reading and listening public. I fear we must now go through a dark passage in which complex, often academic, technical terminology has to be used: for the good reason that it is in these terms that the discussion, if at all, is being conducted. To lead the discussion back out of this terminology into the living language remains, at this point, a task for the future. Some have begun on the task—but in a manner which may be counterproductive, too close altogether to that which it is nominally attacking. We shall have to see.

Discussions on contemporary poetry are very likely, at this moment, to fall under such headings as "modernism" and "postmodernism." As Ron Silliman has perceived, territories are being claimed; "at stake is the framework through which our activity and its products will be received, 'understood' and, most of all, explained."[10] Few agree on definitions, especially of "postmodernism," and the matter is complicated by different reference systems and applications in the different arts and disciplines and in different geographical areas. The terminological confusion probably indicates that we are jumping the gun, attempting to analyze and pigeon-hole a period before we can see it whole. Cultural acceleration is such that we frequently seem to assume the future before the present is safely past, thus raising substantial doubts in many minds as to the depth and value of our appreciation of the present. In any event, I shall use the terms as gingerly as possible and with reference particularly to my main interest here: elite versus general publics, and hegemonic versus universalized poetries.

While the labels "modernism" and "postmodernism" seem to be historically conditioned and sequential, I'm not sure that they do not, perhaps predominatingly, now represent alternative procedures available simultaneously to our practice. We might try a model of some features which appear to be *relatively* acceptable to the critical community, a model which would bring out the *complementarity* aspect of the two labels—for, in effect, most contemporary works will exhibit features from both sets:

Modernist	Postmodernist
Structural (set out in space)	Phenomenological (set out in time)
Ahistoricist (and consequently *trusting* in conventional narrative/information)	Historicist (but, because so, *distrusting* conventional narrative/information to the point of often subverting itself in this respect)
Mythic	Scientific
Gnostic	Agnostic
Gesellschaft oriented	*Gemeinschaft* oriented
Universalist/international	Localist/regional specific
Tradition primes over individual	Individual primes over tradition
Montage	Collage

A possible reading is that *both* "modernists" and "postmodernists" should, in fact, rightly be labeled "late modernists" in a series running from "early," through "high," to "late" "modernism." I am close to thinking that this, not uninfluenced

10   Ron Silliman, "Postmodernism: Sign for a Struggle, the Struggle for the Sign," *Poetics Journal* 7 (1987): 18–39.

by parallel debates in the high-visibility discipline of architecture, remains my preferential view. Another reading would select out certain features of "modernism" as indicative of a "postmodernist" orientation, or trend in "modernism" *toward* a genuinely post-"modern" aesthetic. Any such, I suggest, would eventually find it advisable to change its label—the weakness in any "post" label being only too apparent.

In this reading, we might argue that "postmodernism" is that aspect which now exhibits most fully the *metafunctions* of any medium: its reflections on its own workings and actions taken on those reflections. To that extent, it also reduces the frontiers between culture-producing media (say, here, "creative writing") and culture-receiving media (say critical writing, "theory," etc.). Culture-critics may be achieving the freedom of culture-producers but simultaneously abdicating the adjudicative duties traditionally associated with criticism. The problem here lies with the political implications of such "duties." Until such time as *all* writing can be seen to be, and accepted as, *theory,* there is likely to be unexplicated tension between conservative/traditional (so far, mainly "critical") and radical/progressive (so far, mainly "creative") selectivity in adjudication.[11]

The "postmodernist" orientation, however, in its distrust of "logocentrism," has seemed to some inclined to allow everyone/everything its due expression in a given field with the minimal application of any selective or hierarchical principle: this is often labeled "democracy"/"pluralism"/"decentralization." It seems to carry the implication that an art object has value through the mere fact of its existence and presence in a certain time/space and through no other fact. In the name of an originally historicist distrust of any "*logos,*" "postmodernism" seems to threaten the definability of anything as "past"/"present"/"future."

Guided by various manifestations of "deconstructionism," the "postmodern" argument tends to justify and systematize the delegitimization of any "past," i.e., "original" content, to the extent, at an extreme, of questioning whether it ever existed. The loss of "origin" carries with it a whole series of other losses. If there is no "origin," it is unlikely that there will be any "norm" (nor "ownership"/ "authorship," nor "copy*right*"). If there is no "norm," it is unlikely that there will be any taboo against repetition (such as Pound's "make it new!"). At this point, indeed, we appear to be mired in a grove of grooves, involving an interminable *nappe* of mirrors among the mangroves, such that neo-x gives place to neo-y

---

11   That adjudication can be gotten rid of altogether seems to me doubtful in that I see judgment as a constitutive aspect of a triad—Mentation/Language/Judgment—involved in *any* act of the "self" at the level of "*the Vocal.*" See "Exile out of Silence into Cunning," in this volume.

which gives place to neo-z—and soon, one more time again, we shall be welcoming neo-a, neo-b, and neo-c. While we must beware of taking the toutings of the metropolitan art-market as criteria for art-history, the lack of any direction in the arts today is painfully evident in most disciplines. Whether "anything goes" is isomorphic or not with artistic "liberty" seems to me to remain open to debate.

It is hard to know whether this dereliction arises out of the availability of too much history (media infoglut) or too little (various forms of miserable deficiency in education). Infoglut *may* be coincidental with lack of norms for information selectivity; when there is, or should be, no one to judge what we consume, a superabundance of "choice" has to be the result. At this extreme, information may end up by being treated as the "enemy," as "outside," belonging to "them," to "power" and "establishment." It is then trashed or inordinately appropriated.

Turning to appropriation (self-confessedly and outspokenly "appropriational" art movements seem to be the latest miracle at the time of writing), the subject of collage as our century's single most revolutionary formal innovation turns up in virtually every discussion of these periodizations. It is hard to avoid the generalization that collage is the most appropriative of all techniques. One is attempting to arrive at a product of the imagination by smelting many small acts of acute attention to the data world of all time and space into one vortical image—but this attention does not limit itself to attention: it is constitutively prehensile; it takes rather than borrows; it steals; it appropriates. "*Je ne cherche pas, je trouve*" is one of its best-known mottoes.

Much of "deconstruction"—whether we refer to "graft" or to "mime," "allegory," "parasitism," et al.—seems to justify and systematically extend the charter myth of appropriation in its delegitimization of the original "logos" of any "textual" object. It allows of every kind of imposition upon the text that is "worked off," and it can afford no guarantee whatsoever that neglect and irresponsibility will not characterize such impositions. Since any kind of "origin" implies some form of "depth," "deconstruction" will tend to treat the *surface* of representation or transmission and the surface only. "Content" being unanchored now by any implication, legitimacy goes to formalism *à outrance*: "postmodernism" has succeeded in problematizing reference to the fullest possible extent of its push.

"Allegories," Walter Benjamin has said, "are, in the realm of thought, what ruins are in the realm of things."[12] It has been pointed out that the supreme irony of "logocentrism" is that its *critique* is "as insistent, as monotonous and as inadvertently

---

12   Walter Benjamin, *The Origin of German Tragic Drama*, trans. J. Osbourne (London: New Left Books, 1977), 178.

systematizing as logocentrism itself."[13] Apart from locking us into an iron ring of "theory" proliferation, those artists with the strongest, and in many ways most welcome, stress on "theory" today may be leading us into a greater irony yet. When the logic, and judgment, of any given *polis* is subverted by its arts to this extent, is there any way—assuming, and it's a large assumption, that they are heard at all—for artists to provide a *new* logic by themselves alone, without the genuine revolutionary action of a whole mass of the dissatisfied?[14]

In his recent piece on "postmodernism," Ron Silliman shrinks towering "modernism" to a shadow between "realism" and "postmodernism." In essence, "realism" is that program which attains a unity between "signifier" and "signified" in a manner that conceals the presence of the "signifier": the dream of a totally transparent form. That dream of unity continues into "modernism"—Pound's call for a "splendor" that would "cohere" where the *Cantos* had failed. "Postmodernism" breaks the dream: Gertrude Stein, Louis Zukofsky require a writing "minus that impossible dream."[15]

But is it certain, in fact, that there *can* be, ever, a disunification of "signifier" and "signified"? Linguists agree that every linguistic unit, even a single letter, cannot help having some kind of referential value. "Reader expectation" alone will virtually guarantee that some kind of "signified" will be read into the presence of any "signifier." Is not disunification an ever-receding mirage, as a social fact, that is, and is not co-optation into a previous or ongoing "signified" inevitable this side of revolution and, frequently, beyond?

The *illusion* that this is not so is an imperative necessity to any writing being done at all. In what is an *incest* situation, where no one listens to poets except other poets, writers can create communities of other writers who, aware of that imperative, consume each other's products. This remains a small elite. In any kind of *marital* situation—by which I mean one which continues to recognize the existence of (non-writer) readers, such consumption is going to be extraordinarily

---

13 Edward Said, "Opponents, Audiences, Constituencies and Community," in *The Anti-Aesthetic: Essays on Postmodern Culture*, ed. Hal Foster (Port Townsend, WA: Bay Press, 1983), 143.

14 In addition to the pieces mentioned above, I have found, for a discussion of "postmodernism," the following sources useful: the articles by Habermas and Jameson in Foster, *The Anti-Aesthetic*; also Walter Benjamin, "The Work of Art in the Age of Mechanical Reproduction," in *Illuminations*, ed. Hannah Arendt (New York: Schocken Books, 1969); Rosalind E. Krauss, *The Originality of the Avant Garde and Other Modernist Myths* (Cambridge, MA: MIT Press, 1985); Charles Jencks, *What Is Postmodernism?* (New York: St. Martin's Press, 1986); and Gregory L. Ulmer, *Applied Grammatology* (Baltimore: Johns Hopkins University Press, 1985). The literature grows apace and becomes all-devouring.

15 Silliman, "Postmodernism," 38.

limited. The reader is as permeated by "individualism" as anyone, but s/he continues to see, or want to see, little but the "signified" in any writing: usually through the pressure to obtain *narrative* and (more ideologically) coded *information*. The present predominance in the market, growing ever greater, of "fiction" and "non-fiction," however "difficult," over poetry of any stripe speaks loudly! Silliman insists that "society" is brought in with the programmed admission of the "addressee" into the model. Brothers and sisters are admitted; potential husbands and wives clearly not. As long as this "postmodernist" model persists, the consumption of poetry is likely to remain extraordinarily limited, a highly specialized life-mode in a world of highly particularized specializations.

In another recent piece, Charles Bernstein claims that critics like Jameson have seen all responses to late capitalism as similar when they are *not*. As an example, Bernstein asks us to distinguish between a fragmentation which i) "attempts to valorize the concept of a free-floating signifier, unbounded to social significance, that sees no meaning outside of normative discourse and only convention's arbitrary formalism within it"; and another which ii) "reflects a conception of meaning as prevented by conventional narration and so uses disjunction as a method of tapping into other possibilities available within language."

Bernstein sees, in the evolution of "modernism," not a loss of history, as Jameson does, but a crisis in the representation of history. In another paper, on Pound, this author usefully invokes Eisenstein's distinction between montage and collage. Could we use this to suggest that "modernist" collage is in essence Eisenstein's *montage* (which continues to imply past and sequential narrative—even if only in the thread of the life of a Pound or Joyce), whereas "postmodernist" *collage* would be non-narrative, a-historical (perhaps "schizoid" in Jameson's idiosyncratic sense), non-informative insofar as non-affiliated to any dominant ideology, and open to "pluralism," "decentralization," "democracy"? This is a promising tack. The problem, however, seems to me to be that the "marital" reader is not likely with her/his tools to see the difference. What s/he will see is the product of some kind of collage, the *dislocation* which the artist is presenting; the potential threat to the ever-desirable transparency. From the point of view of *reception* (so much stressed by the community of poets to which Bernstein and Silliman belong), these issues so passionately discussed seem to have limited relevance outside their immediate circles.[16]

Some will also add that we should have attention to the "signifier" by all means (and that there has been plenty of this since forever as a condition of virtu-

---

16 Charles Bernstein, "Centering the Postmodern," *Socialist Review* 96 (1987); also Charles Bernstein, "Pound and the Poetry of Today," *The Yale Review* 75, no. 4 (1986).

ally any poetry worth its salt)—but that the occultation of the "signified" does *not* constitute a disappearance or an elimination. The mysteries they see as justifying the very interference of poetry in anyone's life persist. As Robin Blaser argues cogently, "Proposition: that is, the reason that we cannot, as writers, simply turn poetry *over* to language . . . it is . . . unlike language which, as an object of knowledge, is a construct of philosophers and linguists; whereas poetic language . . . constitutes 'forms of active social interaction and practice.' "[17] The myths of presence, as I have argued elsewhere, remain all-powerful in poetry even today.[18]

On the matter of "origin," too, another point needs making. In "primitive and archaic" societies, the poem has always been *owned:* intangible is tangible; permission/transmission has to be obtained, worked for, begged for, purchased. It may be that we neglect this social implication at our peril: indeed that, in some ways, we *de-value* the poem so, rather than value it.

We know to what an extent the triumphs of our era's arts are due to appropriation. China, Africa, Central America, and others (mostly their pasts rather than their presents—a reunion of poets a few years ago managed to discuss American and Chinese poetry without a *single* reference to *contemporary* China!) are brought into "modernist"/"postmodernist" poetry and jostle there with our own place and time. It is very much as if montage and collage coincided with the decline of one set of empires and the rise of another. I am close to arguing, *pace* Bernstein, that *all* collage is hegemonic, whether conservative or radical, and that this may be a symptom of danger to our poetries today from *whichever* school or quarter they arise. The case, at any rate, may be worth examining.

I go back now to my sense, recorded early, that everyone in America speaks "borrowed languages." William Carlos Williams: "You see in American verse, especially in the modern phase, a struggle to establish itself *formally* among the literatures of the world."[19] My suspicion is that "postmodernism" may one day be seen in the main as a set of regional variations of "modernism," evolved in these States and other western centers of culture under American cultural hegemony, to create and establish a peculiarly American, to some extent isolationist, endeavor. That some of the seeds go back as far as Whitman does not alter the case. Under hegemonic conditions, what universalism or internationalism remains is internalized.

---

17 Robin Blaser, "My Vocabulary Did This to Me," in *A Book of Correspondences for Jack Spicer,* ed. David Levi Strauss and Benjamin Hollander (San Francisco: Acts 6, 1987), 103.

18 See "Exile out of Silence into Cunning," in this volume; and Nathaniel Tarn, "Voice: Ex Nihilo?" in *O.Ars* 6/7 (1989).

19 William Carlos Williams, "Studiously Unprepared," *Sulfur* 4 (1982): 31.

Middle-class English has long been sold out to the British party. The arch-initiators of the American Idiom, enraged by some compatriots' fancied sell-out to the Old World, collect American English from the regional fringes as well as the minorities (W.C.W.: "What influence can Spanish have on us who speak a deriv-ative of English in North America?").[20] Blacks, Hispanics, Indians; then Italians, Germans, Portuguese, Poles, all purveyors of the American Grain. The act of col-lage continues; we piece together our culture with quotations: data quotations, language quotations ("Pin down an American and he utters a quotation," says Pound according to Kenner):[21] it is all one process.

If Williams is correct in his *The American Background* about the role of "wealth" in inhibiting the growth of a "primary" culture made in U.S.A., we must carefully attend to the spread of the wealth into what Ron Silliman calls "the mid-dle strata" and into much of what he would presumably call the "lower strata" as well. My own sense is that we have a consumerization, at the hands of the corpo-rate world of most of whatever "people" might have once existed, dispensing "pop culture" to the masses, with margins of "high culture" and "folk culture" for the very small and basically powerless zones of "aristoculture" at the top and whatever is left of a "people" at the bottom. Such zones link in circular fashion to form the residual amalgam of what used to be "culture," while "pop" or "pap" is fed to the ever-inflating middle zone. Appreciation of "secondary" (non-U.S.A.-made) cul-tures, *external* in the Third World, *internal* among our own "Minorities," then be-comes a major form of the new "wealth's" role among us; an internalization of the orphan fears of our ruler-parents (the search for "roots") which is all-pervasive. In-cidentally, it is also massively destructive of genuinely popular arts and crafts, as we can tell from the ever-growing proliferation of kitsch and "airport art."[22]

And to make sure that we can undermine and escape from the consequences of continued appropriation, we remain "open"—"open" to the universe, "open" to all cultures, "open" to all suggestions, "open" to whatever grows out of the first line on our page (wherever we acquire the first line from, or the subsequent ones), for ever and ever magnificently OPEN—and locked preferentially into the HERE and NOW. This freeze presents a dangerously curtailed and limited attention to the moment in hand, reminiscent, if only on the surface, of certain currently favored interpretations of meditational procedures, but paradoxically ever on the verge of

---

20   Ibid., 28.
21   Hugh Kenner, *A Homemade World* (New York: Morrow, 1975), 84.
22   William Carlos Williams, "The American Background," in his *Selected Essays* (New York: New Directions, 1969), 134–61.

solipsism and tautology, the greatest enemies, one would have thought, of genuine openness. In contrast, the cultural products of the barbarous *others,* our own
past included but, first and foremost, it would seem, the "primitive and archaic"
poetries, remain permanently, and exploitably, *closed.* Which is all a little reminiscent of another impossible ideal, from the European twentieth-century store-
house: the ideal of perpetual revolution.

Such thoughts may yield a very heretical and in some senses tragically painful
view of some of our immediate predecessors. Charles Olson provides a fascinating
"transitional" example. In his responsibility and commitment, his pedagogy, his
effort at structure, his fundamental optimism—even if he goes behind the twenty
centuries to Ur and Sumer—he is a "modernist." Yet, some years after reading
through Butterick's *Guide to the Maximus Poems,* I remain dismayed by the *extent*
to which these marvelous poems are made, without our initial knowledge, of texts
and poems belonging to others.[23]

Jed Rasula has recently introduced the concept of *composting* to define this
process as cardinal in contemporary American poetics.[24] Mark Karlins has written
a fine thesis on Olson, showing how such poetics can be seen as an act of abnegation: the ultimate subjugation of the tedious ego and the ultimate democratization
of the world (problematic as this latter is for Olson) can both be justified by a
poetics which, from one point of view, can be defined as one of universal appropriation.[25] Indeed, it is true that the immense tedium of confessionalism in most
of its forms, including much generated by the Beats, can perhaps only be com-
bated by such means. Anything that can hush the "me-me" generation certainly
deserves a hearing.

There are times when I know that nothing is owned and that borrowing or
outright stealing has been our mark of Cain from the beginning. I hope it is clear
from my own work that, like most of my contemporaries, I would subscribe to the
view that we live in an ocean of language and that it is hard to separate one wave
from another. Nevertheless, the magnitude and extensiveness of Olson's push in
this direction continue to shock. It is not the issue of quotation per se which is at
stake. It is the issue of systematic exploitation of quotation which nags, together
with this further thought: those who own much by belonging to a particular culture *ab initio* may come with relative ease to the idea that nothing-owned,

23   George Butterick, *A Guide to the Maximus Poems* (Berkeley: University of California Press, 1979).

24   Jed Rasula, "The Compost Library," *Sagetrieb* 1, no. 2 (Fall 1982): 190–219.

25   Mark Karlins, "The Derivative Poetics of Charles Olson: A Study of the *Maximus Poems*" (Ph.D.
     diss., Rutgers University, 1982).

everything-borrowed may give us the best of all possible lives. Those who have little at the start may find this idea less appealing . . . and less viable.

Such considerations might lead us to wonder whether the universalist component in "modernism" might not have had its advantages as a starting point over a more localist, and therefore paradoxically hungrier, product such as "postmodernism." But: a universalism of whom? Of the First World clearly. The issue remains stubborn. Also, the "modernist" component in contemporary poetry seems more traditionally oriented and more politically regressive than the "postmodernist." This, however, may be one of the illusions fostered by a "democratic" form of hegemony, in a word by liberal culture making it *appear* that "modernism" was less progressive. On the one hand, not *all* "modernists" were fascists by a long chalk; on the other, fascism is far from having disappeared in our world. At this time it is still very hard to decide.

IV

The scanner slides. Another way of looking at all this may be to change labels. I propose another two macrolabels: "hermeticism" and "primitivism." The former in our "postmodern" times prolongs "modernist" interests in an elite-addressed content, frequently connected to various esoteric traditions with universalistic applications. It also prolongs the "modernist" expectation of exegesis in that its poetries are rarely accessible even to the few, without a battery of critical reinforcements, mostly academic.

In discussing "hermeticism," I would distinguish masters of successive generations like H.D., Robert Duncan, Kenneth Irby, and Robert Kelly, in whom esoteric interests are constitutive, the very breath of life, from the guru-hunters of all persuasions who adopt jargons from their latest enthusiasms and do little beyond muddying the flow of common discourse. That "hermeticism" in the latter case here gives way to obscurantism is one illustration of the problematic aspects of pedagogy and transmission among poets working in a hegemonic context. In any event, "hermeticism" overall is mostly "apolitical" and therefore conservative in its effects if not in its intent. As we shall see in a moment, a more generalized application of the term "hermeticism" stressing its sectarianism rather than its esotericism can lead to somewhat different conclusions.

"Primitivism"—as might be expected *a priori* from the relative simplicity of the poetries which endow it with both its strengths and weaknesses—represents another facet of the "modernist" heritage. Without exhausting the richness of the endeavor known as "Ethnopoetics," it might be accepted as a prime example of "primitivism" in our moment. The father of American "Ethnopoetics," Jerome Rothenberg, leans toward some alternative aspects of twentieth-century European "modernism" often neglected or demeaned by some of our leading American "modernists": Dada, Surrealism, and the like. "Ethnopoetics" has inherited its internationalism from such movements; as far as the expectation of exegesis goes, it is clearly far, far less. To this extent, "primitivism" is far more liberal than "hermeticism" and, constitutively, far more open.[26]

Again, and far too schematically, "primitivism" is no doubt to be allied with the Beat wing of American confessionalism (as distinguished from its high-academic counterpart among the likes of Lowell, Berryman, Sexton, and Plath) and frequently moves away from narrow concerns with poetry alone to the wider, multimedia fields of the "counterculture." It generates a poetry addressed to a larger section of a public far more than any other faction yet considered here. It also appears to be linked to the issue of "performance poetry."

At a World Poetry Conference in Amsterdam a few years ago, ten evenings of "performance poetry" were given, as compared with one devoted to the "poetry of words." It was hard among all the ululations, shouts, howlings, and twangings of electric guitars to remember that, for twenty centuries or more, our poetry, though often sung, had been made almost uniquely of words. Yet it was "performance poetry" with which our western poets responded to non-western poets who were the guests of honor at that particular festival. The linkup of "Ethnopoetics," oral poetry, open poetry, and collage has been made clear to us. Yet, if our response to "tribal and archaic" poetries is for our work to become a subsidiary branch of intimate theater and cabaret, are we really gaining much from the influx of the "primitive" into our writing? For that matter, how genuinely is the so-called primitive able to counteract the immense, irreversible, and murderous technocratic "progress" we have now made on this planet? Grandiloquently as some poets may proclaim the irrelevance to true humanity of the last *x* number of millennia, what can this do for us *practically* and *immediately* in our dying cities, ravaged countrysides, and decimated forests and oceans?

In addition, there have been signs of late that "primitivism" has been following surrealist precedents in calling more and more aspects of contemporary writing to shelter under its aegis. It would get rid of the term "postmodernist"

---

26   For a statement on the American background, see Roy Harvey Pearce, *Savagism and Civilization: A Study of the Indian and the American Mind,* rev. ed. (Baltimore: Johns Hopkins University Press, 1965).

altogether and gather under one banner many continuations of "modernism" from the surrealist and dada lineages especially. (To this view, as I have said, I am fundamentally sympathetic.) Specifically, Rothenberg, in a recent piece reviewing the revised Allen anthology, calls into play Concrete and Visual Poetry, Fluxus, Intermedia, Chance Operations, the New Performance Poetry, the Second- or Third-Generation New York School, the New Black Poetry, Native American Poetry, Latino Poetry, the "Language" Poets, the Poem in Prose, the "New Sentence," as well as many individual poets for whom pigeonholes cannot be found.

Rothenberg's stance, seen also in his *Symposium of the Whole* (with Diane Rothenberg) and the revised *Technicians of the Sacred,* has been immensely and liberatingly influential over the years and is admirable in its continued opposition to all forms of foreclosures and all academic dictates as to the nature of the American canon.[27] Paradoxically, however, it remains open to question when studying hegemonic contexts. Paradoxically, too, this enlargement of the "primitivistic" impulse in the new, revised "Ethnopoetics" may lead us away from non-elite-addressed poetry and back toward a more balanced stance between "hermeticism" and "primitivism." A look at the "Language Poets" may illustrate some of the problems involved.

One intellectual movement at this time could perhaps withdraw some of the stress on "counterculture orality" and put it back into the good old anal-retentive "written/writerly": the neo-structuralist, neo-phenomenological, neo-Marxist, neo-Freudian movements in France of the sixties and seventies. Unfortunately, an obsessive devotion to the sacred "*écriture*" has gone to an opposite extreme. Devotion to the great god Mallarmé has taken much of French poetry so far in its refusal of the oral and the colloquial that, to all intents and purposes, it may have sunk itself into the ground, roughly since the end of Surrealism down to the present day.

Now, a major pastime of twentieth-century culture is the domestication of French thought, especially by the Anglo-Saxons. In anthropology, for instance, Durkheim is "tamed" by a Radcliffe-Brown, Lévi-Strauss by an Edmund Leach. As for us, we now have, in these States, a movement (network? scene?) of poets variously denominated as "Language": "Language-centered" or "Language-oriented" (or, to use individual tags, "paratactic" [Bromige], "perceiver-centered" [Mac Low], etc.). These poets appear to be arguing the death of the "academic" versus "New

27 Jerome Rothenberg, "Keeping It Old: A Review of the New New American Poetry," *Sulfur* 6 (1983): 181–90. See also Jerome Rothenberg and Diane Rothenberg, *Symposium of the Whole* (Berkeley: University of California Press, 1983); and Jerome Rothenberg, *Technicians of the Sacred,* rev. ed. (Berkeley: University of California Press, 1983).

American" controversy, to be replaced by decentralization of poetic activity in the U.S.; an end to sexism; dispersion of poetic production/consumption among various "audience communities"; and the like. There is no doubt that the critical works of Charles Bernstein, Ron Silliman, Barrett Watten, Bruce Andrews, Bob Perelman, and others provide the most sustained articulation of problems in poetics since the twenties and thirties and do show up the *relative* lack of such articulations in the New Americans and their successors.

For my part, I welcome the stress on mind, on intellect, as a cardinal determinant of poetry-making and as an attack on our culture's pervasive anti-intellectualism. I welcome sophisticated forms of "market analysis" as one who has always believed that we badly need a down-to-earth sociology of readership, listenership, and aesthetic consumption. I welcome the politicization of poetics even if I find the Marxism of some of these writers derivative at times and smacking of the twenties and thirties rather than of our own time, and their anthropology antediluvian. I agree with decentralization (although it would seem to me more urgent to address the perennial problem of metropolitan riches versus provincial pauperism in culture), desexism (if that is the word), and the identification and legitimation of audience-communities—even if I do not believe that this will change the overall power structure or validate Silliman's attacks on the "New Americans" for the crime of "commodity fetishism." The poetry community—*pace* our dearest fantasies—is simply too *small;* the movement's books will fall prey to the same "fetishism" sooner rather than later.[28]

My problem, *pace* most "Language" poets of course, is that the theory informing much of the experimentalism of this vigorous movement—as in the case of so many "avant-garde" projects—is almost invariably more interesting than the products: we *do* live, after all, in an age of *conceptual* art. Some of my dissatisfactions are related to the participation of these poets in the "postmodernist" venture and

---

28 An initial formulation of this argument was based on Ron Silliman, "Realism," *Ironwood* 20, no. 10 (1983): 61–121. Note, in passing, that Silliman's identification of feminist culture as *the* major reason for change is challenged, in the final piece of Silliman's *Ironwood* mini-anthology, by Kathleen Fraser identifying the movement as still male-dominated! Among the critical works mentioned, see Bruce Andrews and Charles Bernstein, eds., *The L = A = N = G = U = A = G = E Book* (Carbondale: Southern Illinois University Press, 1984); Charles Bernstein, *Content's Dream* (Los Angeles: Sun & Moon Press, 1986); Bob Perelman, ed., *Writing/Talks* (Carbondale: Southern Illinois University Press, 1985); Ron Silliman, *The New Sentence* (New York: Roof Books, 1987); and Barrett Watten, *Total Syntax* (Carbondale: Southern Illinois University Press, 1984). With reference to feminism, but by no means *only*, Susan Howe's *My Emily Dickinson* (Berkeley: North Atlantic Books, 1985) may be the "Language" community's most influential book of all as well as its finest. On the issue of Marxism, see the correspondence between Jackson Mac Low and Ron Silliman in *L = A = N = G = U = A = G = E,* no. 8 (June 1979) and no. 9/10 (October 1979).

in various manifestations of "deconstruction." Whatever the claims made by these poets, their participation in hegemonic writing as well as the reduction of much of their work to various degrees of manneristic non-, para-, or modified-referentiality (under the touching illusion that this can actually work as a tool against capitalism: is this our ultimate American self-stupefaction?) *also* continue to produce an over-hermeticized poetry which can only be consumed by an elite, usually composed of other such poets.

To the extent that it is heavily influenced by formalism of all stripes, heavily over-intellectualized in its procedures and results, and very close in its bibliographies and lists of recommended readings to the "post-critical" academy, it seems only a matter of time before these poets find themselves in the university, co-opted by its exegetical systems (or, at best, co-opting them)—systems which, like jargons, exist to protect entrance into and performance within a closed universe. How is their revolutionary stance to survive such co-optation? I have here, of course, broadened my definition of "hermeticism" to encompass what I have called "incestuous" procedures in contemporary poetry.[29]

One thing is certain: at the time of writing, the debate is by no means over. The "Language" community of poets may be right in arguing that their quarrels with some of the heirs of the "New Americans" arise not so much out of enmity as out of jealousies provoked by the latter's failing to formulate a poetics of their own.[30] The fact remains that it is still the "New Americans," older or younger, who are the logical sparring-partners of the "Language" poets—both, considered together, are the only alternative to the rampant "gutted modernism," or anti-modernism, of the writing schools, and it is to be hoped that new solutions can arise out of their dialectical interaction.[31]

Some final remarks on "primitivism." If "Ethnopoetics," among other aspects of the "postmodernist" moment, were to have led to a host of relatively under-equipped individuals ripping off traditional knowledge and serving it up to the uninitiated *in competition with* individuals from the "tribal and archaic" world, transplanted or *in situ,* we would not have reason for too much pride. We should ask ourselves whether the symbol of this process is not perhaps the "Yaqui" Don

---

29   See my response to the question "Is There, Currently, an American Poetry?" in "Is There, Currently, an American Poetry? A Symposium," *American Poetry* 4, no. 2 (Winter 1987): 31–34; and Nathaniel Tarn, "Conversation," in *Talking Poetry: Conversations in the Workshop with Contemporary Poets,* ed. Lee Bartlett (Albuquerque: University of New Mexico Press, 1987), 210–26.

30   Ron Silliman, talk at the M.L.A. Convention, 1987. Published as Ron Silliman, "Negative Solidarity: Revisionism and 'New American' Poetry," *Sulfur* 22 (Spring 1988): 169–76.

31   I am working on further papers about this issue. See also my letter in *American Book Review,* tenth anniversary issue.

Juan, the genius of his author being the negative one of forbidding us to know whether this Don exists or not in any sphere that we can still ascribe to the real. And if we do not ask this, the "tribal and archaic" peoples, transforming themselves right now into a very vocal Third World, will ask it for us. I only need quote part of a poem by Wendy Rose to make the point. She says,

> You think of us only
> when your voice
> wants for roots,
> when you have sat back
> on your heels and become primitive
>
> You finish your poem
> and go back.[32]

"Form," we have been taught to believe, "is an extension of content." I am raising the question of whether the question matters: WHOSE CONTENT? However many truisms may be involved, it seems necessary to deal with it if "Ethnopoetics" is to move forward.

The problem is surely this. If, at the time when Mr. Hyde was being invaded by Dr. Jekyll, he felt that the thrust of anthropology and that of poetry were near identical, it may have been because the thrusts were both toward the as yet unknown, the other, the exciting, the new. This thrust toward *the other* is constitutive of the human condition; it is the way in which the organism keeps moving in the world, grows, overcomes conflict if possible, and avoids stasis. There is no way we can keep going without this particular attraction to the exotic.

At the same time, it has been observed more than once that the more one's gaze fixes on the other, the more the other becomes a mirror in which one sees one's own reflection: the better s/he is known, the closer the other looks like the self. The human moves out toward what appears to be the non-human or superhuman and returns to the recognition of the generality of the human. This movement out as process from, and return to, structure, I have taken to be a guideline in poetics and found *both* to be absolutely necessary to completion. It may be time to recognize that there has been an overemphasis on process for too long and that we need to return from an *and/or* position to one in which we can freely say *both/and.*

The care that must be exercised in "Ethnopoetics" has to do with the misunderstandings which can arise on the part of what anthropologists would call *ego:* when

---

32 Wendy Rose, "For the White Poets Who Would Be Indian" in her *Lost Copper* (Banning, CA: Malki Museum Press, 1980).

desire for the other and insistence on his or her exoticism overwhelm the other from his/her *own* point of view. If the other, as ego, or anything belonging to his/her structure is *appropriated,* the other is harmed, wounded, exploited, and undermined by the act and must retaliate. Likewise, if the other as ego moves toward us, taking *us* as the other, we shall feel, according to the manner of it, used and appropriated. The realities of power in the world being what they are (think, for instance, of Mesoamerindians being photographed in a market by (a) professional photographers, (b) tourists, (c) Mestizo fellow-citizens, and (d) their own kind), some are going to feel appropriated more than others, and that for a very long time to come.

In this respect, the situation is similar to that of all poetries in which one side (a minority) has been unjustly treated for too long. Similar to all human relations of any sort when love is capable of being met with hate if it overwhelms the object of its attentions. Until everyone has his or her own satisfaction, this danger will continue. It seems worth stressing when "Ethnopoetics" appears to be moving out toward an ever more inclusive viewpoint, an ever more totalizing vision of its role, even though, paradoxically, "Ethnopoetics" is one of the strongest components of an answer to the "Language" community's sense that there are no "New American" poetics. Nothing will replace breaking down the segregations; nothing will replace true universalism; nothing will be more rewarding than struggling with the *one world.* On the other hand, to forbid ourselves being other to ego, or ego to other, deters any flowering whatsoever on the part of that world. This contradiction too remains stubborn.

I have written at length on the "ego" or "self" as a relatively superficial phenomenon in the area of self–other reciprocity in normal literary intercourse ("*the Vocal*") and its undermining by self–self reciprocity in "*the Silence*" and by non-reciprocity in "*the Choral.*" This is another way of dealing with the problems approached here, and one which may, I feel, provide one possible path out of the impasse.[33]

A final example to illustrate the extent to which our unconscious can go when it is unaware of how sharp the razor's edge can be between genuine love and appropriation: at a recent meeting convened by an anthropologist in New York—a meeting to bring together anthropologists who were, or had discovered themselves to be, poets—I heard one of the panel members suddenly declare that our poetry had "benefited from an immense *blood transfusion*" out of the poetries of the "tribal and archaic" worlds. I asked him in horror how he could bear to use such words when so many human beings were being bled, in the flesh—in Brazil, in Guatemala, in South Africa, in Indonesia; bled for their lands, their forests, their lakes, their seas—

33 See "The Choral Voice" and later papers in this volume.

so that we might continue to live in the style to which we had become accustomed. Bled, because the truth of it is, alas, that, *whatever* the color of the political stripe involved, the "tribal and archaic" world is to be eradicated in our time: politically right or left, the strong want the land. He became extremely irate and refused to look upon the possibility that we might be bleeding such people in more senses than one, or that such a lack of attention had manifested itself in his words.

But, then, everyone is irate at Mr. Hyde. His author created him forever as a nasty piece of work. As Rimbaud, the future African, declared, "*Il faut être absolument maudit.*" I'm sorry. I meant to say, "*Il faut être absolument moderne.*"

V

Another label requires examination in this context.

From the vantage point of the dull seventies and even duller eighties (our decadent decadic periodizations!), the "counterculture" of the sixties was a heroic epoch. It has left an enduring, often beautiful, often courageous mark on our material and spiritual cultures. Yet, the very ease and abruptness with which we passed from those sixties to the present decades show that its urge to make everything new and to give up all past solutions and panaceas was such, when allied to its ignorance of, and frequent contempt for, history, as to make it resign any hopes it may have had for social effectiveness and continuity.

With all its merits, the counterculture could not, of and by itself, replace twenty centuries of human culture, organized, codified, and systematically handed down from one generation to another. While I am at the furthest remove from being a defender of the academy in its present form, academics know that the "counterculture" may well have damaged education so irreparably that much of the academy will have to be completely destroyed as it stands in order to survive at all in a reconstructed mode. In the end, the "counterculture" made America in many ways a better and more diversified place to live in. What it has *not* done is to ensure that American political hegemony cease and desist from devouring much of the earth. It seems paradoxical to say that, one day, America-in-Vietnam (or America-in-Nicaragua) and America-at-home, shopping for, trading, buying, ever acquiring *gurus* of every persuasion from every corner of the earth, from past, present, and even future, may be two facets of one single process. And yet I am not sure that we shall not reach this point.

It is this which seems to be so rarely considered: the *political* coincidence in time of American cultural hegemony and of appropriative techniques in the arts.

This, perhaps, is my main doubt about the future: how we issue from this phase into something which is ever more our own but does not act and survive so largely by the appropriation of what belongs to others.

As one of the relaxing forces at work in our overall culture, the "counterculture" (others are the spread of general, and much diluted, "education"; the media; and the ease with which we travel, communicate, and so forth) would appear, in its ferocious over-valuation of ego, to have abandoned that which, in collage, is witness to an interest in the other. I wonder if this is the case. Where collage enters here, I believe, though now at an unconscious and irresponsible level, is in the all-pervading ahistoricity of people content to write the same poetry over and over again because *they do not know or care* that it has been written before.

Pound's injunction to make it new has vanished in an unparalleled drive toward a pluralism in poetic operations so extensive that the very possibility of any standard of judgment whatsoever seems to have been eliminated from the field. What happens here, of course, is that you are quoting "history" despite yourself: what you ignore you are condemned, as the tag goes, to repeat. When every schoolchild can have, if s/he wishes, a poet's baton in his/her backpack; when, in relation to the market there is for the stuff, naturally, we are overproducing poetry to a previously unknown extent, how do we respond to the craft's immemorial respect for, and evocation of, order? It no longer seems possible, and in this shipwreck some might read the death of the art.[34]

(A parenthesis here in an effort to stem over-generalization by labeling. I have already distinguished between master-"hermeticists" in whom esotericism is constitutive from the *guru*-hunters and jargon-wielders of the entrepreneurial fringes. It is also necessary to tell apart a trained anthropologist from a fantasist who reads outer space into every archaic ruin. The closer you are to "primitivism," the easier, presumably, confusion is likely to arise. What appears to have happened to the "counterculture" is that it has jettisoned whatever political acumen events had taught it and placed all its eggs into one of its baskets: the realm of "spirituality." At this point, the "counterculture" may be transforming itself into the apolitical and frequently vatic-vacuous "new age," characterized, it seems, on most of its fronts, by a more insidious anti-intellectualism and anti-historicism than anything we've seen before. I tend to call it "newage," and it rhymes.

Obviously, again, not all "spirituality" is of this ilk. It does, however, get harder to tell day by day what is hidebound, insipid, and often poisonous fundamentalism;

---

34   See Nathaniel Tarn, "Open Letter Regarding a Proposal for an Order of Silence," in Tarn, *Views from the Weaving Mountain.*

what is just as insipid, if not quite as harmful, "newage"; and what is genuine exploration, on a cross-cultural basis, of the ways in which "spirit" might be kept alive and evolving. A reasonably healthy relativism in attitudes toward belief having more and more given way to a panic fear of any kind of judgmentalism whatsoever on the part of non-fundamentalists, we abide in ever more difficult circumstances in this realm also.)

On the other hand, I have often been told—and I have told myself—that this is far too pessimistic a view. Also that it is totally wrong-headed. It may be that I truly do not understand the nature of "democracy" and totally fail to grasp the implications of general literacy (if indeed "literacy" it is!) for the arts in general and poetry in particular. This is what Williams appears to have been hinting at in linking his struggle to establish an American literature in the world with American poetry's "seeking a new adjustment to a new world—perhaps its final fruition depend(ing) on the entire social-democratic survival or collapse."[35]

Whether this type of democracy will survive or collapse, however, is precisely what is being widely discussed beyond the borders of our poetry world. Despite all possible sympathy with Williams, questions remain as to *what* language (when so much language has become debased among the media and in public life?), *what* people (when it is so hard to identify a "people" now among the homogenized, consumerized mass—the "American People" so dear to the politico's heart?), *what* democracy (when we have such an abyssal record of supporting so much non-democracy the moment we get out of our borders?).

It is here, of course, that the "Language" poets are of importance: in their stress on the signifier against commercialized devaluation; in their political stances, no matter how "utopian"; in their historicism; in their interest in other efforts similar to their own across community boundaries (thus defusing the isolationism inherent in the notion of "community"), they provide an antidote to the worst of "counterculture" laissez-faire, much of which has now rallied under the twin banners of consumerism and "newage."

To draw toward an end with this. On the theme of collage, I have sometimes fantasized about what would happen if, one day, we were constrained to return to our own words: the words only we can invent, to which we have acquired a right by hard work. Or rather, combinations of words I suppose. It may be that thousands would heave sighs of relief. The Japanese, Indians, and Chinese; the Hopi and Navajo; the Chicanos and the Puerto Ricans; the Black musicians and the Polish Jews in our own land might heave sighs of relief. Our own ancestors and

35 William Carlos Williams, "Studiously Unprepared," 34.

our dead father-and-mother poets might heave sighs of relief in their graves. What would be left of "America" when "Americans" had reconquered it?

A fantasy indeed, insofar as such a thing would have to be NOTICED! Insofar too as words have immensely long pasts.

In this situation, as a woman Asian-American poet and a woman Anglo-American poet once pointed out to me, my own experience of racism might seem to be a very mild one. Racism: labeling an individual as X or Y, pinning her/him down there, irrespective of her/his efforts and moves in any direction whatsoever. "British poet and will always remain so" is a form of racism. As the women said, almost *anything* this country has to offer might well be worse.

But is it not a woman who remains one of the most successful Britannic transplants in American letters? Ah, but Denise Levertov reached these shores, I believe, much earlier in life!

VI

Instead of trying at all costs to achieve the "American," I believe we could live up to one aspect of our original mission by extending the rules of our own melting pot to the rest of the world: I mean the *original* rules. It does not seem to me that there is any real alternative to universalism, not once the planet has been SEEN from the outside. In this respect, "Atlantean" poets like James, Pound, Conrad, Eliot, MacDiarmid, Auden, and Levertov in "English" (but also Celan and Rilke, or Césaire and Senghor, and many other examples) could be studied in the effort to find out whether poetry could survive or not beyond national "genetics." We could honor men like Kenneth Rexroth, our most universalist master and, perhaps, our most neglected.[36] It may be, of course, that if we go too far beyond the national word, especially with our computers, our art, perhaps all arts as we know them, will cease and desist.[37] But I have not yet given up the ghost in that direction.

Short of treating the contradictions as hideous instead of beautiful, I cannot, for myself, but take a both/and attitude to most of the diversifications I have outlined here, rather than an either/or one. It does not seem possible to me, in this complex time, for a poet to fulfill her/himself without that extreme attention to language and the craft for which, for better or for worse, elite-addressed poetry is responsible. At the same time, the craft is mocked if it cannot also produce, perhaps

36   See Eliot Weinberger, "Kenneth Rexroth 1905–1982," *Sulfur* 5 (1982): 4–6.
37   See Claude Lévi-Strauss, in Georges Charbonnier, *Conversations with Claude Lévi-Strauss,* Cape Editions no. 32 (London: Jonathan Cape, 1969).

in one framework, perhaps in a variety of address, something available to what is left of the "general reader."

I have tried to stress the perils both of "hermeticism" in which our everlasting struggle for communication is often short-circuited and negated, as well as of "primitivism" with its promiscuous welcome to so much in the universe that any particular thing risks losing its uniqueness. I have also tried to look at what some are seeing as the undoing of the American mind in various forms of absent- or vacant-mindedness. I hope it is possible to go on from there, but that must be in the poetry it is given to me to make—if I am not rendered extinct by the haphazardness of the state of publishing today, surely as uninformed, confused, and disastrous as any we have ever known.

To return to my initial point about English English and American English, Williams believed that the element of *change* within the former was the fertile one that Americans should follow. England had lost it: its poetry did not *use* the possibilities for change inherent in the language as it once had done in the past. True or not, England becomes for Williams the stability/security pole (so attractive to nostalgic Americans hankering after the comforts of the Old World). The desire for security has to be resisted in order to face and deal with the NEW. To do that, the "very bone of English poems," the fixed foot, would have to be sparagmatized.

The English father who refused to become an American citizen is a knot in Williams's being. His love for his father and his despair at his father's not choosing the new are a vortex of contention and conflict, often evoked when Williams discusses the two languages and their poets. Then, note what happens. Pound is saved first from among those who have strayed abroad as the first poet to write in the American idiom. Eliot becomes the great enemy. At a later date, Williams perceives that Eliot's childhood maintains him in his Americanicity, while Auden's keeps him English. Eliot climbs toward an absolution, raised to the company of Pound, and Auden now bears the brunt of Williams's distaste.[38] And, later still, Williams and his idiom gain some measure of recognition. In some sense, Williams displaces the father and becomes a father himself. Around 1960, he is interviewed by William Sutton about Denise Levertov's "closeness [to him] in her way of writing":

> W.C.W.: Oh, yes, very close. . . . She is from England. But she came to this country to seek a freer relationship to the line in our country, and she has adapted herself completely to our way of listening. She is a very interesting person to me. And she is a very skillful poet. She is half Welsh and half Jewish. That's a curious

---

38 William Carlos Williams, "The Poem as a Field of Action," in Williams, *Selected Essays*, 287–89.

thing and must have its influence on the writing of her poetry. But she has
rebelled from England and come to a freer place. Free construction of the line
and has done very well at it. . . .

I feel closer to her than to any of the modern poets.[39]

Astonishingly, Williams has acquired a daughter and she is British (not quite
English, note: Jewish and Celt)! The American idiom now has a daughter and the
daughter comes from the Old World. The maturity of the "American Branch" has
been established.

Williams eventually acknowledges that the American idiom has become
hegemonic:

Next we must establish in our minds the historical fact that the American
Language invaded both English and French in the nineteenth century. . . .

The invasion, the modification of Yeats's corpus by the direct criticism of Ezra
Pound, Joyce (who never failed to read his Paris edition of the *Herald-Tribune* lest
he miss the sayings of Andy Gump), Gertrude Stein, Hemingway, etc., etc. The
thing to bear in mind is that it is the American language penetrating the European literary modes which should be studied.[40]

And, in his description of Stieglitz, he recognizes the necessity for both branches:
the "local effort" and "the forces from the outside":

Stieglitz inaugurated an era based solidly on a correct understanding of the
cultural relationships; but the difficulties he encountered both from within and
without were colossal. He fought them clear-sightedly.

The effect of his life and work has been to bend together and fuse, against
whatever resistance, the split forces of the two necessary cultural groups: (1) the
local effort, well understood in defined detail and (2) the forces from the
outside.[41]

Perhaps there is still some hope that I can yet come home and be at home *here
in America* . . . and all may be forgiven!

1984

---

39 William Carlos Williams, *Interviews with William Carlos Williams* (New York: New Directions,
    1976), 40.
40 Ibid., 60.
41 William Carlos Williams, "The American Background," in Williams, *Selected Essays*, 160–61.

Section Two
Auto-Anthropology

André Breton, Anthropology, and the Limits of Culture

Sitting in an old farm among the Black Mountains of Wales, facing wild hillsides on which André Breton, had he ever reached these parts, might have found arcana kin to those he loved the most, I shall try to send him a brief and naive word of celebration. These Celtic marches have given twentieth-century Britain its greatest poets, the only ones capable of rivalry with the Americans Eliot and Pound: Yeats of Ireland; Mac-Diarmid of Scotland; the Welsh bard himself, Dylan Thomas. England herself, a few miles from here in Herefordshire, seems to belong to a different world.

I am remembering another Celtic country, the north of Cornwall where his school had been evacuated during the war, and a young boy of fifteen or sixteen reading Breton, Eluard, Aragon, Desnos, Crevel, and all those legendary masters he believed dead. In that vast prison which Europe had become (this authoritarian school sometimes seemed to be an infinitely distant and unworthy mirror of that prison)—how could he have believed, this schoolboy, that those who had done so much against the sclerosis of the mind, of beauty, of poetry had not entered, live as

---

Some time after publishing this piece in French, I received a grant from the National Translation Center, Austin, Texas, to translate *L'amour fou,* and was also planning to include Breton's poems in my London Cape Editions series. Gallimard, on the basis of this piece, was instructed by Breton's successors to forbid these endeavors.

certain prophets had, into Legend? And it is on that very coast, whose natives drew shipwrecks to them until shamefully recent dates, that our schoolboy had one day stood astonished at the sight of an immense ghost fleet: the liberation fleet on the way to France which he would have to see again in order to continue living.

That debt, which I believed I owed to André Breton, ironically caused me to attempt repayment precisely at the moment he left his retirement village to return to death in Paris. I was traveling in the Loire Valley with a copy of the *Poèmes*, some of which I wished to translate and discuss with him. I also hoped to get him to in-scribe the book. A travel accident prevented me from even trying for that meeting: in any case it was already too late. Alas, it is *never* possible to say everything to a father and never possible to take one's leave of him.

André Breton always surprised me when he maintained that he did not under-stand English, and I remember smiling again and again when he would, at the *café* sessions, pretend to be shocked by the Cokes which his daughter insisted on or-dering. Did he feel that, in spite of certain appearances, England was not only a country as "reasonable" as France but also one where it was difficult to defend any super-reason whatsoever using the means provided by reason? Are the surrealists not striking to an Anglophone because of their use of enemy weapons: one of the things which makes Breton into one of the greatest of French prose writers being his argumentative logic, lucid and serious, and the programmatic mastery which characterizes his theoretical writings?[1] Now, it seems to be very difficult for the British "national character" to tolerate the defense of the unreal, the para-real or the sur-real by means of the methods used to define and delimit consensual real-ity. The British tradition, not the only but the dominant one, of empiricism and positivism scarcely seems to favor the development of a programmatic surrealism. How many times here do we do scarcely more than domesticate the audacities of Continental thinking! Are we saying that the French surrealists would only be coming to Albion as the anthropologist comes to the "primitives" in order to find a naive or primitive surrealism—to find illustrations rather than interlocutors? The part played by madness, alienation, childhood among the British ancestor-surrealists certainly seems to suggest it.

~

I shall not be so modest as to claim that we in Britain are the only ones who are behindhand in regard to the cultures of other countries: I know only too well, for

---

1   I fail to understand certain Anglo-Saxon critics, like J. K. Matthews for example, who declare that one must never look in Breton for sequential arguments since only passion and intuition regulate his discourse.

example, the extent to which contemporary British poetry is unknown to French audiences.[2] It is still true, alas, that we are terribly lacking here in any systematic intellectual contextualization of literature and the arts. We should therefore never limit the number of occasions on which we tell people here that the confrontation between Marxism and Surrealism in the first part of the twentieth century is (Faculty of Arts and Humanities, needless to say!) the most important cultural phenomenon of our time. This confrontation, in its turn, will have to be studied in the even larger context of the totality of present culture: i.e., a culture dominated by a scientific worldview. Would it be an injustice to say that we would then touch on an important facet of the problem by considering the surrealist movement as a last move of Romanticism face-to-face with science and that Marxism could then be seen as taking on the job of the social control of applied science, whereas Surrealism would be assuming the responsibility for the social control of theoretical science? Far too naive a vision of the problem without a doubt—and yet one which may bring up some questions which we would not be unwilling to look into.

In this perspective we could see the surrealist movement as looking to push back the limits of the possible, in a world prematurely *closed* and disappointed at the ruin of nineteenth-century optimism, by keeping open to the fullest extent feasible the vision of a total liberty of the mind. Proposed political solutions to the problem, in too many cases, soon came to insult the individual to an unimaginable degree, and it is too early to say that this situation is behind us. And theoretical science? It has seemed to me on many occasions that poets have too mechanistic a view of this science, one almost entirely out of date, due no doubt to the ever-widening gap between men of science and poets imposed on us all by a culture in a state of vertiginous acceleration. Surrealism, then, imagining that concepts can be expressed in particular classifications of recognizable objects, related among themselves by recognizable ties, would never have succeeded in going beyond an effort to modify these classifications by making the links and ties, the *relations,* less recognizable. The problem of absolute originality was not resolved by this process. Were there not, in any case, *other closures?* If Surrealism had not recoiled face-to-face with Freud (on the contrary!) and Marx, had it not finally come to a stop when faced with Durkheim, Mauss, and Lévi-Strauss? What, indeed, had anthropology done with the "other" and the "elsewhere"?

2 It need hardly be said at the time of translating this into English (1987) that, had I been looking at the problem from an American perspective, the view would have been mercifully different. The presence of so many surrealists in the United States during World War II was a great catalyst.

Deprived by his international status of absolute originality in any domain, deprived even, through his knowledge of all cultures and the general pardon that this knowledge implies, of the possibility of looking after his own garden in peace—where will modern man go to look for that "other" which is perpetually hiding? Or that "self" which is nothing but the mask the "other" takes off when, along the length of the *Tristes Tropiques,* his face appears after all in its own likeness which is *so* similar to our own? It seems, to be sure, that this modern man must become passive, listless, lazy, must renounce both action and the analysis of action, must even renounce artistic creation itself. Hardly reassuring, this social pudding, this rather formless mass of cultural traits, this *ersatz* man, choosing here and there, as long as they still survive, a few habits, hardly more than a few tics, among exotic populations so as to fill the sad void brought about by too many knowledges and too many conjugated solitudes! What will we have left in a *one* world, a *one* culture, a universe rushing it would seem toward *choicelessness*—and this despite the fake choicefulness of products in late Capitalism?

As Lévi-Strauss realized, we will retain the prodigious wealth of our own archives, of history itself such as we have conceived it, another anthropology if you will, other voyages: in time rather than in space. That history, even if we have to go back to the Neolithic, offers us situations, alternatives still possible perhaps and conforming more to basic human needs than those offered by the hypercephalous societies in which we suffer today. We also have that presentiment of the long narrative of the earth, of those silent societies—plants, fish, birds, animals that came before us on earth and could well remain after us. We have, in these landscapes, a knowledge never sufficiently profound of the natural world's structures capable of taking us toward a figurative art newly conceived, a new wisdom, another humanism based no longer on human supremacy but on a true and just appreciation of man's position here vis-à-vis all other living beings.

We also retain the possibility of another conception of what our relation to ourselves might be. Modern man, deprived of all his quests and of all his travels, finds himself obliged to look for the "other" and the "elsewhere" in nothing but himself. This duty frightens us: the surrealist movement understood this but at the most critical, most weary phase of its career. Had the notion of occultation, announced with such mastery in *Arcane 17,* been truly understood and postulated with the rigor as well as the freshness characteristic of the first surrealist revolution, the movement would have given to the second half of the twentieth century, but with still more nobility and depth than the first had done, a springboard, an enthusiasm, a responsibility, a *path.* Disappointed by politics, bothered by certain recent developments in psychology, the movement, confronted with the frightening *absence* of originality in all things postulated by anthropology, fell headlong into what one can only call a *magicism* as banal as it was sterile since it had suffered the most tragic defeat: that of no longer being in relation with the genuine sur-real. What a beautiful platform to lose!

Was it really in transforming relations between things apparently well-known that one was to discover a new reality? For sure, if one is looking—like Michel Carrouges for instance in his fine work *Les Machines Célibataires*—to the structures of certain modern myths. But we are dealing with more than that. In spite of the poetic majesty of the "beautiful *as*" of the surrealists, implying, as Octavio Paz pointed out recently, a prophetic understanding of one of the two fundamental aspects of language according to contemporary linguistics, it still seems to me that the movement has forgotten something essential. It has forgotten that things as they are must remain *unknown* on this side of a total revolution in the human spirit against the very notion of *reciprocity*. As long as we are dealing with relationships—on the social plane as on any other—we only have a closed circle inside which the understanding we believe ourselves to have regarding things tempts us like quicksand. Most of our contemporaries will say that nothing exists outside such relationships. It is not difficult to live with that.

But he who becomes what he observes and is become by what he observes no longer finds himself on the plane of reciprocity. And this, I believe, was understood by Breton. In that place where the individual and the collective cease to be contradictory and where the most tenacious liberty of the poet's voice detaches itself from silence and falls back into silence—as do the beings of our earthly domain, ourselves included—we shall accept the price this earth requires of us still, this earth we seem determined to bring down about our ears so that it blots us out and destroys us altogether.[3] He who destroys his own home—is he not the maddest among all madmen?

~

So it is here perhaps that Romanticism of nature and psychologism of mind and spirit can come together. Breton, the poet of genius I honor here, saw, both in *Arcane 17* and in his *Ode à Charles Fourier*, the true reach of Utopia, the great responsibility at the heart of *le gai savoir*. The good is incapable of not conjugating

3 It seems strange to me that Claude Lévi-Strauss, in his brilliant comments on issues I have only been able to deal with naively here, seems to forget, in discussing the revolutions of Impressionism and Cubism and their relations to the problem of individuation in artistic production, that the *surrealists* had at least expressed the hope that art should be made *by all*. The reference is, I believe, in his *Entretiens* with Georges Charbonnier.

and being conjugated with the good—but the drama which tears us apart today, that of facing up to human social problems without losing ourselves, is a difficult and wrenching drama whose solutions are nowhere open to a single simple life. Breton lived the drama with very great nobility: the most living light will lead him to relive it again.

As a poet, I offer to him who for me is not a past but a future these hills, these metamorphoses of light, these humble jewels made of moss and lichen flaunting the colors of his beloved Quetzalcoatl, these grave winds traversing the larches, and this hawk, queen of the valley, who is once again flying her lengthy spiral toward the zenith. And this silence, where the great faces of the earth are dreaming, which his face receives and gives back, in perpetuity.

1967

Newly Saying the Already Said

An Attached Comment in Honor of Keiji Nishitani

1) An "attached comment," I read in Nishitani, is a "pithy comment attached to the utterances of Zen masters or to passages from sūtras, meant to express in a free manner one's own appreciative interpretation." As neither theologian, nor philosopher, nor scientist, I am astonished as well as stunned by this immense spiral staircase thrown over the void. I apprehend, if only dimly, the immeasurable importance of *Religion & Nothingness* but I despair of ever beginning to do it justice. I can see that by engaging with the language of the West, it brings about a situation in which we here no longer have the slightest excuse to avoid consideration of the serene majesty of 2,500 years of Eastern philosophy, aka Buddhism. Each in our own way, we must wrestle with it. This "attached comment" then bears the subscription: written by the lowest, youngest, and most ignorant of all possible listeners in homage to a master.

At first sight, I tell myself, this book seems to be made of words. Perhaps I was asked to talk, I continue, because my vocation is to deal with words—but I am aware that the poet's vocation in our culture is a residual one and no longer as

---

This lecture was given at the Amherst and Smith Colleges conference on Nishitani's *Religion and Nothingness*, April 1984.

highly prized as it once was. Now the way a poet deals with words is s/he takes them after everyone else has finished with them, when all the *use* has been gotten out of them, by theologians, philosophers, scientists, and so forth, and s/he makes them into his/her toys. Perhaps s/he has the hope that, used by so many now, words may have recovered a sort of renewed innocence. They are playthings now, toys if you will, to be used for their own sake, without any utilitarian motive whatsoever. The poet seems to be less of a hero than a fool because s/he tries to do something valuable with words when all the value has been drawn out of them, when they are at their most reduced and reductive. But it has been my habit to think of reality this way: as what is left after everyone else has had his ploy and his play and has gone home for the day. Then the poets, like ants or termites, worry at words in the dark. In the preface to *Lyrical Ballads*, Wordsworth, still writing early enough in the nineteenth century to retain some optimism about the brave and complex new world evolving all around him, presented the poet as the most *available* human being, available to what is important to us all when we have done being theologians, philosophers, or scientists and are simply human creatures. This may be our leave to take poetic play as representative of all "construction of reality" at its most disinterested—if disinterest is still a possibility in this fallen world. The being-at-doing so graphically described by Nishitani is most purely and most unarguably the poet moving from verse to verse and from poem to poem. Thus I console myself.

Poets worrying at words in the dark. It had always seemed to me that words, when traced to their uttermost origins, had to be accepted as arising out of an unspeakably mysterious depth to which I ascribed apparently negative characteristics: darkness, incommunicability, silence, death. Or I would call the depth "The Great Silence." The most interesting characteristic of the mystery was that the more deeply and unimpededly one listened to the voice welling up from this primordial silence, the more this voice appeared to exhibit general characteristics, the more it *appeared* to be the collective human voice rather than the individual voice of the poet. But this was a matter of trust or faith. I could do nothing to explain the conviction that, blessedly, something beyond one's insignificant subjectivity could be called into being in our vocation of listening to the voice while staying at home and playing, with nothing in particular to do.

2) Now, put in its simplest and most innocent form, the way categories of opposition appear to be exploded in Nishitani is that, under whatever ground can be known and named, an underground opens up which is the real ground and subsumes all the apparent contradictions in previous formulations, resolving them by allowing them to live in deeper, more harmonious co-existence. I sense, while reading,

that wisdom may appear when *all* the grounds and undergrounds, even unto the "real ground," finally explode, but I cannot pretend to know the way home yet. So let me stay for a time with what now appears to me to subsume the unspeakably mysterious depth I had conceived of before.

I was asking before whether the ground of poetry does not seem to be silence, out of which mysteriously arises what appears to be an individual voice.

I ask now whether there may not be a deeper ground still and whether this ground may not be voice again but, this time, collectively.

Collective because it is the voice of all things, both human and non-human and even other than both human and non-human, as they truly are, as they undifferentiatedly are on their own home-ground of all grounds as we might now have license to say: the *void-voice* or universal *mantra* if you will.

I ask further, if we are to follow Nishitani, whether this *void-voice* is not also the noise of the world that we hear immediately around us, that noise to which we used to try to add our own poems in an effort to insert our art into the world of nature or give our art objects the status and authenticity of objects in nature.

In that case, however, we would have to question what the silence is from which our poems appeared to us previously to arise, whereas now they arise out of the *void-voice* once they have pierced this undercoating or underlayer of silence.

Perhaps the silence is the illusion we have that our poems come from some distant realm—some *far side,* as Nishitani might call it. Perhaps the silence is the illusion that we have something to do, tasks to perform, difficulties to overcome, when we write poems—since we appear to have to create some kind of noise out of a *nihilum* we call silence and that this seems to be hard work rather than the play I spoke of playfully before.

Perhaps the silence we appear to have to wrest the poem from is the illusion not only that the poem is being *wrested* from something but also that it is *we* who are wresting it.

Does this mean that this silence is intolerable? That the chains of this silence are intolerable? Yes, yes, it means that the chains of the poetic condition are intolerable. And that we are born free, free not to work but to play? Yes, free, and already here, with nowhere else to go. Nowhere to go. And I who had been thinking all my life that I had to run somewhere, to get to somewhere! Where is that *there* which has always been here? And, if it has always been *here,* how can it be a *where* or a *there*?

Likewise: I have been constantly impelled by the practice of poetry to produce something that appears to need to be said. It appears to be rising inside me out of some unfathomable silence in a hungry need to be said outside of me, to be placed out there, as if the answer could somehow survive the question! When it has come out, however, and stands out there, it always seems, to my impatient and vengeful ears and eyes, to be something that has already been said; that is, "*said*" in the sense in which I have used the expression "it is *here*" or "I am *here.*"

But to stay with the moment of saying a while longer: what I say, as I say it, never *seems* to be the already said but that which needs to be said. If it were not for that illusion at the moment of saying, I might be led, or misled, into giving up the attempt to say anything at all. If it were not for that illusion which arises out of the unfathomable silence whence that which has to be said appears to have to be wrested. Are these not the "chains" of the poetic condition: that we have to pass through the promise of saying what appears to need saying only to find before us the last year's harvest? Why can we not reach the already said immediately without all this suffering through saying?

In some sense, then, the "said" or "already said" seems to be an unattainable because we cannot attune ourselves to the idea that the poem has already been written before we began to write. And we might then ask: if the poem is already written, what use have I for myself and in what sense would it not be better for me to put an end to my life in poetry, to throw myself away and to die?

Now if years ago, without knowing what I was saying then, I put into print the view that "poetry is the religion of language," perhaps I can now ask not only "What is the purpose of religion for us? Why do we need it?" but also "What is the purpose of devotion to poetry? Why do we need it?" and humbly disagree with Nishitani only to this extent—that, on the first page of his book, he states, "learning and the arts . . . can be considered a kind of luxury."

3) If we follow Nishitani to the possibility of saying that, because there is a ground which is wider than time and space, the existence of time and space is grounded in that ground and the possibility of the uniqueness of every single thing truly exists, then perhaps we can ask a few more questions regarding the need to newly say the already said.

I have long thought that, from the point of view of production, we need at least three aesthetics: the aesthetic of the individual poem, the aesthetic of all the poems that any poet writes in his or her lifetime (the aesthetics of *opus*), and the aesthetic of all possible poems or possibilities of poetry (the aesthetics of *page* or *text*). The life of a poet is an interminable conversation with these three aesthetics, all conversing with each other at the same time as s/he is conversing with each in turn. It is this multi-stranded and multi-levelled conversation that gives the poet some illusion of operating within the widest available time-frame: that of her/his own each-and-every act in poetry, that of her/his life's work in poetry, and that of her/his life's work in poetry in relation to all other lives in poetry, past, present, and to come. In particular, it has seemed to me that the sense of *opus* has not been sufficiently attended to in the aesthetics of reception and that, properly looked into, it would yield clues to critics about a certain kind of *foreknowledge* frequently found in a poet's individual act in poetry. Things appear to happen as if the poet knew, well before a poem, that s/he would write that poem, or as if s/he knew that one poem would, perhaps much later, call another into being. Whence, also, the apparently mysterious experience of destroying certain lines or certain poems and finding them reappearing many years later in another context altogether—as if nothing could in fact be destroyed, as if time, for the poet, were an illusion that could be dispensed with. Talk current since the "death of God" that art is now our religion and the poet its priest often hinges on such apparently "prophetic" or "shamanistic" possibilities within a poet's experience.

Following Nishitani onto the greater grounds beneath all ground for whatever is ever said may allow us some insight into the question of how it appears that something needs to be said when, in fact, it always reveals itself when once said as the "already said." If the widest possible circle of Nishitani's ground of grounds contains within it the simultaneous arising and ceasing of everything and anything that is to be said, whether by the human voice or the voice of all other sentient and non-sentient beings (the rocks and trees that heard Orpheus and were heard by him as well as gods, demi-gods, heroes, ghosts, and animals), any act of true listening in the always-here cannot but catch echoes of what has been and what is to be as well as of what is. In particular, the manifesting of the voices of the dead has always been one of the deepest responsibilities of the poet, wherever the dead are or whatever they are on their way to. In the place where all things that have been, are, and are to be speak together, the poet's effort, always one to strain most purely against the illusion of primordial silence in the act of listening to the one, choral, voice, cannot but catch echoes of the true discourse behind the contradictory static set up by myriads of individual voices in the contentiousness of noising abroad the myriad selves. The difficulty of saying anything "new" in poetry arises out of the difficulty of conjugating what is said by the myriad selves with the harmony of the *void-voice,* of conjugating that which is said all around us with the one deep sound of the *world-mantra.* The miracle of exquisite balance, the guarantee that this has to be attempted, is that we are occasionally granted—perhaps once in a lifetime— the true poem, the poem which sounds and looks exactly right, the poem which is both new-born and immeasurably ancient, the masterpiece, which is both primally alive and plunges its roots into the realm of death. The masterpiece arises when the myriad voices and the one deep sound are heard as one identical voice and there is no difference between the clash of battle cries and the universal hymn of peace.

Religion & Nothingness is a masterpiece of almost overwhelming proportions built in the clearing where the human city is menaced as it has never been before by the clash of dissidence and nihilistic despair. The form which this crisis has taken in poetry bears the selfsame stamp of the Reign of Quantity as that which afflicts all other deep-sounding human activities. Today, in innumerable writing schools which affect to bypass the living of a life, every student carries in his/her backpack the baton of Emperor of the Poets and is more likely to try to use it than not. Apprenticeship is virtually dead; the market alone survives. The contenders enter the field with the greatest conceivable ease and begin at once sounding off their individual pipes and drums according to the latest mode in martial music. The fratricidal nature of the ensuing carnage, with individual liberties at their most naked, stark, and poignant, is blatantly visible to all, yet rarely alluded to. The contenders fight for the ears and eyes of a group of listeners which gets smaller and smaller by the year—our culture having reached the point where the only people who read, record, review, publish, and diffuse poetry are poets themselves; the general reader, gentle or not, being as extinct as the dodo. Quality is drowned by quantity and literally cannot find any foothold in the ever-narrowing world. Small world or not, this world of poets, and I have indicated that I hold no great illusions as to its present scope, faces a scandal of unbelievable proportions: one in which *everyone* wants to sing and *no one* wants to listen to the song: the will-to-will at its most abhorrent and grotesque.

And then we ask, "What is poetry? What is the purpose of poetry for us? Why do we need it?" And it seems that we only need it in order to shout louder ourselves in the evermore deafening clamor made by everybody else.

If this were not in the image of many other human enterprises of possibly deeper import, I would not have troubled you with mention of it.

4) I have tried to suggest that there is another way of viewing and going about our life if we are to avoid destroying poetry and our human universe. Nishitani has given us an awesome demonstration of the fact that "only on the field of emptiness does all this become possible. Unless the thoughts and deeds of man one and all be located on such a field, the sorts of problems that beset humanity have no chance of ever really being solved." We must learn the archetypal action of non-action, the non-coercive sourcing, the gentle, spiral circling of the adamantine hawk. We need patience, immeasurable patience, if we are to hear the sound of "that which is spread out under all the things of the world."

1984

Pablo Neruda and Indigenous Culture

To make some sense of this in only fifteen minutes, I'll concentrate on the first sections of *Canto General.* This was written on Neruda's return from the Spanish Civil War at the height of his commitment to the Communist Party of Chile. Personal, poetic, and political pressures conspire to structure a fascinating set of contradictions in Neruda's project. Looking at these from the point of view of Ethnopoetics may be suggestive and even useful for us now. I can group my hunches, and they are little more than that, under three paragraphs.

1) Neruda is Hispanic in culture, but the root of enablement he requires is Indian. I am far from being a Neruda scholar but in virtually nothing I have come across is Neruda's ethnographic environment looked at in any detail or with any precision. The Chilean scene is not as massively and obviously Indian as are Peru, Bolivia, and Ecuador (cf. in Mesoamerica: Chiapas, Yucatán, and Guatemalan Indians versus "Mestizo" or "White" El Salvador, Honduras, Costa Rica, etc.). Brand, around 1941, estimates the Central Chilean population at 10% Indian, 25% White, 65% Mestizo. In hard fact, most everyone is biologically mixed: "Indian"/"Non-Indian"

This was presented as a paper at the 1986 Conference on Latin American Literature held at Fort Lewis College, Durango, Colorado.

categories are mostly determined by cultural, political, and economic self-definition, as is the case, indeed, in Mesoamerica.

The Indians of Central Chile are the Araucanians who call themselves *che* (people); *re-che* (real people); or, now, using the name of one sub-group, *Mapu-che* (people of the land). Those of North Central Chile (Río Aconcagua—Río Bío Bío) were invaded by the Peruvian Inca around 1450 and Incanized. Around 1550, Spain replaces all of this. Neruda is born in Parral, inside this area.

But he is taken almost immediately to Temuco in South Central Chile (Río Bío Bío—Island of Chiloé). This is an area of extremely heavy rain forest, with wood as a major industry. The Araucanians here were extremely fierce and blocked both the Inca and the Spaniards for centuries. In 1877, they were finally placed on reservations. Reservation acculturation and politics have determined them ever since: a case which has drawn comparisons with our own Southwest. In sum, these people were fairly simple hunting, fishing, and gathering tribes with adaptation to Andean civilization in material culture and crafts, while social, political, and religious life remain close to early patterns (one example: the predominance of shamanism rather than an evolution of priestly castes on the Inca model).

In Temuco, Neruda could see Indians, especially in the market. It is hard to say how distinctive they were. Most sources talk of wholesale adoption of European dress, though you can find photos of the 1920s showing women's dress of an Andine appearance. Silver jewelry became ever more highly developed (again, an echo of our Southwest). Country Indians used Temuco as an economic and politico-legal central town. Anthropologists disagree. In 1951, Titiev (who worked at Hopi) sees reservation Mapuche as virtually indistinguishable from Mestizos. Faron, in 1961, regards them as an internal colony of Chile, having preserved many distinctive ethnic characteristics (patrilineal-based political activity and ceremonialism, belief in their own gods and spirits, witchcraft and shamanism, many crafts, etc.). This does happen among anthropologists: if you look for cultural continuity, you find it; if you look for discontinuity, you can find that too![1]

---

1   See M. Titiev, *Araucanian Culture in Transition,* Occasional Contributions, no. 15 (Ann Arbor: Museum of Anthropology, University of Michigan, 1951); and L. C. Faron, *Mapuche Social Structure,* Illinois Studies in Anthropology, no. 1 (Urbana: University of Illinois, 1961). Gonzalo Rojas, a major poet also from Central Chile and present at the conference, tells me that Indians can still be distinguished by dress at the Temuco market, although a majority appear to have melted into the crowd. Jewelry goes from strength to strength; it is more and more inventive and saleable to visitors and tourists. Mr. Rojas notes that Neruda's mother "was indubitably Hispanic," while his stepmother, the one who really brought him up, could have been perceived more easily as an "Araucanian mother."

But Neruda may not have looked as closely as Faron did. I get no sense of a strong interest or personal concern, on Neruda's part, for Indianity as such.

In "*La Lámpara en la Tierra*," section one of *Canto General*, the Indian, if he emerges at all, tends to do so generically as "*el hombre*" (man); "*el pobre*" (the poor); "*el pueblo*" (the people). Later, in *Alturas de Macchu Picchu*, he comes as "*el antiguo ser*" (the ancient being); "*el servidor*" (the servant/slave); "*el dormido*" (the sleeper); and, of course, "*hermano*" (brother). Indianity strikes me as adjectival in Neruda, if it is at all, rather than substantive: "*Yo, Incásico del légamo*"; "*entre flores zapotecas*"; "*la dulzura chibcha*"; and so forth.

The section "*Los hombres*" is a totalization composed of a series of vignettes: the men of the islands, the Tarahumara, the Aztecs, the Maya, the Tarascans, and the Araucanians (standing for Chile). In between, as if Neruda were more comfortable with matter than with men (an impression not infrequently created by his work): Chichén Itzá, Machu Picchu, Cuzco. The elements of the totalization seem to be selected without any demanding sense of organization, almost lackadaisically, and do not persuade me.

In fact, Neruda's interest is far more geographic than ethnographic. The work begins with a kind of seven-day genesis: "*Amor América*," "*Vegetaciones*," "*Algunas Bestias*," and so on: his triggers are nature, the land, the rain, the forest, timber—not man. His ethnography as such is almost bathetic. When man, Indian man, appears, we almost have anti-climax. We have to await the *conquistadores* who *do* arouse his ire and his inspiration.

2) I derive a few propositions from all this: as always, they need testing.

A) As Monegal points out, Neruda—mostly unconsciously perhaps—identifies with an indigenous mother figure, "*mi madre araucana*" (my Araucanian mother), opposed to a Hispanic, conquering father figure (who can, however, modulate into an oppressed Mestizo worker).[2] I believe, however, that the mother moves south, from Parral to Temuco, into Indian *land*, not into Indianity as such. Neruda is inspired by the South: it is southern geography, not ethnography, which triggers him. He worked hard to move himself into a brotherly position vis-à-vis the Indian, but the hard work shows. For instance: against evidence that most ethnic admixture derived from the union of Spanish men and Indian women, Neruda argues that Chileans are born of Araucanian men and Spanish women. He is in direct contradiction with himself and his mythical Indian mother.[3]

2   E. Rodríguez Monegal, *El Viajero Inmóvil* (Buenos Aires: Losado, 1966), especially pt. 3, ch. 7.

3   See an interview with Neruda in Rita Guibert, *Seven Voices* (New York: Knopf, 1973), 51.

B) Neruda is a Chilean but his Indians are not as symbolically visible as the Andine Inca are. This might have provided one good reason for him to jump as he did from an original project of a *Canto General de Chile* to a *Canto General (de América)*.

But, there is a further problem. The Araucanians were mortal enemies of the Inca. Also, incidentally, the Inca were feudal and could have been criticized for imperialism (as nothing is simple, note in passing that some have argued this to be a socialistic kind of "feudalism" . . .). Neruda tends to ignore all this by concentrating not on Indian-Indian conflict but on Indian-Spanish war and, later, on Mestizo-Yanqui exploitation.

Monegal argues that Neruda is so anti-Spanish that he neglects Indian feudalism. This seems unfair, as Pring-Mill points out. In Pring-Mill's reading, only the primitive Caribs and the Araucanians go uncriticized: the "brother" in *Alturas de Macchu Picchu* is, after all, a slave of the Incas.[4] I suppose one could argue, along this line, that *Alturas* is a paean to people like the Araucanians, although I think that the intent of hymning *Inca* Machu Picchu is pretty clear.

What actually happens, I believe, is more generalized than all this and, politically, very effective. Neruda can use an Indian object (Machu Picchu) as a "human root," but Indian humanity itself is disregarded in its rich variety and subsumed under the category of "people" or lower classes. For Neruda, in short, "*Indio*" is "*Pueblo*" before being "*Indio*": there is no clearer contrast with Vallejo. We remember that for many, perhaps most, Latin American Marxists, Indians should be subsumed under proletariat. This is a Pan-American problem: that revolution does not involve continued Indianity when seen, that is, from a non-Indian point of view.

C) The use of the Indian *ruined city* of Machu Picchu was a brilliant intuition for Neruda, a profoundly elegiac and nostalgic poet whose political duty was to look forward and upward.

Not long ago, I wrote a study of the Orpheus myth, especially its back-looking and forward-looking aspects (descent into Hades / return to upper earth and light) as the constitutive, enabling myth of a double process in writing: the *elegiac* looking-back at all previous poems in order to recognize the present poem as poem, and the *lyric* push forward and upward of the poem to position it in the lifework sequence or *opus*.[5] I went on to look at various ways in which archeological ruins so often appear as diacritical indices of the elegiac process. Then, I

---

4   R. Pring-Mill, *Pablo Neruda: A Basic Anthology* (Oxford: Dolphin, 1975), esp. xxxiii–xxxix.
5   "Archaeology, Elegy, Architecture," in this volume.

looked at such ruins in Rilke's *Duino Elegies,* contrasting them with Neruda's *Macchu Picchu.*

The argument was complex. But, briefly and simply, it appears that, symbolically, we go down and backward to the past, up and forward to the future. This process can be seen in its orthodox form in the first part of *Alturas.* In the second part, an exciting, heterodox jolt is generated by the simple ecological fact that Machu Picchu lies way up a mountain in the air. We have a ruined past which is, symbolically (and Neruda makes it into an *archē,* whereas, in fact, it is quite late), the future of all of Latin America. Equally propitious is the transformation of the Eurydice motif into the slave buried under the ruins whom Neruda calls to "arise to birth with me as my own brother." We do not, of course, require that Eurydice should be female: think of a Dante-Eurydice fetched by a Beatrice-Orpheus through the patroness of music!

Neruda, perhaps, hardly even notices when he says, "I come to speak through your dead mouths," that his enablement as a poet arises out of the enforced silence of the Indian, an enforcement in which he cannot help participating as a non-Indian. Indians have to have been oppressed, enslaved, and killed *in order that* he can speak. As with the rest of us, a useful Indian, alas, is a dead Indian. Or, perhaps, one who has disappeared into the faceless masses: if not genocide, then ethnocide.

Neruda is a good ethnopoet, i.e., one who, as I have come to believe, sees and uses the symbolic value of the Indian root of Americanicity while continuing perforce to dwell in his own non-Indianness. I am not arguing here, need I say it, that not being an Indian makes one an Indian-killer. I am saying that we need to be perpetually on our guard in what we say about "the Indian."

Here is a passage from Neruda's *"Algo sobre mi Vida y Poesía"* ("Something about My Life and Poetry"), dated 1954:

> I was not able to segregate myself from these buildings. I grasped the fact that, if we trod the same ancestral earth, we had something to do with those high efforts of the American community, could not ignore them—and that our doing so, or our silence, was not only a crime but also a continuation of a defeat.
>
> Aristocratic cosmopolitanism had brought us to worship the past of far-off peoples and had bandaged our eyes to prevent us from seeing our own treasures.
>
> I thought of a great deal after my visit to Cuzco (and Macchu Picchu). I thought of ancient American man. I saw his ancient struggles bound up with our own struggles.
>
> That is where my idea of a *Canto General de América* began. Before that, I had persisted in the notion of a *Canto General de Chile* as a chronicle. That visit to Macchu Picchu changed the perspective. Now I saw all of America from the

heights of Macchu Picchu. This was the title of the first poem from that new point of view.

The sentiments are worthy. *Alturas* is a marvelous poem. But may not Neruda have been *too* high? "The same ancestral earth"? "The American community"? "Our own treasures"? "His ancient struggles bound up with our own struggles"? Are we that sure? Can Neruda be that sure?

A total identification, à la Whitman, with "my people" is fine, but it masks a great deal of conflict and unresolved trouble within that people. First: there has been intra-Indian conflict and this continues. Second: while many Indians are no doubt patriotic citizens, it seems to me we have very far to go before we can take for granted their view of us as belonging to the same people as themselves. Too much of Ethnopoetics has been bound up with the confusion of the geographic and the ethnographic: it is *not* because the non-Indian lives on an Indian continent that he can appropriate Indianity. It is understandable, this search for roots in a new land. We desperately need them. But, whatever we do, there are old roots and new roots. They must not be confused.

1986

On Paul Celan

1) Adorno's view that, after the unspeakable, no poetry can anymore be spoken; that it is, literally, unspeakable, fought lifelong by Celan. After Babel, language being the only place where we are or are likely to be, where anyone is or can be, but, precisely, *in* or *on* Babel. All communication perforce linguistic, thus *ipso facto* deficient; even the paralinguistic does not survive the doubt. How then shall language be spoken, after Adorno, where nothing else can be spoken? Language then to be taken from its usual site and placed elsewhere, allegorized, *translated,* so that it can still, if only at the zenith, be heard. An unspoken language heard, extracted *in toto,* from the stone of silence, that tongue sticking out, not speaking but the smoking air hearing it. Care that there should be someone to hear (*Shemah*) far more than that anything should be spoken: if not, turn aside and break the Tables. All bastions of *I* collapse; *You* still stand to hear there, or float. George Steiner's "all Celan's poems are translated into German." Yes, as long as all German is translated into *your* ear, listening to the silence of German. Ears of

This piece, originally entitled "Survolant Celan: Quelques sursauts sociologiques supplémentaires au sujet de *ACTS 8/9*," is a review of the following: Benjamin Hollander, ed., *Translating Tradition: Paul Celan in France* (San Francisco: *ACTS: A Journal of New Writing,* 1988).

dead smoke in air more live than silence of German and ready to speak. Where else has the God-Aweful Jew ever been?

2) Hollander: Bukovina's "refined, middle-class German-Jewish culture."[1] A Jewish nightmare not all that well-known to outsiders: the particular horror of Holocaust to German Jews who, before the Fall of Germany, had snubbed all other Jews for not being German. And may still do, somewheres.

3) Dangers of snubbery on Mt. Babel. Horror-struck to stone though we are by Holocaust, is this matter of the "butcher's language" *so* unique? All Native Americans speak the butcher's language; all Native Australians; all Afroamericans, *ad infinitum*. Milder: minute nations make poems for translation just as many nativisms make art for airports only. No mystifications of this needed in nether nether lands.

4) Silencing of the word in minimalist directions. The more you charge the less with moving *you,* the greater the loss of the more in that cardinal of silence. A suggestion: no minimalists save *ex infernos.* Portentousness the minimalist sin. Down from Mallarmé, French, Celan's sinecure, addicted to minus. Celan's turn against Char not for being later than Resistance but for this "self-centered cele-bration"? Böschenstein, again, on du Bouchet: "all valences drown in a neutraliz-ing extinction of the individual voice, even where this still says 'I,'" "so that we neither can nor must look for a key to his texts: they are no longer written out of the tension of a meaning to be deciphered, a tension Celan maintained to the end." Of this whole lineage Celan lived by, only Michaux seems to endure for him, Michaux who took "language to task for lacking penury. But those who ex-pressly seek it there lapse into artifice": "*Séparé de la séparation / je vis dans un im-mense ensemble*" and ". . . *et le monde effroyable et immense de la souffrance jamais loin, qui ferme la bouche à tout le reste.*"[2] After C. who gives a D for Ds and *tutti quanti*? Silence certainly cannot. Except for M1 to M2. Silence is *not* saying yes.

5) Heidegger, in this hell, a minimalist philosopher? On the whole, writers in *ACTS* still salute uncompromised Heidegger. But, Pierre Bourdieu: *L'ontologie politique de Martin Heidegger,* ed. de Minuit ([1975] 1988): H. as only getting away with the expression of *Völkisch* ideology in minimalist language because it is phrased in an elite dialect which cannot be challenged by any other code, philos-ophy being both Crown of Academe sociologically *and* the Metacode of all Codes in the Realm of Discourse. Joel Golb, perhaps the only academic in the *ACTS*

---

1   Benjamin Hollander, ed., *Translating Tradition: Paul Celan in France* (San Francisco: *ACTS: A Journal of New Writing,* 1988), 2.

2   Ibid., 184–87, 194, 196.

issue who is aware of this, in a dazzling analysis of the poem *"Huhediblu"* from *Die Niemandsrose*. He sees the poem as a comment "not only on the fallen status of all poetic discourse . . . but more specifically on the relation of this 'date' (i.e., 09.01.1939, Nazi invasion of Poland) to the modern, ideologically-tainted history of Hölderlin interpretation—as well as . . . to Celan's own late, postmodern role, along with Heidegger and Blanchot, in carrying forward this tradition in Paris, *while trying to bring it to an end.*"[3] See also the *Critical Quarterly* "Special Feature on Heidegger and Nazism."[4] Supplement Blanchot in *ACTS*—that same Blanchot tagged by Golb as "a propagandist for the French right" before the Occupation[5]— with Blanchot in *Critical Quarterly:* "Allow me after what I have to say next to leave you as a means to emphasize that Heidegger's irreparable fault lies in his silence concerning the Final Solution. This silence, or his refusal, when confronted by Paul Celan, to ask forgiveness for the unforgivable, was a denial that plunged Celan into despair and made him ill, for Celan knew that the *Shoah* was the revelation of the essence of the West."[6]

6) The codes: Golb again: "C.'s language repeatedly flees from its own linguistic matrix, estranging itself into an idiom that both pays tradition its due and strives for an ideally complete break."[7] Bringing several languages into his own German so that it should have friends and the old German be deleted, say by the key "backspace." This bonding of the bottles thrown out to sea in one glass to land on the shores of the heart perhaps: *"an Herzland vielleicht."* Push all forms of ambivalence to their uttermost states to secure shots of "the spectral analysis of things," no dream but a *reality* made of "unabashed ambiguity"; "overlapping relationships"; "conceptual overlay."

Overall, looking at the corpus of Celan's translations will help spot C.'s idiosyncratic terms of speech more directly perhaps than by looking at his own poems. Various academic experts show the value of this working model: Felstiner, Wortman, and Blue on Emily Dickinson; Bernhardt Böschenstein on Daive and French from Char to Dupin. In much less space, and demonstrating that "not much cackle is needed,"[8] two poets—Robert Kelly with Celan via Marianne Moore, and Pierre Joris with Celan via Artaud—show deictically and impressively what can be done here.

3   Ibid., 179 (my italics).
4   *Critical Quarterly* 15, no. 2 (1989).
5   Hollander, *Translating Tradition,* 180.
6   *Critical Quarterly,* 479.
7   Hollander, *Translating Tradition,* 173.
8   Ibid., 122.

Now compare the Spicer (*ACTS* 6) and Celan issues. Celan has, to a great extent, already suffered his way down the academic maw; Spicer has not: the Spicer issue is the saucier for it. The following remarks because *ACTS* is by far the most serious, thoughtful, and valuable of the younger magazines something outside of the "Language" community and one which can only go from strength to strength. The academic code-juggling merry-go-round is interminable. Scholar X or Y presents his/her vision of what C.'s interpretation of poet A does to his translation of her/his poem. *But,* scholars X and Y differ in their interpretations of the poem in question and, in turn, differ from all other scholars, then differ about the translation. One seems to feel that C. almost improves on Dickinson;[9] another (admittedly dealing with different poems) thinks C. is "domesticating" her.[10] We hear at great length about not only compound word coinages (frequent in the old German) but also radical compressions and displacements (perhaps less available in the fallen tongue): the stuff of most studies of translation. While aware of the subtitle, it seems unfortunate that we are not given *something* on translations of Celan into English. Despite the pieces by Bonnefoy, Huppert, Cioran, and Jabès, we get only the most tenuous of holds on C.'s life and death here. In that respect, Jerry Glenn's *Celan* in the Twayne series seems well worth checking out.

7) The Celan-industry maw has been German for the most part and expands at light speed. It happens I have French, alas not German: less there, but some (sometimes from German into French) a most worthy supplement.

E.g., *Contre-jour: Etudes sur Paul Celan,* Colloque de Cerisy, Martine Broda, ed., Editions du Cerf, Paris, 1986:

A) Beda Allemann: Problems relating to concordance in a complete Celan: comprehending first, out of chaos, a catalogue of particles of C.'s material world (*Weltmaterialen*). This close look at the realia infrastructures reminds me of Gadamer's study, partly translated in Michel Deguy's magazine *Po&sie* (number 36, Paris, 1986) and worth knowing, not to mention a great deal more on Celan throughout the magazine's career.

B) Martine Broda: *La Leçon de Mandelstam:* Mandelstam as an emblem of Judaicity for C. and the *amicus par excellence* of these and future times; implications of C.'s translation of "no-one" (*Niemand*) from an absence into a presence, a negative into a positive; on exile as dialogue and the bringing into being of the Thou—the end of monologic Romanticism, as in "*Es gab dich Dir in die Hand: /*

9 Ibid., 113–18.
10 Ibid., 136.

Ein Du, todlos, / an dem alles Ich zu sich kam" ("He offered himself to You in the hand: / a You, without death, / beside whom all the I returned to itself ").

C) Renate Böschenstein: on possible sources in Freud, Novalis, Nerval, Keller, Kafka, Breton. Early poems constantly speak of dream, never reveal their content, are never "contented." Terror of self-betrayal by dream under tyranny (conscience must never fall asleep) and the growing cancer of anxiety (cf. C. H. Beradt: *Das Dritte Reich des Traums*, Frankfurt, 1981). Escape from dilemma of dreamer unable to dream by (a) concentrating on the moment of waking (cf. W. Benjamin: *Das Passagenwerk*, Frankfurt, 1983, p. 580: "utilization of dream elements at the moment of waking is the canon of Dialectic") with resulting *apparent* "incoherence" and wide semantic gaps, and (b) by translation of dream structures into poetic structures (cf. T. Todorov: *La rhétorique de Freud*, in *Théorie du symbole*, Paris, 1977; & E. Benveniste: *Remarques sur la fonction du langage dans la découverte freudienne*, in *Problèmes de Linguistique Générale*, Paris, 1960). Implications for word-play metonymy, and allegory in Celan.

D) John Felstiner: Hebrew words in Celan denoting what cannot, at any price, go into German (and, therefore, into *any* other language). Hebrew as the root, *Ursprache*, original language of the kabbalists, discovered by C. to be *utterly* his, however hard it cost him to use it. (*Radix, Matrix:* "Root of Abraham. Root of Jesse. Root / of no one—o / ours"). That which remains, above persecution and triumphant in the State, against neo-Nazism, against his own anguish and Tsvetaeva's, Mandelstam's, Nelly Sachs's. "Perhaps I am one of the last who must live out to the end the fate of Jewish spirituality in Europe" (letter of 1948 in *Zeitschrift für Kulturaustausch*, volume 3, 1982). He cannot stay in Israel (cf. "Address to the Hebrew Writers' Association," Tel Aviv, 1969, in *Collected Prose*, R. Waldrop, tr., Manchester, 1986), needs all the tension of Diaspora even though, only in *Eretz*, could the paternal tongue assume the intimacy of a maternal one. Search for a light, *Ziv*, that can embrace mother; Rachel & all sisters; *Shekhinah*, collective she whom Celan has caused to wait for him ("*dich / ließ ich warten, / dich*": Almond-like, you who only half spoke, / still shaken from the bud, / you / I left waiting / you." In *Last Poems*, Washburn & Guillemin, trs., San Francisco, 1986, 177).

Only half the book, but, already, we are told so much. The Felstiner piece: I have read little recently by a Jewish critic on a Jewish poet more perceptive and more moving than this.

8) When all is said and done, Celan did not suffer lack of recognition, that plague of most "difficult poets": two of the highest prizes that can be granted to a poet writing in German were his (he doubted them, of course) and his work had been studied in Germany before he died. There was more. Richness of Sartre on

poetic "suicide" in his unfinished *Mallarmé: la lucidité et sa face d'ombre* (Paris, 1986). After M1, poets get more and more serious about God's demise. Everyone wants to be dead, everyone vies with everyone else as to who can be more dead than he. Salt gets lost from poesy, hangs out in science only. M1 achieves greatness by being the most dead of all, by living death more than in dying until dying itself: he is the arch-dead, the real dead, the honest to goodness fried-fish dead, the maestro of absence: *l'absente de tous bouquets* that tricks all presences into surrounding her void. And "not for one instant does M1 doubt that the human species, if he were to kill himself, would come to die entirely in him; that this suicide would be a genocide,"[11] with extraordinary implications for the Holocaust child who died the hard death in his body. The greatest difference of all, however, is between God being dead and not being dead but unable to be said. Weight of history as language minus the which there is no memory (cf. Jack Marshall's excellent review of *ACTS* 8/9 in *Poetry Flash,* January 1989). Translation from the past obliterates forgetting so that time cannot comfort but only slowly kill. That is the silence smoke listens to, ready to speak.

9) On the "obscurity" of Celan. Certainly Primo Levi (*Survival in Auschwitz,* New York, 1969) shows how linguistic violence, yet again in history, is almost unsurvivable in camps: not designed as communication but as extermination—and how obscurity has *always* been an instrument of political oppression. From there to speak *more* clearly, *most* clearly, and of Celan's defeat? Hard to say. Some have *only* silence to swim to. Often, the dues simply cannot be paid. Much obscurity may be the cheapest drug of all.

10) Suddenly, out of *Muttersprache* and for no rhyme or reason, after, what, fifty years, the name of Iasi as the root-place, the mother-root. Moldavia, not Bukovina, but close. It could have been in the sixties, both for C. and M2, had there been world enough and time, and less fear. What is the date of page 15 here? That head bent forward, the tentative lift of those eyes: *"Ailleurs, bien loin d'ici! trop tard! jamais peut-être!"*

Gratitude to *ACTS* for a beautifully and bountifully produced symposium.

1989

---

11 Ibid., 155.

Vicente Huidobro

Some Notes among Altazor

1) It's not often a new collection, Cecilia Vicuña's *Palabra Sur,* kicks off with a masterpiece, Vicente Huidobro's (peer to Vallejo and Neruda) *Altazor.*[1] Eliot Weinberger's magisterial translation, joy to read, superb piece of American poetry, shows, besides great sagacity for rendering the "untranslatable," a magnificent elegiac breath. Here you have it complete at last, after large helpings in David Guss's fine New Directions anthology of 1981.

2) Elegiac, yes, because: a poem of *flight?* E. W.: "The century's great paean to flight . . . the airplane as a vehicle for ascension." Later: *"Altazor* is a poem of falling, not back to earth . . . but out into space." E. W. also calls it "Einstein space." I find almost unbelievably little ascension in *Altazor.* The sub-title, *A Voyage in a Parachute,* clarifies *fall* but not rise. Without counting, I bet there are ten or more times as many *boats* in *Altazor* as planes; perhaps fifty times as many mentions of *sea* as any kind of air. There is extraordinarily little here of the exhilaration of flight, virtually nothing on the manifold experiences of being up in the sky. The overwhelming direction is *down*—not, I think, in space but in

---

1 Vicente Huidobro, *Altazor,* trans. Eliot Weinberger, *Palabra Sur* series, series ed. Cecilia Vicuña (St. Paul, MN: Graywolf Press, 1989).

water/sea/ocean, also signifying psyche. Like Neruda, Huidobro is Chilean enough to be devoured by ocean.[2]

3) Criticism, I am told, agrees on the subject being the fate of poetry in Huidobro's time, but oscillates between a downbeat and an upbeat interpretation of Huidobro's own attitude to poetry's future. Maybe these basic directions in the poem can help decide? Is the fairly systematic review of referential dislocations (mainly, be it said, at the lexical level) running from Cantos 5 to 7 and ending with an "untranslatable" (now translated) trio of pages an optimistic surge towards the future? Or is it (as the only critic I've read so far, René de Costa, thinks) a rehearsal of the avant-garde's failure and a Rimbaudian abdication of all hope for a visionary language (itself, of course, a matter for heated debate)? I don't find much encouragement for the positive view in a poem which often seems to me to read like *A Season in Hell.*

4) "Rosicrucian" suggestions: birth of Huidobro on the day of Christ's death (traditionally at 33); "alone in the middle of the universe" (Dante: *nel mezzo*); the Blakean search for the hour that Satan cannot find; man as replacing God; reference to the "hidden rose"; a fall through *self* rather than space, an initiatic fall of a self "who watches himself at work and laughs in his (own) face," falling from "the heights of his star" (the star it seems to which one is always [astrologically?] chained), "hanging in the parachute of his own prejudices" (trapped in ego?), to "an endless voyaging in the interiors of the self." If "we must change our luck," it is only, repeatedly, through drinking the "pale lucidity of death" to the dregs, the death of the "failed experiment," for "Everything is pain": the Buddhist *dukkha* perhaps which marks the exhaustion of all conditioned things, the picture of the world's future being dismal and contemptible. It is said, yes, that the greater the height from which you fall, the higher you'll rebound, a transformation is possible from *paracaidas* (parafall, parachute) to *parasubidas* (literally, pararises, E. W.'s parashot), but the poem never dwells long on rising while doing so, abundantly, on falling. It is only at the very bottom of "shipwreck" fall that the poet sees the hidden rose, and even in the one truly ascensional sequence in the poem, when the earth gives birth to a tree (rooted, of course), Huidobro continues "falling across your body from your heights to your depths."[3]

The fear of giving way to any ascensional hope is constantly re-iterated. "The airplane carries a new language / To the mouth of the eternal skies" but, only a few lines later, the plane is "drowsy" and "the clouds turn to stone," or "The sky waits for an airplane / And I hear the dead laughing under the earth." Indeed, any-

---

2   For the implications of this kind of entrails-reading, see "Archaeology, Elegy, Architecture," in this volume.

3   Huidobro, *Altazor*, I, 15, 41, 9, 21, 25, 41, III, 39, 43, 57, 65, 23, 27, 25, 29, 35, 42, 47, 45–46, 113, III, 57.

thing rising seems unthinkable without being linked to the sea-fall: "My swallow anchors / Its sources in the sea"; "And waves are the wings in my blue"; "My lies smell of heaven / And that's all / And now I'm the sea." In turn, the death through whose spaces the parachute interminably falls (as far into the poem as page 109, Huidobro is still talking of "aerial burials" because all of air is absorbed into sea), this death is indissolubly associated with dream and with the sea: death "sitting by the edge of the sea," the sea in the depths of the tomb, and so forth.[4]

5) Huidobro's critique of avant-garde poetic procedures (cubist, dada, surrealist, etc.), if this is being read right, appears to follow the same pattern of fear of ascensional success. The "remedy" passage begins with a call to "revive the languages," put "circuit breakers in the sentences," "cataclysms in the grammar," "beautiful madness in the life of the word"[5] leads through an exaltation of the "pure word and nothing more," "The simple sport of words," appearing to end in "Single combat between chest and sky" (note "combat," but indicating freedom one would assume). Then, however, there is something which seems very ambivalent to me: "Then nothing, nothing / Spirit whisper of the wordless phrase."[6] In the same vein, the passage at page 87, "The sea waits to conquer / So there's no time to lose / Then / Ah then / Beyond the last horizon / We'll see what there is to see" (curious echo of the bear-over-the-mountain, repeated at 105), seems heavily ironic, as well as "so sad,"[7] indeed tragically dangerous: "There's no time to lose / The steamer has the day marked / For the dangerous holes stars open in the sea / It could fall into the central fire"[8] and the Jouvian "Goodbye one must say goodbye" of page 101. Straight after this, a promise of sap springing up, yet, again, immediately: "The tree is afraid of going too far / It's afraid and looks back in anguish"[9] and "It's afraid I say the tree is afraid / Of going too far from the earth"[10] and, again, "Aviator be careful with stars / Careful with dawn / Lest the astronaut become a sunicide[11] / The sky has never had as many roads as this / Never has it been so treacherous."[12] The poet is lost in night, sea, and splendor of "blind death" which is what there is to see "beyond the last horizon."[13] It may be that Huidobro is

---

4   Ibid., 73, 75, 149, 157, 143, 3, 115, 119–21.
5   Ibid., 81.
6   Ibid., 83.
7   Ibid., 95.
8   Ibid., 99.
9   Ibid., 101.
10 Ibid., 103.
11 "Sunicide" is E. W.'s translation of "auricida," no doubt from *auro*ra (dawn) of the previous line, also echoing *aerona*uta in the same line.
12 Huidobro, *Altazor*, 105.
13 Ibid., 105.

simply pointing to the massive difficulty of doing anything new in this age of the new, but I don't see him raise a single cry of real hope out of any of it.

6) The question of whether the ever-increasingly "untranslatable" text is indeed so or not must be linked to whether Huidobro wanted some degree of referentiality to be present to the very end of the poem, or not, and this would also reflect on his hope, or lack of it, for poetry's future. E. W. clearly feels that Huidobro was not after pure sound in his search for a new language: "the 'untranslatable' poem is simply one which has not yet found its translator." On the other hand, the statement that, in the neologisms, "no two Spanish readers could ever agree upon" the various components of the word—so that another English version could be "utterly dissimilar to this one"—leaves us free to feel that, less than any other poetry, this kind of poetry has a definitive translator. E. W. agrees: "The game of *Altazor* has an infinite number of moves, and I look forward to its next translation match." This is perhaps one place where poetry can be made by all—as Surrealism wanted it to be: while admiring the brilliance of E. W.'s own solutions (it would take far more space than is available to unpack his extensive labor in detail), a dictionary and a knowledge of Spanish will allow any poet to try for another "match" with the neologisms.

7) Can we deny Huidobro's claim to have found the key to "*eterfinifrete*" (the word can be read backwards or forwards; E. W.'s "infiniternity" cannot, though it gains in precision)? It occurs to me that the degree of ambivalence is such throughout *Altazor* that it will always be possible to take opposite views of its intentions. This may be the genius of the thing: we may be in the presence of a both/and situation. The ambivalences are constitutive, however, and not due, as so often in Neruda, for instance, to a simple lack of linguistic energy. *Altazor* would be a triumph if only because, while being without any ostensible "subject," it manages to give such a sense of energy and purposeful direction. This is so especially in its totalizations: the Rimbaudian poet as total man; indeed as total world; woman as a remembrance of other lives/worlds and guiding spirit of this one; the all-embracing shipwreck of the tomb;[14] etc. The old truth: that great tragedy is mysteriously uplifting prevails as in all major elegiac work: I am moved at the fact that an early title of the poem seems to have been *AltAZUR.* More than this, however: the language is taut at all times and completely surmounts, as Vallejo's does, the sentimentality and vapid rhetoric endemic to so much Latin American writing. This is a poem to live with, in both its original and its English versions.

1989

---

14   Ibid., 3, 7, 39–41, 137, 141, 69–71, 119–21.

Michel Leiris, Timor Mortis, and the Peopled Self

A Reading of "L'Afrique Fantôme" as Auto-Anthropology

Maintenant je pardonne à ce plaisant labeur,
Puis que seul il endort le souci qui m'oultrage,
Et puis que seul il fait qu'au milieu de l'orage,
Ainsi qu'auparavant, je ne tremble de peur.

—*Joachim du Bellay*, Les Regrets

—d'où ma tendance . . . à fuir . . . attitude
d'ensemble que j'adopte à l'égard de la vie (qu'on ne
peut vivre qu'à la condition d'accepter de mourir)

—*Michel Leiris*, L'Age d'Homme[1]

Richard Sieburth has asked me to comment on Leiris's *L'Afrique Fantôme* from both my professional viewpoints: that of a poet and that of an anthropologist. I should stress that I am not a Leiris scholar and have not found it possible to read all of him or all that has been written about him. If I repeat others, my apologies. Let me begin with the view from fieldwork.

～

Paper delivered at a conference on "Leiris Fantôme" organized by Richard Sieburth, Denis Hollier, and Eric Fassin, Center for French Civilization and Culture, New York University, April 18–19, 1991.

1 Joachim du Bellay, *Les Regrets* (Paris: Pleiade, 1953), 421; Michel Leiris, *L'Age d'Homme* (Paris: Gallimard, 1946), 231.

L'Afrique Fantôme is the record of a Trans-Africa French expedition from Dakar to Djibouti lasting a total of thirty-three months (May 19, 1931–February 16, 1933), i.e., somewhat longer than the average anthropological fieldwork period. As French museums are governmental property, the brief for forming an Africa collection seems to have been as, or more, important than fieldwork (perhaps the group was doing fieldwork in the interstices of their official pursuits) and to have led the expedition into a probably inexcusable theft of objects, many sacred.[2] It also involved the expedition in interminable political hassles which Marcel Griaule, the mission director, appears to have treated with imperial high-handedness. It is hard from Leiris's record to tell, especially in Ethiopia, whether Griaule and Co. were virtually obliged to be high-handed by political obstructionism or were in fact blameworthy and the obstructionism partly or wholly justified. Natives, of course, are mostly depicted in the book as *avida dollars* but colonials get short shrift too. The whole colonialist situation has to be taken into account as well as Leiris's "disloyalty" to his "mission."[3]

I get little sense of what the other researchers were doing—this includes Griaule—but for Leiris there were ten months of fieldwork *stricto sensu* with the *Zar* or Spirit cults of Abyssinia. While the *Zar* stuff has its own fascination, far more than Ethiopian officialdom's *marasmus,* Leiris, still an apprentice, reveals himself, when at work, as a strictly old-style, fact-collecting ethnographer. Virtually all interpretation at this stage (much later, he wrote an analytical book on the cults) is directed upon his own reactions to field, to people, to his own feelings and behavior. In that sense, this record is an extension of *L'Age d'Homme,* whose dates, December 1930–November 1935,[4] reveal it as being written *around L'Afrique Fantôme,* which he claims to be a virtually *unrevised* field diary.

L'Age d'Homme makes it quite clear that Leiris took the trip as an effort at distancing himself from psychological problems acute enough to have led him into analysis—an analysis which is, of course, carried out in his whole literary production far more than on the couch itself and certainly begins, at large, in *L'Afrique Fantôme.*[5] Travel journals were more publishable then than now, and there had always been, in France, longer than elsewhere perhaps, a kind of self-glorifying adventurer to write them, to the intense horror of "real" anthropologists (Lévi-Strauss is on record). Which adds to the suggestion that Leiris's record needs to be taken far more as an autobiographical (and hence, no doubt, literary) document

---

2   Michel Leiris, *L'Afrique Fantôme* (Paris: Gallimard, 1934), 30–31, 82, 87, 89, 125–28, 331, 338, 473, 496.
3   Ibid., 453, 511, 517.
4   Leiris, *L'Age d'Homme,* 226.
5   Leiris, *L'Afrique Fantôme,* 246, 249–50, 321, 332–34, 347, 358, 380, 390, 407, 432, 455, 488, 497–99, 504.

than as an anthropological one. Perhaps I can take it as an early crack at an Auto-Anthropology (or Autoanthropology), the term I have used since the sixties about my own productions in this interdisciplinary activity.

Certainly a field anthropologist, with perhaps less "scientific objectivity" than is ideally demanded of such, will recognize, with fellow-feeling and pleasure, a whole fan of familiar reactions. Initial attraction to the exotic;[6] anxious anticipation as to how Natives will react to one's arrival and work; initial reactions to the field, often negative;[7] attempts, sometimes a little desperate, to find points of contact and identification such that this field can become "my" field, "my" village, "my" people;[8] despair when unable to find informants and sudden, even abrupt, mood swings,[9] as well as acute boredom;[10] joy at sudden bursts of revelation, and dejection again when these cease;[11] frequent sense of being overwhelmed by data,[12] fury and frustration at never completing data, and burnout vis-à-vis data;[13] despair and frequent rage at being duped or misled in regard to data or timing of events in the field;[14] energetic attempts to differentiate and distance oneself in one's own mind from local colonial personnel, non-Native locals, or Native officials, plus contempt for the latters' ways[15]—but desperate suspicion that one is, in the end, no better than they are—thus tending toward a critique of colonialism;[16] resulting over-identification and emotional involvement with certain informants or groups of informants, as well as overreacting antipathies for them when the work is over;[17] pride at achieving ritual grades and/or savvy or other attainments praised by Natives;[18] desperate and often sentimental nostalgias for both the people and places left behind, the home base,[19] and the present context which will relatively soon be the past, dead and gone;[20] re-entry anxiety;[21] etc., etc., etc. To this

---

6 Ibid., 127, 130, 208–11; cf. Leiris, *L'Age d'Homme*, 105, 135.
7 Leiris, *L'Afrique Fantôme*, 17.
8 Ibid., 25, 336, 342.
9 Ibid., 24, 48, 71, 127, 131, 200, 249, 312, 315, 321, 324, 498.
10 Ibid., 37, 43, 95, 162, 169, 216, 222, 324, 350–53, 359; cf. Leiris, *L'Age d'Homme*, 30, 147, 168.
11 Leiris, *L'Afrique Fantôme*, 51, 70, 447.
12 Ibid., 111.
13 Ibid., 105, 109, 117–18, 173–74, 359.
14 Ibid., 88, 95, 399, 447, 453.
15 Ibid., 20, 65, 136, 495.
16 Ibid., 21, 38, 118, 172.
17 Ibid., 338, 399, 401, 408, 447, 453.
18 Ibid., 36, 342, 452.
19 Ibid., 41, 169, 171.
20 Ibid., 122.
21 Ibid., 323.

extent, Leiris's honesty with the record would recommend him as initial reading for anyone's first field trip preparation.[22]

Regarding the text qua text, signs are that Leiris probably had rewriting opportunity: rough notes followed by one-time revision journal entries. Substantial evidence of stylistic refinement. Virtually no reading throughout the trip (books apparently not carried as equipment!) so that the journal could be the essential literary vehicle for a man determined *ab initio* that writing alone would save him from *timor mortis*. No evidence I could find that he was writing anything else (do we have a chronology for his poems yet?) so that the journal may have been his only investment. Continuity of confessional style between this work, *L'Age d'Homme*, and most later work, placed at the start, *n'en déplaise à certains*, under the sign of Jean-Jacques Rousseau.[23]

Thematic study of the self as if it were another, indeed a tribe of others when *je est un autre* is the rule, this seems to be the way of any Autoanthropology. How to describe the main topic? I would venture: constant battle of autonomous Angel of Creation (poetry) against the dependence of the Angel of the Record (anthropology) on data-donors—the struggle, incidentally, tending by saturation of effort and personnel to inhibit yet further distancing by using fiction. A thematic study of *L'Afrique Fantôme* as part and parcel of the literary work would take hours and I have but the half of one.[24] Among the many threads I would choose to follow, almost arbitrarily, the following seem to me to be linked and to form the major pattern in this complex web.

1) Theme of escape from the immense monotony and boredom of all existence; its radical unsatisfactoriness because all life is death-tainted; all beginnings irremediably ruined in that beginning implies end;[25] death the ruin of life in that it cannot be entirely *lived:* i.e., one cannot by definition be present at, and in, *all* parts of it[26] (a series on *dukkha* which should, some might think, have made of Leiris a candidate for Buddhism). Link this with the very prompt realization that "departure" *à la Baudelaire ou à la surréaliste*, exoticism in short, offers nothing

---

22 Reading this book was a pleasure for me in that, long before my first field experience, I had worked with Griaule as my very first teacher and been minutely caught up in the Griaule-Dieterlen & Co. extended study of Dogon/Bambara initiatic systems, systems so intricate and sophisticated in relation to the technological milieu they came from that, for some time, many social anthropologists—predominantly the British—were unwilling to accept their results as valid.

23 Leiris, *L'Afrique Fantôme*, 9.

24 Remember that Leiris chose to distinguish later in toto between his (perhaps deliberately dull?) ethnographic work and his literature: this is something to return to.

25 Leiris, *L'Age d'Homme*, 51.

26 Ibid., 93–94.

whatsoever to comfort such pain. Anthropologically: source of much rage and exasperation in the optimist/pessimist dialectic; inability to reduce the symbolic world to order; inability to find an alternative in the "savage" to the Decline of France and the West.[27]

2) Theme of the classical self-hatred of the bourgeois, abundantly documented by Leiris;[28] link of this self-hatred with a profound masochistic and shame-ridden personality in which the other is a constant provoker of sado-masochistic confusion;[29] beginning of a linkage between sexuality (first erection at the sight of a small pauper child climbing a tree with bare feet), poverty, social consciousness, and the Native as other;[30] eroticism implied in almost all contact with Natives, coming most to the surface in the relation with the *Zar* priestess Emawayish, whom only in *L'Age d'Homme* does he openly admit into his paradigm of love objects,[31] a woman who has all the characteristics of his fetishism, first and foremost the ruined beauty and the antique, wax-like aspect.[32]

3) Theme of the near-impotence, often converted into full impotence by the weight on the author of themes 1 and 2, which invests all his activities in whatever personal domain he chooses to act or, more frequently timorous, retreats from action. Applies to his great difficulties with getting writing done; his relations with women, mostly disastrous (actual accounts of Leiris's apparently contented marriage, in later works [other than the four major volumes I have not yet read], are significantly rare or absent altogether);[33] his attempts at taking political positions and virtually all his anthropological involvements, riddled with self-questioning, self-accusation; self-impairment; and interminable anxiety and sheer *frousse*, perhaps we should coin, in his glossarizing style: *frousse de brousse*. Rather fundamentally, and one is surprised he continues in this *métier*, he is constantly contemptuous of scientific research for holding one back from participating, for being such a cushy job when the world is such a hard place for the Poor and the Natives. One notices, right through his account of the *Zar* cults, that he never *wholeheartedly*

---

27 Leiris, *L'Afrique Fantôme*, 95, 130, 164, 185–87, 195, 198.

28 E.g., Leiris, *L'Age d'Homme*, 137, 141, 167, 202–3.

29 Ibid., 155, 160–64, 187, 190.

30 Ibid., 42.

31 Ibid., 217.

32 Ibid., 56–73, 88. References to Leiris's analysis of his own sexual problems and psychological status are usually clearer in *L'Age d'Homme* than in *L'Afrique Fantôme*. In the latter they are often downright obscure, if not coded. See Leiris, *L'Afrique Fantôme*, 115, 125, 147, 219, 225, 231–34, 243, 288. Clearer observations come later in the book, e.g., 330–34, 347, 358, 380, 407, 432, 455, 488, 497–99, 504.

33 Leiris, *L'Age d'Homme*, 212.

participates—and indeed mourns that fact. Fear of apparent "subjectivity" in accounts which should be "objective" (it *was* a fear in his and my time), or ridden by his own obsessions? It is fairly clear that we deal with the latter mostly.[34]

Lightheartedly, in *L'Age d'Homme*, Leiris suggests his analyst told him to go abroad as a cure for not having led the hard life for a while (in France, typically, for most: military service).[35] Elsewhere it becomes clear that the main motive was an escapism which led him only deeper into his own vortex of self-fulfilling prophecies and circular angst. And so we are brought to wonder (abetted by Leiris's self-confessed fascination with initiation, esotericism, and the occult) whether this is not, yet again, a journey into the interior masquerading as a journey into the exterior, of the self under the mask of the other and, ultimately—note the fact that he ends up fascinated by Spirit cults and that (I would like to check this) *all* of these spirits seem *malevolent*—a classic descent into hell.

Here, we are confronted by the paradox of Leiris's religious stance. Early in *L'Afrique Fantôme*, he tells us, "All of this is religious and I am decidedly a religious man."[36] Clearly, he is very happy when wrestling with a symbolic system (his immediate liking and respect for the Bandiagara people on whom Griaule and his colleagues will later concentrate are very clear), exasperated when never getting to the end of it, yes, but delighted and immediately "in love" when in the thick of solving the riddles. His lifelong defiance of religious belief, however (not uninfluenced by his horror of the Catholicism inflicted on him during his upbringing, a common French predicament), and his fundamentally negative stance of "'t'were better never to have been born" stand in opposition to such pleasures in both the early writings and the late ones; definitely in the late ones.

Perhaps the clue lies in another passage of *L'Afrique Fantôme* where he confesses that he is only religious "when he is shown the god."[37] This, surely, has to be linked with his ultimate rejection of Surrealism and his later claim to being a "realist" writer, one for whom the facticity of any given fact or objicticity of any given object (no doubt the classic "Why is it that this thing is such and not other-

---

34   Participant observation has several degrees ranging from the fieldworker being present at and observing at close range, as distinct from sitting in an armchair back home (Malinowski's "revolution"), to varieties of wholesale *tatamisation* or "going native." James Clifford, incidentally ("The Tropological Realism of Michel Leiris," *Sulfur* 15 [1986]: 4–20), does not seem to distinguish between these. Does Clifford ever take enough account of Leiris's apprentice status: did he write about himself so much partly because he did not yet fully know how to deal with the "other"? That he was under Griaule's direct orders in the field is clear from the start, a situation not frequently met within Anglo-American anthropology.

35   Leiris, *L'Age d'Homme*, 214.

36   Leiris, *L'Afrique Fantôme*, 86; cf. 97, 374, 389, 401, 443.

37   Ibid., 374.

wise?" extending to the whole of creation) is both the joy of poetry and the guarantee that poetry is an alternative creation, that other utopian order which the human opposes to order-less (external to order) death.

Is this perhaps for him the ultimate fascination of the anthropological "other" and the activity of recording (and deciphering) its "*other*" code? Is it a desperate search for the possibility that, somewhere in human origins, or in the variety of human potential, there is an answering echo to this magic of the fact, another poetry being architectured and built or already edified inside an age-old tradition? Is the frequent despair linked with the fury one meets in oneself when that whole "*other*" structure is revealed as nothing else than one more poor and deficient set of those little things any given self is made up of and repeats over and over?[38] Is Leiris bound and tortured by that statute of self-limitation which drives one back to the sine qua non of self-liberation . . . (or none), the primal liberation movement: poetry . . . (or not), ultimate and only triumph of human solitude?

~

In this second part, I will react to *L'Afrique Fantôme* as a poet.

I wrote the first part before reading James Clifford on Leiris, then read Clifford.[39] This allows me a point of entry into critical debate by looking at this author's pioneering and admirably subtle account of the French School of Anthropology's relations to the arts and commenting on some aspects of that account which, as a poet, I cannot help finding difficult.[40]

A few questions. *First,* why is it that Clifford never discusses the most fundamental of all field problems, namely, whether an elementary level of truth and adequacy to observed facts on the ground is, or is not, delivered by an "informant" to an "anthropologist" and/or recorded by the latter?[41]

---

38 Ibid., 218–19, 231.

39 Clifford, "The Tropological Realism"; and James Clifford, *The Predicament of Culture* (Cambridge, MA: Harvard University Press, 1988).

40 Confessionally, I suppose I would have to acknowledge that part of the sorrow of growing older is the realization of how many fields of activity one has had to give up because of the limitations in time and energy of *one* existence, fields that have been taken over by others. I would have *liked* to be the introducer of the French school into the Anglo-Saxon world (I had lectured on Leenhardt, Griaule, Lévi-Strauss, and others as a graduate student at Chicago in 1951–52); *liked* to do pioneering work in the theory of Ethnopoetics; *liked* to translate so many French poets into American English; *liked* to write the definitive work for our time on *initiation*—the list could be extended. . . . In the event, re the first of these, Clifford has made a brilliant job of it.

41 Leiris's own sensitivity to this is recorded almost as soon as *L'Afrique Fantôme* starts (20). He is showing himself to be a good student.

Second, why is it that Clifford, for all his knowledgeable appreciation of matters artistic, chooses deliberately never to stray outside the borders of anthropology proper so that, in his writings, *novelists* are only of interest as factual recorders or narrative strategists in comparison to anthropologists doing the same thing, but not as writers of fiction, while poets do not appear as *poets* but also as fact-recorders, translators, or critics? Further here, why is it that Clifford sees only reflexive anthropologists as potential candidates for the position of anthropology's Joseph Conrad while totally ignoring the by now rather substantial experiments of Ethnopoetics? (I may have some answers to this, but it would be nice to draw Clifford out. . . .)

Third, how much do these lacunae have to do with a salient strategy of Clifford's analysis, i.e., the separation of what he calls "ethnography" from "anthropology"? Does he not allow his "ethnography" to transcend academic disciplinary boundaries and to englobe or manifest itself through the arts (in the guise of Surrealism, say) when he is stressing its essence as *creator* of negotiated worldview agreements between informants and investigators? Does he not thus jump over the problem of elementary veracity and also appropriate away the *creative* factor from the "creative artist"? And does he not admit his "ethnography" *back* into anthropology's bosom when science is powerful enough to lord it over any kind of fiction? *That* is usually treated historically, i.e., by arguing that French research of the 1920s and 1930s (which participated in the magazine *Documents* and was housed in the Musée du Trocadéro) was closer to his "ethnography," whereas French research after 1945 at the Musée de L'Homme was more kindred to his social scientific "anthropology."

It is not that such distinctions are invalid; indeed, they are highly illuminating, as when he finally sums up by distinguishing schematically "anthropological humanism" as making the different appear familiar and "ethnographic surrealism" as making the familiar appear different (both, therefore, aspects of one process).[42] It is that, in his emphasis on ethnography as *creative,* his consequent stress on *collective* authorship of culture-as-texts, and his avoidance of distinctions between that kind of "creativity" and the creativity of the poet or novelist (by avoiding these latter *as such*), he conspires with much contemporary theory in disenfranchising the "creative writer" both in Leiris himself and in the rest of us poets. In short, it seems to be one more example of our academic culture's present widespread empowerment of the critic at the expense of the poet. While much contemporary poetry has lovingly embraced this critical empowerment, I must firmly record a belief that such

42   Clifford, *The Predicament of Culture,* 145.

an embrace, while extremely stimulating in many intellectual respects, will ultimately turn out to be *political.* And, I happen to think, mortally dangerous to the heart of poetic endeavor. I believe it can be sociologically demonstrated that the poet is more and more the *slave* that the critic and the academy keep in their own basement.

Since there is little time, let me take the lyric poet as prototypical of the "creative writer" and go further into Clifford's treatment of Leiris as poet.

What I have long called Autoanthropology (published variously since a first fragment in *Boundary 2*),[43] Clifford later seems to call "personal ethnography." In his *The Predicament of Culture* chapter on Leiris, he writes, "By excess of subjectivity, a kind of objectivity is guaranteed—that (paradoxically) of a personal ethnography";[44] and, in his work at large, he mentions Leiris as one of the main promoters, at the Collège de Sociologie and elsewhere, of the notion that subjective matter should enter anthropology on the same footing as allegedly objective matter. "In Africa Leiris begins to keep field notes on himself or more precisely on an uncertain existence. These notes, on carefully collated cards, will form the data for *L'Age d'Homme* and *La Règle du Jeu:* not autobiographies but collections of 'facts.' "[45] Tellingly, Clifford quotes Leiris on fact in *L'Afrique Fantôme:* "To be in facts like a child. That's where I'd like to get."[46] And he comments, "Desire for a regression to existence before the need to collect oneself, to account for things and one's own life."[47] Later, Clifford writes of the extraordinary *innocence* of *L'Afrique Fantôme* maintained, as is all of Leiris's work, against the devastating pressure of a sense of universal futility, where the miracle of continued writing, the tenacity of it, is that every entry promises something but never gives it: *"L'Afrique Fantôme* is only a pen starting up each day."[48]

"Never gives it"? Is this the beginning of a very subtle derogation of Leiris as poet? What if the "pen starting up each day" is all of Leiris that Leiris *can* be and, hence, *wishes* to be? Clifford describes the narrative in *L'Age d'Homme* and *L'Afrique Fantôme* as drawing "on both the intimate journal and the novelistic fiction while falling into neither genre."[49] What Leiris makes of himself is an

43 Nathaniel Tarn, "From Atlantis: An Auto-Anthropology," *Boundary 2,* 4, no. 1 (1975): 36–48.

44 Clifford, *The Predicament of Culture,* 167.

45 Ibid. This Leiris quotation continues as follows: "and images *which I refused to exploit by letting my imagination work on them; in other words the negation of a novel. To reject all fables . . .* nothing but these facts and all these facts" (my italics).

46 Leiris, *L'Afrique Fantôme,* 234.

47 Clifford, *The Predicament of Culture,* 168.

48 Ibid., 173.

49 Ibid., 171.

"*objet fabriqué*"; not "an identity but . . . a personage."[50] In his *Sulfur* piece, Clifford had put it this way: "The subject . . . is less an intimate or private self, an inner soul revealed, than it is a kind of personal 'culture,' a collection of meaningful
artifacts to be connected, understood and rewritten."[51] "The 'sincerity' Leiris
seeks," Clifford adds in *Predicament*, "has as little to do with the romantic notion
of confession (an unmediated true speech) as the 'objectivity' he cultivates has to
do with scientific detachment." (I would, at greater length, question both these
statements.) In the end, Leiris's sincerity is *style*, not speech from the heart.[52]

But, the poet might ask, do we not hold that style may be *all there is*? Constitutively all there is of *us*—and that given the nature of the stuff we use in our art,
that is *all for any poet that there can be*? Is Clifford contradicting himself here without noticing it? He is all for "creative construct," yet when he comes nose to nose
with the monophonic *individual* rather than a polyphonic *collective* construct,
even in someone whose cause he is upholding, he tends to underplay and under-
value the former's autonomy. As I see it, Clifford occults Leiris the *poet* behind
Leiris the avant-garde auto-anthropologist and prophet ethnographer—*both* creative naturally, but in very different senses. The very complicated problem, of
course, is that Clifford may be conspiring with Leiris or . . . Leiris with him.[53]

Is Clifford going against, or with, the grain of Leiris himself in disregarding the
poet and presenting him, for his own purposes, as more of a homogeneous entity
than in fact he is? He talks of Leiris and other anthropologists, such as Alfred Mé-
traux, as coming to distrust Surrealism's "fast-and-loose way" with ethnographic
fact, a distrust which takes us right back to the question of "elementary veracity" I
referred to earlier.[54] It also takes us forward to Leiris's decision, after *L'Afrique
Fantôme* and *L'Age d'Homme*, to keep completely separate his two jobs. Clifford
(and others) tend to put this to the account of Leiris's politicization when Leiris,
criticizing (as he does in the preface to the 1951 re-edition of *L'Afrique Fantôme*) his
own early "excessive aestheticism and radical chic posturing,"[55] finally allows its full
liberating weight to the political polyphony of his "informants." This is perfectly
justified. But, thinking back to my early distinction between Creative Angel and

50   Ibid., 171.
51   Ibid., 11.
52   Ibid., 172.
53   This occultation could be further shown up in Clifford's comparison of Joseph Conrad and Bro-
     nislaw Malinowski, where Conrad, it seems to me, almost disappears as creative writer. It is in
     this chapter and in the following one on ethnographic surrealism that Clifford's ambivalence to-
     ward *creation* manifests itself most abundantly. I have to look at this more closely.
54   Clifford, *The Predicament of Culture*, 125.
55   Clifford, "The Tropological Realism," 12.

Angel of Record, I wonder too whether it is not *also* related to Leiris's evolving (or devolving) view of himself as lyric poet and his desire to withdraw a vulnerable, even damaged, and possibly collapsing, vehicle from what he sees as one of our time's most humanly important grounds of conflict.

As Leiris makes abundantly clear in his interminable record of daily battle between despair, fear, and hope, he eventually, Clifford claims, abandons "imagination, both surrealist and romantic, in favor of a '*parti pris de réalisme.*' His oeuvre is a cenotaph, the tomb of an impossible poetry, a silent oracle."[56] Of course, Clifford has too much invested in Leiris to avoid adding immediately, "But in mourning his lack of inspiration, Leiris produces another kind of poetry." But Clifford—since he avoids discussing poetry (except, one guesses, that of the dead; see his 1988 introductory chapter on W. C. Williams)—does not tell us exactly *what kind* except to say that "a poetry of visionary imagination is replaced with a poetic prose."[57] Looking at Leiris's record in terms of production within given genres and, naturally, without detracting for a moment from his stature as a writer, it may be that we should try to take him more seriously in his avowal of failure and agree, even if only experimentally, that where he may have failed is *as a poet.* Which confirms Clifford in his basic view.

What remain complex and undiscussed, however, are the full scope and implication of a struggle within a poet-anthropologist between her/his two vocations and what exactly it signals for one vocation to win out over another. Here, to give a true reaction, I have to go into some of my own stuff which has worked in the teeth of a great deal of contemporary assertion that the individual author, like the individual God before him, is dead. Also against the contention that all previous poetics or Defenses of Poetry and the Poet must sink below the weight of auto-creative and auto-enacting language. To underline what I feel up against, let me here quote Clifford's devastating view of poetry seemingly implied in his description of the "surreal" as "all too easily co-opted by romantic notions of artistic genius or inspiration."[58] God forbid, ha? that anyone should be *inspired*!!!? Does a manifestation of Blakean jealousy have to be invoked here yet again?

I have tried to evolve a model which, while by no means denying its origin in romanticism, seems to me to be a sheerly biocultural sine qua non of poetic *survival.* In the model, *initiation* as a passage back and forth between individual and collective grants an ethical disposition to the lyric mode of apprehending, and acting in,

---

56   Ibid., 15.
57   Ibid. For the Williams essay, see James Clifford, "Introduction," in Clifford, *The Predicament of Culture.*
58   Clifford, *The Predicament of Culture,* 134.

the real world.[59] I do not ascribe to chance Leiris's interest in initiation and in its "secret languages."[60]

For my present purpose, the importance of such a model is that it is capable of defining an autonomous stature for the lyric poet as archetype of the individual stance in a world generally more and more hostile to individuality. The polyphonic dimensions dear to Clifford figure here. They figure, however, in a manner that, for the purposes of this stance and this stance alone, ensures they are firmly under the control of the monophonic and firmly within the domain, not of ethnography or anthropology, but of *poetry*—the activity typical of all writing which is totally committed not to the recording of fact but to its creative transformations, whether alchemical or semiotic matters not a jot.[61]

This runs parallel to my argument that the genre so long looked for which would assure a complete union of the poetic and anthropological enterprises (should such be desirable) lies *not* in the keeping of the anthropologist who cannot, for all his/her efforts, get beyond *belles lettres,* but with the poet who, in theory, still can. This is the question of a language which, without turning away from scientific veracity, abdicates not one jot of its literary potential. Undoubtedly utopian, the search is at home in poetry, incurably utopian, and probably nowhere else.

Autoanthropology is one of my activities: I am convinced that it should not be my major. I believe that Leiris was an extraordinarily brave victim (for which his time, his historical position, was partially responsible) of a belief that he could replace poetry by, or lead to its destination in, Autoanthropology. Thus, he either chose the latter, perhaps believing that his constitution allowed of no other path, or, ultimately, in his truly epic fight against *timor mortis,* the ultimate and determining fight as I suggested some time ago in a comparison between elegy in Rilke and Neruda, he lost his balance: the hope and energy for the atrociously long haul died in the miasma of his sense of futility.

It is a fight we all, in poetry, fight: more and more as our stance and position deliquesce in Western culture. It is strange to me that the overwhelming question

59   On this model, see many essays ranging from "The Choral Voice" to "On Refining a Model" in this volume.

60   Leiris, *L'Afrique Fantôme,* 16, 314, 320, 446.

61   In my model, the collective is first and foremost dealt with at the level of the "*vocal,*" that of the often cruel give-and-take of literary life, while building an *opus* to stand among others as one's *praxis* in one's times. This alone guarantees nothing without "descent" to the "*choral*" which, like all initiations, is a matter of death or survival. Listening to the "voices of the dead" (culture, tradition, and the accumulated "securities" of human existence, even if only as utopic *desiderata*) may vivify or deaden a poetry according to the initial stance the poet has vis-à-vis Eros and Thanatos.

in my mind so often becomes "Well, after all of that, how *did death come upon him?*" more so, perhaps, than "Well, after all of that, how *did he go out against death?*" But that it does so reads to me as if the *Choral*—my own model's *voice of the dead,* as it happens—triumphed over his individual voice and as if the struggle for poetic survival, however nobly, dignifiedly, and impressively, was indeed, if related to the full potential, inevitably and ineradicably lost.[62]

1991

---

62 It was only at the conference, after writing this paper, that I began acquaintance with the work of Jean Jamin. I may unwittingly have repeated some of his criticisms of Clifford and other historians. See especially J. Jamin, "L'ethnographie mode d'inemploi: de quelques rapports de l'ethnologie avec le malaise dans la civilisation," in *Le Mal et la douleur,* ed. Jacques Hainard and Roland Kaehr (Neuchâtel, Switzerland: Musée d'Ethnographie, 1986).

The Search for the "Primitive" Outside and Inside

The Ethnopoetics of Antonin Artaud, with Notes on William Carlos Williams

I am going to be talking about two poets, one French, the other American. The French one will be my main subject.

Antonin Artaud was born in Marseille in 1896 and died in Paris in 1948. He led one of the most tortured lives ever experienced by any poet. Reaching Paris in 1920 he began, three years later, an epoch-making correspondence with Jacques Rivière of the *Nouvelle Revue Française*—an exchange about the mind of a poet, what it could do and not do, what it needed in order to survive at all. This, when published, was regarded by many French writers as a complete break with poetry as then conceived. From 1924 to 1927, he took part in the surrealist movement and worked as an actor and director. He had an impressive appearance as a priest in Dreyer's famous movie *Joan of Arc*. In 1927, he broke with Surrealism and began work on what he called a "Theater of Cruelty," a theater freed from text and depending greatly on voice, cries, and movements, a theater at the origin of most twentieth-century avant-garde drama. He suffered all his life from extreme poverty, slavery to heroin and opium, and appalling mental visions and tortures. He is supposed to have been in Mexico in 1936. In 1937 he traveled to Ireland but was arrested after threatening to do himself damage and sent back to France in a straitjacket. From 1937 to 1946, he had many stays in psychiatric hospitals (Rouen,

Paris, Rodez) undergoing what he claimed to be murderous episodes of elec-troshock. A famous lecture-performance at the Vieux Colombier Theater in Paris on January 13th, 1947, graphically exhibited his lifelong hell to all of literary France. Artaud died in 1948 in a hospice. Gallimard has published over twenty-five volumes of his *Complete Works* so far. Much of his work is available in English.

My second poet is an American, William Carlos Williams, a physician by pro-fession, who lived most of his life in Rutherford, New Jersey. I'll come back to him at the end.

I open a parenthesis here to say a word on the context of this present talk. It is an exercise in Ethnopoetics. "Ethnopoetics" in the United States is based on a variety of literary activities linking poetry and anthropology. An ethnopoetic cri-ticism as such does not really exist in the strictest sense: when we talk of Ethno-poetics, we are dealing rather with a vast body of translation of "primitive" poetry into a Western language and with a search for the roots of poetry—beyond the canons and ethnocentric criteria of the West—in order to get closer to and to bring on what Robert Duncan called a "Symposium of the Whole." A sympo-sium, that is to say, of all cultures and all members of any culture, including the members which any culture keeps on the margins of what it defines as "normal" and "acceptable."

My own efforts, being at the same time poet and anthropologist, have been di-rected to confronting the results, more or less "objective," of a social science with the ideas about such and such a "primitive society" formed by certain poets—attracted by the idea of closing in on the apparently most ancient forms of human thought and behavior. Let us admit right off that this confrontation can be mostly unflatter-ing even to the most genial of poets for it is more than probable that the thinking of such a poet will carry, even more acutely than usual, the ethnocentric prejudices of the culture to which s/he belongs. Let it be said, then, that the admiration one har-bors for a poet, qua poet, does not necessarily have to suffer from this kind of analy-sis and must never be taken in any way for a devaluation of her/his work.

Another way of putting this is that I am studying the way in which a given poet has looked at what he or she conceived to be the "primitive." Traditionally, in this search, the poet has, like the anthropologist, looked toward the other, the for-eign, the exotic. In this talk, which is based on what is very much work in progress, I want to begin comparing a poet who, for reasons very much his own, may have extended the vision of the "primitive" as far as it can go with a poet who would probably not be considered by most people as having looked for the "primitive" at all—largely because he was looking at his own people in his New Jersey home area. The former poet is Artaud. The latter is William Carlos Williams.

Most of my work so far has been on Artaud and I have concentrated on his alleged voyage to the Tarahumara Indians of Mexico—along the way voicing some doubts as to whether this ever actually happened or whether Artaud did not invent a great deal of it or, possibly, all of it. I suggest that it not having happened would in fact strengthen the view that Artaud had placed the "primitive" so far out that it would end up, in truth, by being completely out of reach.

In this talk I limit myself to consideration of his Mexican journey. Because of the very weak library resources which I dispose of in New Mexico, I am limiting myself, more or less entirely, to the section called "*Les Tarahumaras*" in the ninth volume of the Gallimard edition of Artaud's *Complete Works;* to some parts of volumes 4 and 5; and to books by Carl Lumholtz and Wendell Bennett and Robert Zingg on the Tarahumara Indians that I happen to own. I did not have access to the work of Carlos Bassauri (1922). I must also indicate that I am neither an Artaud nor a Tarahumara specialist. Despite whatever I say here, please be assured that I continue to believe in two possibilities: that Artaud did reach the Tarahumara and that he did not reach them.

The works of the poet which I will quote suffice to indicate, however, that Artaud's trip to the Tarahumara—a Uto-Aztec people of some 40,000 souls living in the extraordinarily dramatic canyons of the Sierra Madre, comprising something like the southwestern third of the Mexican State of Chihuahua—is extremely sparsely documented.

Cardoza y Arágon, Artaud's translator in Mexico, tells us that the poet was "on a mission" with money from the Fine Arts Department (Mexican, one assumes) and with some help from the University of Mexico. The trip lasted from the end of August to the middle of October 1936. On the 7th of October, Artaud was back in Ciudad Chihuahua. So we are dealing with a period of only six to eight weeks which is very little for a "mission" and even for a trip which he claims he had wanted to do for a very long time. In the various pieces or articles themselves, spread out over some twelve years, stretching from the moment of his alleged stay until fifteen days before his death (for the poem entitled "*Tutuguri*"), he gives us no dates, no itinerary, no place names (with one exception), no informant's name—in short, none of the basic data which one usually expects as the basis of most ethnographic accounts or even of most travel narratives.

It follows that the characteristic events of his trip and, more problematically, the most elementary information about the people he is supposed to have studied are obliterated. One is therefore entitled to suspect that, from the start, Artaud eliminates their historicity. This is a fact worth noting: the thirst to find a people who have escaped from history sometimes leads an author to take away from them the little history that they possess. It is difficult, reading Artaud, to realize that the Tarahumara, even if their lifestyle remains simple, have known us for some 400 years like all other Mexicans and that their culture has been influenced by us for all that time. I quote an example. Artaud writes, "They sometimes come into the towns, moved by who knows what desire to roam around."[1] To which one must answer: the Tarahumara, by God, come into the towns for economic and commercial reasons, is that not so?

Additionally, *in the texts which I refer to here*, especially those more or less contemporaneous with the trip, I find no information on Artaud's intentions, his exact interests, the aim and purpose of his journey. All of this, of course, could eventually be illuminated by other texts. I have just found, for example, a 1984 issue of *Europe* magazine containing articles by Le Clézio and Cardoza y Arágon: but find neither of these in any way conclusive. But we are missing, more instances, the reasons for the poet's following such and such a path among his hosts or the identity of individuals in Mexico City, there were some certainly, who could have given him advice on the choice of his destinations. It seems to me that we do not know—and this is really a mystery of some importance in the light of what was known in his time and what is known in ours—*why* he had chosen the Tarahumara instead of, for example, the Huichol, geographically closer to Mexico City, whose symbolism, aesthetics, and religious and mystical ideas relating to the hunt and the use of peyote are infinitely more developed and interesting than those of the Tarahumara. Cardoza writes about this in *Europe* but it seems clear that he gives us his own hypotheses on the question and not those of Artaud.

In our reading, we then ask how, in such a short time, he would have been able to understand the Tarahumara tongue, until, as expected, we learn that he had a mixed-blood guide and interpreter (although questions remain even here).[2] We also ask ourselves how the Tarahumara, excessively shy and very reluctant to give away their secrets according to all those who have studied them, so quickly and readily allowed Artaud to witness a "secret" ritual (his expression), leaving us wondering whether, in fact, the ritual was as secret as he claimed. However this may be, we learn (and a host of details are lacking) that he was able to insert himself as "protector of the Indians" in a quarrel between Indians and mixed-blood

---

1   Antonin Artaud, *Oeuvres Complètes* (Paris: Gallimard, various dates), 9:79, and cf. 9:80. After a French original given at a Montreal conference, this text was read as the Toyota Lecture at the Art Center, Pasadena, CA, in 2002. All Artaud references, except those specifically noted, are to the ninth volume of Artaud, *Oeuvres Complètes*.

2   Ibid., 9:14.

administrators who intended, in the name of the Mexican government, to forbid the use of peyote at the very time of Artaud's arrival. The local bureaucrats, he says, had just destroyed a field of the stuff.[3] Interesting question: the peyote is searched for, or "hunted" as the Huichols would say, from seven to ten days' march east of the Tarahumara territory but, as far as we know, is not cultivated locally. Where, then, was that "field"?

Artaud's claim is that he was an initiate: an initiation was necessary in order to see the ceremony and the Indians gave him that initiation. We remain uncertain, however, as to whether the ceremonies he describes were actually prepared and enacted serially for his benefit. He complains about a wait of thirty days (not much of a deal for an anthropologist!) because of a death which had taken place locally, and it is at least possible that he was in fact inserted into a funerary rite for that person, a question of keeping Artaud (not the most easygoing customer one could imagine) happy with as little trouble as possible. All of this said, with full respect for Artaud if he did do the trip, regarding his problems with heroin, his suspicions that he was being mocked and taken advantage of, his idea (virtually an *idée fixe*) that the Indians no longer knew exactly the reasons for what they were doing—the famous "need-to-remember-without-knowing-what" well-known to all Mesoamerican anthropologists and other students of conquered peoples.

Did Artaud see a "peyote rite" as opposed to any old rite (a death rite, a healing rite, who knows), or were all rituals peyote rituals: ritual behavior in this area being after all not highly particularized? It would seem, indeed, that several rituals, a death ritual for instance, included a "peyotl rite" or part of one. Artaud's "*Tutuguri*" for instance, which he identifies with "the One" or with "The Sun," must refer to one of the two Tarahumara ritual dances, the one called *Rutuburi* (Lumholtz) / *Dutuburi* (Bennett and Zingg), a very common dance in the whole Tarahumara area.[4]

A place name, Norogachic, the only one that Artaud mentions in his story, tells us indeed that he found himself fairly close to a geographical center where *peyotero* shamans were still dominant at the time.[5] We are probably dealing with the place called Nararachic by Lumholtz. But Artaud does not help us much by using expressions like "the master of all things[6] who touches him with his knife in order to initiate him" or "the road where the priests of the *Ciguri*" (probably the peyotl *Hikuli* mentioned by Bennett and Zingg) or "the priests of the *Tutuguri*."

3   Ibid., 9:18.
4   Ibid., 9:12.
5   Ibid., 9:72.
6   Ibid., 9:11.

Nor in leading us to believe that the rituals of the latter were, without fail, to lead to a deeper understanding at the hands of those of the Ciguri. Certainly, a more extensive investigation should consolidate and compare the three main descriptions that Artaud gives of his rituals with the scenarios detailed in the ethnographic literature.[7] It will not be easy because links and recognition marks are often lacking in Artaud.

But, here I only have a rather narrow window. Let's admit right away, then, that Artaud projected from whole cloth onto the Tarahumara the clichés that one still heard from ethnographers, and especially French ethnographers, in my student days. How about "These men supposed to be uncivilized, these dirty people . . . how struck one is by the heights of culture to which their minds were able to attain"?[8] How about comparing that to statements made by the Griaule expeditions, criticized by the poet-anthropologist Michel Leiris in his *L'Afrique Fantôme*?

Let us also admit that Artaud projected fantasies which were not exactly complimentary for American indigenous peoples onto the Tarahumara, fantasies of certain nineteenth-century diffusionists (still current among some science-fictioneers of our time) which were at the base of his own passion for esoteric literature as composed by the likes of Fabre d'Olivet or René Guénon. Let us choose one phrase among others: "And it seems strange to me that the primitive Tarahumara whose rituals and beliefs are older than the Deluge might already have been in possession of that science well before the Legend of the Grail, well before the formation of the Rosicrucian sect."[9] The bulk of Artaud's texts is rife with such occultist interpretations. Older than the *Deluge*?

For the rest, it is often hard to know on what level of reality one should place things, and it is too simple—from our point of view—to abdicate by talking about one single "poetic" reality. In the text entitled *The Mountain of Signs*, for instance, are we dealing with pictographs cut into the rock such as are found in the whole region up to New Mexico—or with less concrete forms, as the following would lead us to believe: "yet, I was able to realize that I was dealing not with sculpted forms but with a determined play of light which added itself to the relief of the rocks," this followed in turn by remarks on a kabbalistic "music of Numbers acting on Nature in order to direct the birth of forms, which it extracts from chaos."[10] And if Artaud did not *see* the pictographs (illustrated very precisely by Lumholtz for Artaud's area), should we not be asking why?

---

7 Ibid., 9:20–23, 44–47, 72–75.
8 Ibid., note, 9:230.
9 Ibid., 9:39.
10 Ibid., 9:37.

Further, what are we to make of a phrase like "If the major part of the Tarahumara race is autochthonous and if, as it pretends, it fell from the sky into the Sierra"? What would this "race" be if not "autochthonous"? Where does Artaud get this qualification "the major part"? What ethnographer or traveler would not establish some sort of difference between truly falling from the sky, *saying* that one fell from the sky, and *believing* that one fell from the sky? A tribe, Artaud continues, still speaking of the rocks, which fell into "a Nature already prepared. And that Nature wished to think as a human being. As it evolved human beings, it also evolved rocks."[11] Very fine, all of this, but where exactly does it leave Tarahumara reality which Artaud claims he is so proud to give us *exactly* as he always perceived it?

What we have to note carefully is that Artaud did not pretend to do scientific work to reach, as he puts it, a doctorate. But, like any man of his time respectful of science and scholarship ("I do not believe," he says, "in absolute imagination, I mean that which makes something out of nothing"),[12] he takes care to indicate to us the rigorous nature of his reportage—even if, as he goes along, he leads us to understand that the poet always primes over the ethnographer. Artaud writes, "These are the very words of the Indian chief and I am only reproducing them faithfully, not as he spoke them to me *but such as I reconstructed* them, the fantastic illuminations of the *Ciguri*" (my emphasis).[13] Or else: "These words of the Priest that I have just quoted are absolutely authentic; they seemed to me to be too important and too beautiful to allow me to change anything and, *if we are not dealing with an absolute word to word translation,* nevertheless they do not go far from them." Note on this that the priest has just said, according to Artaud, "this obscene mask of he who cackles between sperm and shit," a phrase which, knowing Artaud's other works, it is extremely difficult to attribute to the priest as opposed to the poet.[14]

There is also the long litany of the witness: "it is not I who invented this / and I can't help it if / it is puerile if you like but it exists / I saw six times / What can I do if / I saw / and was I not told that . . ." on the same pages where Artaud speaks of the doctorate. The quote on the doctorate is worth giving as a whole, for it is a good indication of the spirit of these texts:

> Much less was needed by novelists and poets to recover and precisely delineate myths invented by their imagination alone. I did not pretend in recording my trip to write a doctoral thesis, rediscover the path of a genuine tradition and furnish

11   Ibid., 9:36.
12   Ibid., 9:101.
13   Ibid., 9:12–13.
14   Ibid., 9:25.

proofs to corroborate it. Believe whatever you wish about these meetings of mine—no matter. And still less important to me is it to believe that the Three Kings made a detour to get back home through the uninhabited mountains of Mexico. All I know is that, arriving up there and looking down over nearly infinite kilometers of land, I felt strongly moving inside myself reminiscences and strange images that nothing, on departure, would have led me to foresee.[15]

This gives us fairly remarkable insights into the state of mind of a poet who, just recently, had come to urgent conclusions about the theater as a vehicle for the "Great (Esoteric) Tradition"; who despaired at the slowness of the publishers Gallimard in getting his book out into the world; and who felt that what he called "Another Man" was soon going to emerge from his corpse whose willpower and wisdom would depend on an absolute and unconditional poetic fiat.

What is most interesting about Artaud at this point is the way in which he observes and thinks about his observations colored by interpretations which he alone imposes on his field data while demanding for these observations a value equal, if not superior, to that we grant to relatively objective anthropology. I am not referring only to the extraordinary ritual authority (noted by Artaud)[16] often occurring in someone when taking certain drugs, mescaline or psilocybin for example, but also to arguments which are very striking because of their quasi-scientific character. As in this argument for example: "the forms are natural, I agree, (natural and ritual objects are referred to) but it is their repetition which is not natural." From this, Artaud deduces that the symbolic repetition undergone, whether among the rocks ("The Mountain of Signs") or in the rituals by the senses of a body "whose obsessions are enslaved especially to the obsession of counting," is not born of chance but of one same "secret mathematics" which he ties in with the Jewish Kabbalah.[17] Had he been an anthropologist, this kind of reasoning (the predetermined mathematical secrets aside) could have led Artaud to establish a lexicon of Tarahumara symbols in agreement with informants' data and opinions or even reach the site of a true proto-structuralist "savage mind," to use a Lévi-Straussian term.

However, these possibilities dissolve at every step. One can actually follow changes in manuscripts, especially in relations to the piece entitled "The Peyote Ritual of the Tarahumara," always moving from a more or less ethnographic stance to a description completely colored by the poet's personal mythology.[18] Artaud does not let go for a moment of the game of scientific persuasion. Let's see:

15 Ibid., 9:102–3.
16 Ibid., 9:21.
17 Ibid., 9:36.
18 Ibid., note 35, 9:18 and 9:220; note 46, 9:20 and 9:221; note 50, 9:22 and 9:226; and elsewhere.

"But Traditions unbelievable perhaps but which scholarly digs little by little demonstrate as reality (of an alleged "Great Solar Tradition . . .)."[19] *What* scholarly digs, we have to ask, while pointing out at the same time that, regardless of the fact that most Mesoamerican religions are solar in a general manner of speaking, we usually find no specifically solar cults? Or, on the following page: "but if you recall in addition that the Tarahumara Sierra is the place where the first giant human skeletons were found and that they continue to be found as I write"[20]— *What* giants!?! we gasp out in the role of a Sancho Panza, recalling obscure and now totally forgotten texts about giants penned by a Dr. Blanchard around 1909. . . .

In the absence of substantial documentation, one is perhaps entitled to ask questions regarding the exactitude of Artaud's Mesoamerican expertise. Let's take as an example the list of an "inconceivable mixture of races" in Mexico given in a letter to Jean Paulhan of Gallimard on April 23rd, 1936.[21] It does not start too badly but it ends as "Zapotecs with Kakchiquels, Kakchiquels with Creoles . . . Yaquis with Ki-Ka-Pus. . . ."

Even with the help of enthusiasm and humor, this can hardly be called very brilliant. Who knows what Creoles are doing in that list? Further, not only are the Kakchiquel Guatemalan rather than Mexican, living fairly far from the Mexican border, but the Ki-Ka-Pus (Kickapoos in the anthropological literature) do not only belong to the United States rather than Mexico but also are inhabitants of the American far North: that is, in Wisconsin! But perhaps, I'll be told, I am not here to convert Artaud to anthropology.

Or else, following suggestions already located in the first texts, we must have recourse to observations made by Artaud after his time in the field. "I went (to Mexico) to find a race capable of following me in my thinking," he writes in a letter from the internment hospital of Rodez of October 6th, 1945;[22] or, in another letter of November 27th, "as I went to the Tarahumara to put an end to certain magical practices whose victim I have long been";[23] or again and already in an extremity in 1936–37, "It had to be from now on that a certain buried thing . . . should be extracted and render service precisely through my crucifixion."[24] In order for us to realize, not without sadness, that the Tarahumara existed in the poet's intention uniquely to serve him, his art, his theories, but that he, in that same intention and

19   Ibid., 9:64.
20   Ibid., 9:65.
21   Ibid., 5:201.
22   Ibid., 9:173.
23   Ibid., 9:188.
24   Ibid., 9:50.

leaving aside his one-time "protectorship," was of no use whatsoever to the Tarahumara.

It is certain that one cannot accuse Artaud of directly and consciously serving the forces of colonialism: among others, the text on the Theater of Cruelty will testify on his behalf.[25] We also notice that Artaud is perfectly capable of seeing what is harmful to native peoples in Mexico when Mexicans insist that "their Indians" "are still racially inferior" or "savages."[26] But something tragic remains in all this if we feel that there is, or would be, some merit in attempting the conjugation of a poetic vision on the one hand with another vision made up of the true pronouncements of a people whose guest one happens to be and toward whom, or toward a description of same, one might feel a certain responsibility.

Artaud was reading at the time, and probably much before that time, works on universal esoteric knowledge, works forming a codification of a Western tradition, basically Christian in inspiration. We can recognize that what Artaud says about "the Tradition," *from that tradition's own viewpoint,* is well said and very clearly set out: see, for instance, the text *Une race-principe.*[27] He is also adept at keeping secrets (a basic initiatic requirement) and did not give away, with one exception, what he had seen or felt under the influence of peyote.[28] But this codification, we have to admit it on the political plane, rendered no disservice to the colonialism and imperialism of his time. This in the sense that so-called primitive peoples, being as it were autochthons of eternity, had no use whatsoever for our "progress," did not know what to do with it. This primitive state, admired but sempiternally *other,* before acquiring a human face had to be parahuman if not superhuman if the larger nations were to be able to feel completely unresponsible in their regard.

All of this continued alive to the end among the surrealists, for example, as well as (I have pointed this out) among the early ethnographers—it is not for nothing that in the sixties, anthropology came to be defined as "daughter of imperialism." Let no one believe that we have done with this, for our societies, whether of the right or the left politically, have now gone from theory to practice. In an ever-shrinking world, where competition for land and resources increases with every passing day, what this signifies is quite simply the *extermination* of this primitivity, whether by genocide or ethnocide. Whether it be through destruction of habitat by logging, over-fishing, global warming, or whatever form of outright theft, this continues on a daily basis. If there is one thing that can be

25   Ibid., 4:122; 5:18–19.
26   Ibid., 5:202.
27   Ibid., 9:68–71.
28   Ibid., 9:25.

said in favor of present-day Ethnopoetics—the set of concerns evolved by some poets among us to try to combat through plus-value this deadly process—it is that by being the forerunners of multiculturalism, some poetic activity today favors an egalitarian view of humanity rather than the phantasmagoric view that poor Antonin Artaud saddled himself with—whether or not he ever truly reached the Tarahumara.[29]

Without a great deal of time at my disposal, I would now like to give you a quick sense of what I am trying to look at in regard to the American poet William Carlos Williams—someone I am sure I should not have to introduce as I had to in the case of Artaud.[30] First, it so happens that, around the time Williams wrote his early work, anthropology was finding good reasons to study the anthropologist's own society rather than, or in addition to, exotic ones. An extensive study known as *Middletown* is a good example. Second, I believe that a case could be made for looking at the extremely realistic uses in literature of his own Paterson, New Jersey, area as if it formed, in fact, an anthropological study. There is an interesting travel book element in his treatment in the stress that he puts on using his car, not only as a doctor but also as an observer, to get around. Third, for any careful reader, there is in Williams a constant search for some kind of ur-ground in America which, if it could be contacted (*contact* is a most important word for him via his friend the poet Robert McAlmon), would serve as a basis for the "making it new" which Williams wanted for American culture and literature. The critic Harry Levin put this very well, albeit for Williams's one incursion into foreign parts, in his introduction to Williams's "A Voyage to Pagany":

> Pagans had originally been dwellers in rural villages; the early Christians used the term at Rome for those who still practiced idolatry; more neutrally, a *paganus* was a person who did not share the prevailing beliefs. . . . The novel charts a return,

---

29 I'd like to propose another two questions. First: in *The Theater of Cruelty*, Artaud is very keen on defining in a very striking manner the theatrical act as being totally unique *par excellence*, and totally unrepeatable. Among the Tarahumara and elsewhere, he defends the great value of ritual. But ritual is essentially repetitive. How do we reconcile these two attitudes?
    Second: Vincent Kauffman has tried to show how we can, from the point of view of a "pure" poetry, avoid certain criticisms of Artaud's feeble hold on so-called reality. Fine. But Artaud himself ("I do not believe in an imagination . . . which makes something out of nothing"; see Artaud, *Oeuvres Complètes*, 9:101) seems to choose a view of poetry which is not at odds with the realia. I am obliged to note that any idea of a "pure" poetry renders impossible any true interdisciplinary work between poetry and anthropology that would be followed by a critical endeavor such as ours.

30 Re-reading this, I realize that James Clifford has been hereabouts before. See James Clifford, "Introduction," in his *The Predicament of Culture* (Cambridge, MA: Harvard University Press, 1988).

via "Old Pagany," to primal forces antedating both Europe and America. The central section, "At the Ancient Springs of Purity and Plenty[,]" seeks to revive a sense of power and beauty through communion with "a resurgent paganism still untouched." Long obscured by Christianity, and by the Renaissance, the pagan gods survive as stone images in the cathedrals.

Immediately following Williams's trip to Europe came *In the American Grain,* which book makes it very clear that our poet was interested also in the pagan in his own country. I do not think it would take us long to demonstrate that the word "pagan" here is synonymous with "primitive" or that the continent of America envisaged as a female Earth, a Gaia, with Indians as her original children, is what any American poet worth his or her salt is ordained to love and sing. A final point for right now: any reader of Williams on the people of the Paterson area will quickly be struck by the poet-doctor's interest in, and compassion for, the poor folk. In our context here, might this not be because the poor "are always with us," that they are, as it were, an ur-reality as against the upwardly mobile who have created, with their wealth, their bourgeois values, their Puritanism, and their political stasis, everything that Williams most cordially detested in his own country?

I have to leave the matter there for the moment but it seems to me that, for this and other reasons to be adduced at some later date, Williams is a good candidate for the position of the poet who looks for the primitive inside, about as far inside as it is possible to go. In this, he stands as an interesting contrast to Antonin Artaud.

1992

Translation/Antitranslation //
Culture/Multiculture

Some Contradictions?

1) I would like to lead into this talk with a few personal considerations. First, I must admit that, for many years now, I have avoided paying great attention to writing about translation—being under the strong impression that very little new was being said and, indeed, could be said about translation as a craft: what we had here was academic self-perpetuation, not more. I felt that translation should be *done* as opposed to being talked about. As a result of this misapprehension, I have missed some new information about the field. It is not irrelevant here to note that when I tried to get some ten recent books on translation out of a provincial university library recently, I could not find a single one.

Second, I have felt a connection between my lack of interest in Translation theory and my waning interest in anthropological theory itself, a waning which, of course, went with the loss of any desire to do anthropology. Perhaps the turning point came with an interview of Gary Snyder done at Princeton in the early seventies. It was much more of a conversation than an interview but, for publication purposes, in *Alcheringa,* I erased my own contribution. It was Snyder I believe who chose the title—"From Anthropologist to Informant"—but it corresponded

This paper was given at the Bard College Translation Conference, October 1992.

very strongly to a deep longing of mine: that is, no longer to ask questions but to put myself into an activity in which there was a chance of giving answers: this activity being the constantly sought, ever-receding possibility of being a poet and nothing but a poet.[1] I mention this here because it is going to have something to do with what I might say about Antitranslation.

A couple of other, possibly related points although the relation may not appear at first sight. The first is that I have had growing doubts throughout my "career" about the advisability of any poet, young poets especially, taking on translation jobs on "major" authors if their own intent is firmly to be totally committed to poetry, what I call in several places "married to" poetry. This is because, quite simply, in this society, if you translate a major poet, perhaps a Nobel Prize winner or one in the running for such, you will be held all your life as married to *that* poet rather than to your own work; the "your work" which others want to discuss with you is, nine times out of ten, your translation of that poet, *not* your own, and, whatever merits your own may have, an infinitesimally small number of people will actually bethink themselves to consult it, even after having admired your translations. It goes without saying that the work of that poet (being a Nobel) is more important than yours; but that it frequently negates, erases, or totally obscures yours, however, is another matter indicating something about the sociological standing of poetry on the one hand, translation (even of poetry) on the other, and implying that, even in the case of translating non-Nobels, the same principle applies. I am far from Novalis here saying that "there is hardly a German writer of importance who has not translated, and who does not take as much pride in his translations as he does in his original works"[2] and it may well have to do with our American habit of fawning on foreign poets in order the better to ignore our own. In any event, I would advise young poets to consult older poets they wish to translate and ask them if they are considering winning the Nobel. If they are, turn around and run for it.

The final point: while everyone today in the academy pays lip service to interdisciplinary work, such work only has to appear on the scene for it to face almost insuperable difficulties in being consumed, respected, taught, published, and generally treated as a part of culture. Our specializationism, to coin an awful word meant to double-underline the depth of our classificatory disease, is that strong. I

1 See "Child as Father to Man in the American Uni-Verse" in this volume. For the Snyder interview, see Nathaniel Tarn, "From Anthropologist to Informant: A Field Study of Gary Snyder," *Alcheringa* 4 (Fall 1972): 104–13.
2 As quoted in André Lefevere, *Translating Literature: The German Tradition* (Assen, the Netherlands: Van Gorcum, 1977), ix.

will continue to be personal by saying that, but for the insight of one particular editor with what amounted to an imprint of his own, Lee Bartlett of the University of New Mexico, my *Views from the Weaving Mountain*[3] could never have been published without very considerable mutilation. I have similar problems with finding a scientific language which would retain literary quality. The absurdity of the situation is underlined when you realize that any amount of interference with linear narrative, to take one instance of complaint, can be published in a work of *fiction* nowadays (and earn big bucks) and even the hard-to-consume poetry of certain communities of poets can get published—but God forbid there should be any such thing in Holy Science: the public, intone the suddenly all-wise publishers, would not stand for it a single instant! This too is not unconnected to the subject of translation.

2) I now hope to switch off the personal. Those of you who have not turned a blind eye to what was going on in Translation theory, say some ten years ago, will have recognized by now that you must not expect any originality here at all in that I must be coming from at least two major innovative stances. The first is that of George Steiner, in his *After Babel*, where he shows with a massively erudite deployment of phenomenal fans of encyclopedic knowledge (his poetry) that virtually all acts of cultural communication, whether in time (usually the dimension of one's own culture) or in space (the dimension of inter-culturality), involve a transformative activity which in essence is what we mean by Translation.[4] The second is that of Edward Said who, following Gramsci, Foucault, and Schwab, demonstrates in his masterly *Orientalism* the extent to which the construction of apparently apolitical systems of representations in all the disciplines of our knowledge in fact constitutes cultural hegemonic mechanisms which inform, strengthen, and perpetuate the political oppression and/or control of he who is studied by he who studies.[5] Both these contributions lift discussion of Translation into an altogether different realm from that in which it is usually carried on.

It is not my business here to critique such major works. I would however say that, as of this moment, I cannot see much attention to Translation as a discipline and particular craft, rather than as a category of political action, paid by Said, nor do I hear him suggesting that, given all the years in which Islam had some hegemony over parts of Europe, we should at some time have a study of how Islam interpreted the Occident. This, however, brings me to risk widening my discourse

---

3 Nathaniel Tarn, *Views from the Weaving Mountain: Selected Essays in Poetics and Anthropology*, an American Poetry Book (Albuquerque: University of New Mexico Press, 1991).
4 George Steiner, *After Babel* (London: Oxford University Press, 1975).
5 Edward Said, *Orientalism* (New York: Pantheon, 1978).

and getting to my own possible contribution, a very humble one, by risking two statements. The first would be that *all* communication is political in any direction whatsoever and that its passing from a sender to a receiver, whoever s/he may be at any moment, constitutes every single time a translation. This would imply, for one thing, that the study of a hegemony of *x* over *y* can never be separated from the study of the reaction of *y* to *x*'s hegemony: there should, ideally, be no privileging of *x* or *y* because of a temporary, however long, situation of dominance of one over another. Second, we clearly need a discipline which would study the code of hegemony (or of anti-hegemony) in the very stuff or matter of the translational process itself, thus reinvigorating the central branch of our study as translators: translation as activity, craft, politico-cultural action. Whether this is covered in such proposals as James S. Holmes's call for a "sociology" of translation or not, I have not yet been able to find out.[6] Lawrence Venuti's work on resistancy versus domestication, which he was kind enough to send me recently, certainly seems to be a major step in getting "to that very stuff," raising a host of questions I am not dealing with here.[7]

3) We are not likely to question, at this time, the fact that hegemony and anti-hegemony are the two dimensions or facets of the problem which interest, or should interest, us most: especially at this moment when power in the world is reorganizing itself to an astounding, almost hallucinatory degree. This brings me to trying to explain why the terms Translation/Antitranslation figure in my title as they do. What I am trying to say is that there are forces which resist translation as much as there are others which elicit, require, or demand it. These apparently negative forces, those of Antitranslation, should be of as great interest to us as those, apparently more positive, of Translation itself. By association, you will doubtless have guessed that I am asking whether we can associate Translation with Culture and Antitranslation, not with Anti-Culture of course, but with something I'll here call Multiculture, in itself a positive transform, in its neutrality, of what we all discuss nowadays, often pejoratively, as Multiculturalism.

4) To an anthropologist, the study of translation is not new. It was what appeared on the syllabus in my student days some forty years ago under such headings as acculturation, transculturation, cross-culturalization, and so forth. Power, to anthropologists, was not something discovered during the sixties (though, of course, anthropology as "daughter of imperialism" revealed her full dance of Salome at

---

6 See James S. Holmes, "Translation Theories, Translation Studies and the Translator" (paper presented at the seventh World Congress of the International Federation of Translators, Montreal, 1977).

7 See, inter alia, Lawrence Venuti, "*Simpatico*," *SubStance*, no. 65 (1991): 320.

that time): it was understood that Mesoamerican Indians would be directed and constrained in their behavior by subordination to Spain; Native North Americans by subordination to the United States; many Africans, Asians, or Australasians by subordination to France, Germany, England, etc. Of course, in most instances studied, it was understood that conquered *Y* would have to accept and adapt to the culture of conqueror *X*. But, whether because of cultural relativism, instilled as a virtue and guiding light in all students, or because of inherent sympathy with the *Y*s, whatever later critics have said, anthropologists quickly understood that such acceptance and adaptation were never completely one-sided. Many, if not all, *Y*s would accept only to some extent and adapt what they accepted to their specifications. Syncretism of one sort or another—the religion of the great masses, for only elites can ever afford "pure" religions—was almost always to be found. And in many cases, anthropologists came to have great admiration for the brilliance of these adaptive mechanisms. To be personal again for a moment, I have come to believe over the years that what the Highland Maya peasant has done with Christianity actually gave richer tints to that religion in its folk manifestations than it had had in Spain. There had been a retroactive translation, as it were, a translation into Maya which has enriched or bettered the Spanish original if, that is, one may be so unrelativistic for a moment as to risk such a value judgment.

∼

From there, it should not be many steps to another statement. The path is facilitated by the adversarial stance which Native Peoples as well as many other "Liberation groups" have taken in the last forty years, realizing that now the question is one of sheer biological (anti-genocidal) as well as cultural (anti-ethnocidal) survival. I mean the statement that an Antitranslational stance is a perfectly valid antithesis to a Translational one and that it is manifested, empirically verifiable I suppose we would have said once, in a great many human groups today. Further, it is a striking aspect of the ideology of many groups in what I have come to call the Internal Empire of this country, an aspect which may be more covert and implied than overt and bluntly stated but is nevertheless massively powerful. For the subjects of the Internal Empire are now flying the banner of something called "Multiculturalism" and the whole cultural world in this Republic is in turmoil over that term. If, instead of the old banner of "Don't tread on me," we were now seeing one proclaiming, "Don't translate me," we could not be clearer on such points once they are formulated.

5) I believe I am going to say more about Antitranslation than about Translation, but let's start, traditionally and because it is much better known, with the latter.

Again, let me stress that I am dealing with Translation not so much as a craft or art but as a socio-political phenomenon. Translation occurs, at its simplest, when a culture is built on a society with the material strength and extension to acquire, almost interminably and without limits, the cultural products of other societies. A culture has to feel very secure about itself and its self-possession before venturing into the luxurious course of taking an interest in other cultures and, since the acquisition of other languages is not something most people can afford the time for, backing this interest by bringing the products, say here texts, of those other cultures into its own sphere of discourse, say here language. By the way: as you know, we here in the U.S. are in especial trouble because we are lazy and unproductive. (I stress text and language here because of our own primary topical interests but much the same could be said of other items of culture, say cooking to take an obvious one. You'll say, "But cooking is not translated!" I'll reply, "Watch what becomes of French, Spanish, or Italian cooking in this country. Or, in more detail, watch what becomes of *tapas*, for instance: in Spain, very small mouthfuls of fish usually to go with aperitifs; in the U.S., invariably full-scale dinners.")

It should follow that small and weak societies would not have such resources and would not, therefore, translate much into their own language. But, you'll immediately object, it is very precisely small societies that do! Think of the Icelanders, the Dutch, the Hungarians. Well, first, I would answer, I was thinking of the *really* small and weak: Papuans, Pygmies, Highland Maya for instance. The smaller European societies are not "small" and especially not weak in that sense. Inbricated into an areal Western economy of huge proportions, they cannot afford not to translate, and you will find that such small European societies actually spend a great deal on translation into their own language with much governmental support. The other side of the medal which is the most revealing is the extreme anxiety of such societies in the matter of having themselves translated into the language of dominant partners. I have heard Hungarian, Dutch, and Icelandic poets, for instance, speak of the feeling of extreme constraint they experience when living solely within their own language and how they consider translation into the "great" languages a matter of sheer survival. And you can bet that there is a hierarchy here: most make it clear, to take the most obvious instance, that English is now top bride. I am willing to wager that other secondary preferences would reveal much that is not immediately obvious: a whole aspect of sociology at present submerged. The question of size alone then is not necessarily a pointer to subordination. And if you are a willing partner in Empire, what is happening is not even subordination.

We need not think alone of our own time and circumstance. India, China, and Japan, at various times in their histories, virtually made culture-heroes of translators by sending them out, often at great danger to themselves, on immensely long missions to acquire texts for translation. That these were religious or spiritual texts, rather than technological ones, need not concern us overmuch when we note that religion can be an instrument of political power (think of Asoka in India) or even, very directly, techno-economic development: Jacques Gernet has shown how Buddhist monasteries were at the root of banking in China during the T'ang Dynasty.[8] Certain other figures are worth dwelling on in this domain. Think of Egyptian Pharaoh Akhenaton's translations of doctrine into his own system, or the great Mughal Emperor Akbar's search among religious systems to find a synthesis, causing to be translated Jewish, Christian, Hindu, Buddhist, and other texts into the language of his own Empire when he himself was actually illiterate! Throughout history, there are many fascinating examples of such encyclopedic reaches for a knowledge commensurate with the sublime political role a society saw itself as playing. Again, on Venuti's wavelength: might it be that India translated domesticatingly whereas China translated resistantly? Much in the varying welcomes accorded Buddhism might have been thus determined.

6) If this is Translation, what would Antitranslation be? It is tempting to pass straight from Translation as just described to Antitranslation as sheer political resistance: what I described above as "Don't translate me!" This would leave out a vital consideration about those I've described as truly poor—the Aborigines of the Third World. We must not forget that if those Natives are too small and poor to translate other cultures into their own, it is probably as much as anything because, in so many cases, they themselves have "been already" translated. Most of Latin America is already, as it were, in Spanish or Portuguese; most of Africa and Australasia and much of Asia are already in English or French. And, of course, what I have called the Internal Empire in this country: the ethnic minorities, African, Hispanic, and Native American mainly, have been already translated. Does this exclude them from Antitranslation? I think not.

Steiner, in his very first chapter, points out that "the agonistic functions of speech inside an economically and socially divided community possibly outweigh functions of genuine communication," and goes on to list a number of ways in which subordinates will resist, actively or passively, the linguistic onslaughts of the dominant.[9] He talks of the way in which language events assume the nature of a

---

8   Jacques Gernet, *Les aspects économiques du bouddhisme dans la société chinoise du Vème au Xème siècles* (Saigon, Vietnam: École Française d'Extrême-Orient, 1956).

9   Steiner, *After Babel*, 32.

duel with incommunicativeness; apparent misunderstanding; thickening, blurring, or other distortion of speech; confusion by slowness or rapidity; false obsequiousness; resort to dialect; and many more being the modes of resistance on the part of the subordinate faced with the ever more exasperated "clarifications" of the dominant. I remember a Kipling quote very current among Europeans during my study time in Burma that ran something like (I have not found the source) "The Christian swears and swears and swears; the Buddhist smiles and smiles."[10]

In that there are, for instance, women who are Black or women who are Gay and, likewise, Gays who are women, or Black, or other, their resistances are not as clear-cut as those of ethnic groups. However, I have often, in my writing, included, in the Internal Empire, the various Liberation movements and their texts in that they shared with ethnic groups the status of being oppressed by the dominant culture. It would probably be possible to demonstrate that there are, as it were, Women's dialects, Children's dialects, or Gay dialects which oppose Antitranslation to the dominant culture. Much of the fiction concerning what used to be known as the war of the sexes reveals the history of these evolving and ever-changing resistances. And there is, of course, an extreme form of translation, especially in sexual matters (but not exclusively—cf. the recent history of certain rap groups), that is the absolute negative, or nadir, of Translation when you bring a subordinate group totally under your control by absolute suppression. The name of that one is censorship, pure and simple when dominant, manifesting as self-censorship when subordinate.

Glancing at other aspects of this, I should note that subordinate does not necessarily imply politically laudable, embraceable, or correct. In fact, perhaps, it may also englobe just the opposite. At the time of writing, I have just watched a two and a half hour trial in video transcription: the case of two Human Rights' groups in Portland, Oregon, against the Metzgers, father and son, leaders of WAR, the White Aryan Resistance. In this case, I am thinking of the double-speak which characterizes such subordinates. When seemingly free and unfettered, their racist discourse is brutal to the point of incitement to murder. When under any form of constraint or examination, Antitranslation here manifests as a purified language in which violence, for instance, becomes "violence only as self-defense"; "all Xs are mud" becomes "some Xs are mud"; a racist murder becomes a "tragic event brought on by two people fighting in the street"; and so forth. The double-speak of a David Duke was widely noted during the recent elections for governor of Louisiana. No doubt such processes stretch back into the history of the Ku Klux

---

10   Rudyard Kipling (exact quote unobtainable at this writing).

Klan, America First, and many other organizations, back to the first immigrations into this Republic, all demonstrating censorship and self-censorship in plenty. In the case of "decent people," I happen to be thinking of Charles Lindbergh's diaries as an example: self-censorship attains such degrees of subtlety that it strains our analytical talents to the highest degree, and we despair of ever being able to uncover the exact dimensions of the opinions held.

Other examples of resistance. Anthropological cases in which a tribe or other sub-group of a society—a religious sodality, say—refuses to act as informants to anthropologists are very frequent: there are many such groups among the Eastern Pueblos right around my present home. I read this as Antitranslation, stating, "I will not let you translate this sacred information into your empirical, quantifiable, so-called scientific language." The case of such groups who, after a certain time, seem to break down completely and, against all precedent, seek out those who would so translate their secrets parallels the case of the Dutch, Danes, and Hungarians I spoke of before: such seeking out occurs when the fear of extinction arises: better these survive in translation than not at all: "better we give up on autonomy and merge into Empire rather than disappear altogether" seems to be the message.

~

I read another example of Antitranslation in the behavior of some Minority artists who exemplify in their attitudes the maximal contempt for would-be translators (and actual translators in the case of, say, White rip-offs of Black music). I think of Miles in music or, more subtly but just as directly, of Gwendolyn Brooks in poetry. After decades of publishing with Harper & Row, Brooks, as I gather, deliberately turned her back on the world of dominant publishing in order to give all her work to small African American publishers mainly in Chicago. A variant of this, it seems to me, is the belligerent attitude taken by some Chicano poets I once heard state to a dominant audience, "Stop paying attention and lip service to poets like Paz, Neruda, and Vallejo and listen to us for a change." While this would seem to be saying, "Translate me!" rather than "Do not translate me!" I think it says primarily, "Stop translating those you think to be, rightly or wrongly, at your level and pay attention to *our* uniqueness for a change! . . . but, incidentally, that uniqueness is not available to be co-opted or taken over by you!" Years ago, I pointed out how English poets in the dominant schools translated other poets whose parameters seemed to equal their own.[11] Other poets, both English and foreign, whose parameters were different, usually far more experimental and exciting,

11   See "The World Wide Open," in Tarn, *Views from the Weaving Mountain*, 32.

were marginalized if English, and ignored and not translated if foreign. Similar phenomena occur right now among us. But, watch it! A marginalized poet of only yesterday has a book from Harvard and a named chair today. Things move fast and furious in this field!

This, I trust you understand, is also a response to a situation in this country in which the dominant Anglo/White poetry community (however much itself divided) knows virtually nothing about the Black or Hispanic poetry community and cares still less: a radically scandalous situation which cannot be allowed and will not be allowed to continue if only because the ever-increasing specialization of the Anglo/White elite's products will ensure dinosaurial disappearance and the triumph of the non-Anglo/White poetries is virtually a foregone conclusion if any kind of genuinely popular support for poetry continues to be part of the landscape.

7) These are obviously variant facets of the huge debate going on at present in this country. Are we far wrong if we say that Translation, as read here, is equivalent to Culture if we take the latter as an imperial, hegemonic, dominant entity confident that its traditions, canons, and values are *the* traditions, canons, and values that count and that none other can be held to stand at that level: the level of God-Almighty-Western-Culture itself? And that Antitranslation would then have to be the transform of, not Anti-Culture, definitely not that, but Multiculture defined as (since we are talking here in this Republic) the culture of these United Mistakes seen, no longer as the melting pot transforming all ingredients into one soup, but as an aggregate of the cultures which have entered into this land and now compose what, for better or for worse, has become the eternally invoked "American People"? Which would then leave Multiculturalism for that body of socio-cultural policy which respects, honors, validates, defends, and puts into action such policies as will uphold Multiculture instead of Culture.

In the last few years, just as we have heard the White Racist arguments both overt and, alas far more extensively, covert that invading colored hordes are taking over White jobs and White country, we have heard the Liberals' arguments in favor of Multiculturalism and, knowing Acanaemic Burrocrassy as I do, I have been scarcely surprised to hear that Multiculturalism is being decreed by dominant Administrations down to subordinate Professoriat very burrocrasstically indeed, which helps no one to understand or be sympathetic to anything ongoing. Obviously, very little is going to be achieved if quotas are the name of the game—if every time you mention Plato, you have to mention Confucius or Ogotommeli; if every time you talk Joyce and Kafka, you have to bring in Soyinka or Achebe. That is mere tinkering. What the situation is asking us to achieve—and not being in the academy at present, I find it hard to say how much genuine response there is, or not—is a re-evaluation greater than ever before in our constantly re-evaluating history, a re-evaluation that amounts to a philosophical earthquake of mega 10 on the Richter scale.

Obviously, in the time available, I could not give the detailed, patient answers necessary here even if my small wit were able to stretch to that. As is my custom, I'll continue and end by following the path I've followed all my recent life, that is, back and away from the sociological viewpoint and into the poet's vision or as much into it as my small means allow. In a recent volume of essays, representing some thirty to forty years of prose work by an incremental, intuitive thinker painfully training himself into some kind of rationality, there are the specifics of a gradually evolving theory of the poet's role in society which I like to test, by incremental procession, against a variety of subjects as they arise. The aspect of the theory I would like to test here relates to a view of the poet (remember my Snyder interview) as the Arch-Informant and Antitranslator par excellence. That is the view which sees poetry as the deliberate, technically astute to the highest possible degree, attempt to produce an absolutely untranslatable language, as untranslatable and "pure," if you will, as music—the test case to most critics. However, and this is why we cannot leave it simply at that, the very same view, by deploying a perchance more sophisticated model of the poetic self or ego than seems to have prevailed to date, is capable of leading us to Multiculture *as well as* Culture and thus, if anything as unempirical as wisdom may prevail, go some way toward resolving the most excruciating social problem we now have before us. As so often, I have found my personal views to come down on the side of a both/and rather than an either/or. So, to end this talk, let me depart the anthropological runway and make a smart left-turn in the pattern back to the poetic.

8) In the interests of this book's overall length, I am shortening this conclusion. I refer here to a model of poetic production, comprising the *Vocal,* the *Choral,* and the *Silence,* detailed in essays of the third part of this volume.[12] In the *Vocal,* a poet, competing with others, tries to find, in language, something so unique to her/himself that her/his writing can never be mistaken for anyone else's. The poet *never* wants to hear that s/he is influenced by *x* or *y,* forms part of a school *x* or *y,* or even reminds a given reader of *x* or *y.* Not unlike the musician's, the poet's stance here is Antitranslational. S/he is saying, "I am not even telling you not to translate me: you could not; such a thing is impossible."

---

12   The reader at this point may wish to consult the later essays in this volume, especially the last one before the interview, for a detailed explication of the model.

Most critics see poetry as arising out of, and falling back into, Silence. In my model, there is a *Choral* function *under* or *on the other side of* the *Silence*. *Choral* because, however many parts a chorus may have, the essence here is unity, homogeneity, the merging of a part into a more important whole. There is something ecstatic about this. You can think of everyone singing, "Yes, translate me! Translate me!" or "Don't even bother, we are all *already* translated!" You can think of Dante's "*Guardame ben, ben son, ben son, Beatrice!*" or of the figures stretching out their arms to each other, almost passing through each other, in the *Paradiso* of Giovanni di Paolo.

Regarding the model, I argue that the *Silence* is the only reality therein, the place where the poet enacts the *praxis* of birthing the poem. Looking at each other, the competitive *Vocal* and the co-operative *Choral* cannot believe each other: I call them reciprocal illusions. Do they not exist? They exist as much as *Samsara* and *Nirvāṇa* exist, for instance, in Buddhist philosophy, and they are part of one and the same existence in the same way as, at the extreme, *Samsara* is *Nirvāṇa* or *Nirvāṇa* is *Samsara*. They exist as much as the two faces of Janus exist, on the one body of the Roman deity, or on a coin so thin its two sides would be one.

∼

And they exist also in a seeming contradiction arising out of what has been said about Translation and Antitranslation, Culture and Multiculture. In what I've said about Translation and Antitranslation, Culture and Multiculture, you may have detected a suggestion of villainy in Translation and Culture, a suggestion of politically laudable worthiness in Antitranslation and Multiculture. Likewise, you might have felt a breath of disdain tarnishing the struggling *Vocal* in contrast to the paradisal *Choral.* How logical it would be, then, to have Translation and Culture as part of the same classification as the *Vocal,* under the same totem, to speak Lévi-Straussian if you wish, while Antitranslation and Multiculture fit in under the *Choral.* But, we have seen that that is *not* the way it goes!

The world of Multiculture is right now a world of intense competition, heterogeneity, antithesis; it is very clearly the world of the *Vocal.* The Liberal world of Culture, however, is just as intensely non-adversarial, homogeneous, and apolitical. Clearly, this is not what we might have expected.

We can all relax, however, in reminding ourselves of the illusory character of the *Vocal* and the *Choral.* Or rather, we must call to mind that they are reciprocal illusions: they are both as important as each other in the overall process: it is simply impossible, in fact, to have the one without the other. I said earlier that I had always, somewhat to my surprise, found myself to be a both/and person rather than an either/or one. To my surprise, because it seems to me that the whole weight of our cultural scene and the media which carry it favor, and for obvious political reasons (Divide and Rule!), either/or positions over both/and positions.

We are constantly presented, it seems to me, with the relation of Culture to Multiculture as an agon, as a struggle. We are told that we are in the profoundest of troubles because we must decide and decide quickly, critically, between the tradition of Culture and the new of Multiculture.

I see no such agon. It is clear that we must have both Culture and Multiculture and very seriously work toward that earthquake measuring 10. It was being said in the sixties that anthropology had to go all the way from the Self to the Other only to find, as it got closer and closer to the Other, that the Other had the same face as the Self. Similarly, we have to go to the extremes of each cultural Other and accept the extremest implications of Antitranslation in Multiculture if we are to measure the full extent of human possibility. Without measuring that full extent, we measure very precisely nothing at all and we put ourselves on the socio-cultural level at the same point in which we are putting ourselves biologically by allowing the atrocious diminution taking place every day in the extinction of species after species. Multiculture is as important as that. As I tried to put it years ago in *The Beautiful Contradictions,* the daughter remains blind before and until we fully know the mother.[13] I am, of course, talking of the ancient ideal of human unity, one without which humanity will not be saved and this planet will not be saved. The *Choral,* which may be a transform of Benjamin's "true language," however illusory, is as important as that.[14] Culture is as important as that. There are no contradictions. It is as stark as that.

9) In practice, of course, it is easier to say this than to see it done. Can the social equality required by Multiculture ever become a reality when social inequality remains as blatant as it does today? Can Culture ever be purged of its appalling weight of guilt when social inequality remains as blatant as it does today? We are all in the furnace on those questions. Perhaps a beginning can be made if we can persuade ourselves that we have, quite literally, no alternative. Perhaps we can begin if we understand that.

As I have often claimed before, Poets' Liberation is the most primal and profound of all Liberation Movements. I urge those who are out of the movement to join it. Those on the inside never will.

1992

---

13 Nathaniel Tarn, *The Beautiful Contradictions* (New York: Random House, 1970); reprinted in Nathaniel Tarn and Janet Rodney, *Atitlán/Alashka* (Boulder, CO: Brillig Works Press, 1979.)
14 See Walter Benjamin, "The Task of the Translator," in *Illuminations* (New York: Schocken, 1969), 69–82; and Lefevere, *Translating Literature,* 102.

Octavio Paz, Anthropology, and the Future of Poetry

I take as my text today a passage from Octavio's "*Corriente Alterna.*"[1] "If imitation becomes mere repetition, the dialogue ceases and tradition petrifies; if modernity is not self-critical, if it is not a sharp break and simply considers itself a prolongation of 'what is modern,' tradition becomes paralyzed. This is what is taking place in a large sector of the so-called avant-garde. The reason for this is obvious: the idea of modernity is beginning to lose its vitality. It is losing it because modernity is no longer a critical attitude but an accepted, codified convention . . . it has become an article of faith that everyone subscribes to . . . all this raking of the coals can be reduced to a simple formula: repetition at an ever-accelerating rate. Never before has there been such frenzied, barefaced imitation masquerading as originality, invention, and innovation."

If this is a correct reading, it has deep implications for the future of poetry. I will look at this question in my habitual persona as anthropologist. Be warned, gentle audience, that the social sciences do not often console. I offer a hypothesis in the form of a reduced model of an extremely complex situation: there is no

This talk was given at the Mexican Cultural Institute and Library of Congress Octavio Paz Memorial Conference at Washington, DC, in October 1999.

1   Octavio Paz, *Alternating Current* (New York: Viking, 1973), 18.

time for more. The reason for a sociological approach? It is nonsense to talk about poetry, as most poets and critics today continue to do, without accounting for the socio-economic context of poetry production and reception.

Let us suppose that the ancient art of poetry reposes on certain ancient foundations which are being eroded or destroyed with ever-increasing rapidity. Take three such foundations: (1) Non-Human Natural Species; (2) Human Natural Species; (3) one I shall call Cultural Exemplars.

1) Now that we are environmentally conscious, we hear every day of disappearing species—many unknown to science—in the dwindling forests of the Amazon, Southeast Asia, or Africa. Likewise in the oceans, suffering to their very depths through over-fishing, pollution, global warming.

2) Those of us who care hear every day of underfed, poverty-stricken, culturally deprived, endangered, and oppressed indigenous, "tribal," archaic, or traditional peasant peoples, whether in the Americas: the Amazon; the Maya of Central America; our own Northern Native Americans, or in other continents: i.e., genocide and ethnocide. After managing two world wars of unparalleled proportions, our century continues on its merry way with the horrors of Guatemala, Tibet, Kurdistan, Cambodia, Rwanda, Nigeria, Sierra Leone, the Congo, Kosovo, Burma, East Timor. The truth is that, whether of the Left or Right politically, elites need land and will kill to get it.

3) Along with the effects of the world wars (I think of Dresden and Warsaw, for instance) there is unparalleled and ever-growing looting and destruction of cultural exemplars whether, again for instance, at Angkor, or Egypt, or in the Northern forests of Guatemala or, equally bad, there are the various renovations and the drowning of historical centers by high-rises and bulk projects of every description. Belonging to both (2) and (3), there is the destruction of and backyarding of languages.

Nature Poetry is as old as mankind; so is that regarding human species: think of Homer or the Mahābhārata. For the poetry of cultural exemplars, we evoke Dante's Florence or, more recently, Wordsworth's London and Baudelaire's Paris. It is my hypothesis that poetry consciously or unconsciously anchors itself in, and is nourished by, the existence of these traditional natural and cultural treasures and that when these latter suffer as much as they are doing, poetry is herded into becoming purely elegiac or into turning to other endeavors. What it turns to, I'll argue, is no longer poetry but something which is increasingly being called, simply, "writing."

I am not unfamiliar with many of the internal arguments for this: those, for instance, attending to the changing mutual relations of poetry and prose, the evolution of genres, and a great mass of "so forth." Here I continue to focus on the external and, because we are here and this is where we live, I focus on our country. Let me also stress, once and for all, that there are always exceptions in any theory or hypothesis.

As I have stressed many times, the end of World War II witnessed the insertion of the creative arts into the academic universe with extraordinarily dramatic and transformative results. Let me go on dealing with creative writing—leaving aside music and the visual arts—while adding in passing a footnote to the effect that the sovereign reign of "installations" in the latter seems to me, for many reasons, to parallel the accession of "writing."

The transformation has proceeded along many different lines. The sheer *danger* and life-shaking, lifelong risks inherent in being a poet; the interminable alchemical process of conjugating intellect and emotion, in order to produce a life-*opus*, has become in these institutions, since the head develops faster than the heart, one of the *fabrication* of a product known as "writing" using academic "theory" rather than life experience to, as they say so elegantly nowadays, "write off of." This, I have found, often gives rise to bodies of theory from young practitioners infinitely exceeding in interest their actual "writing" production. The normalization of "poetry" production (I have here to use the word "poetry" in quotes) has led to the transformation of a vocation into a career, a profession.

Our young student practitioners do not follow their life-experience, meager as it is; they follow their *guru* teachers. "At the end of the day," it is impossible for the teaching *not* to assume that anyone in a class can become a writer (a variant of the Napoleonic "every soldier has a general's baton in his backpack"); impossible for it *not* to foster competition—first for the *guru's* favor, next for chalking up achievement in reading, publications, grants, awards, and the like. Competitiveness, reducing the writing career to a simulacrum of other "late-capitalist" careers, ensures a stultifying and extreme degree of unpleasantness, rudeness, irresponsibility, and lack of community and mutual help in the writing population. Above all the result is a frightening overproduction of writers in a society which, in part because of the nature of "writing" as opposed to that of poetry, is underproducing readers, is in fact losing readers by the droves every day. I have described this in Lévi-Straussian terms as a prevalence of incest (the relation of poet as producer to poet as consumer) over marriage (the age-old relation of poet to "general" reader). Regular incest is not particularly good for any species. Yet another aspect of this population pressure is generation-related. In the Age of Information, the fashions and fads of culture move extremely fast (as a new book's title has it, *The Acceleration of Just about Everything*): one's creations may be judged to be "out of date" more than once in a lifetime. There is also the principle that each and every time "late capital-ism" claims to make one's life easier, it makes it, in fact, more complicated and time-consuming. How *does* the average writer survive while aging?

A moment on the question of difficulty and obscurity. While it is true that the great discoveries of modernism preceded the academization of "creative writing," my sense is that the progression of "writing" toward unreadability has been helped by that academization. Many have commented on the disappearance of a true avant-garde and its replacement by avant-gardism: remember my quote from Oc-tavio at the beginning. I see this as a prolongation of experimentation usually lead-ing further on from collage and montage into ever-increasing fragmentation and eventually into a degenerative disease which, adapting an already common usage, I call "disjunctivitis." The argument, used by some producers who, correctly locating the seats of available power in the academy, have ensconced themselves therein every bit as much as the establishment "mainstream," to the effect that the disrup-tion of the common linguistic coin is part of a war against "late-capitalist" dis-course is singularly inept: I do not see oppressed workers of *any* kind devouring the products of avant-gardism. The death-of-the-author thematics, as commonly adapted, are another inanity: when society does its very best to homogenize us, what is wrong with a strong, knowledgeable, and responsible ego crying in the darkening wilderness? The expectation of exegesis in a constitutively backward-oriented academy (I am salaried to explain the previous generation; the next gener-ation explains me, but, excepting "celebrity," no generation explains itself) fosters a belief that significant writing is writing that needs explicating by critics, thus ever strengthening the hold of "theoreticians" and canon-formulating critics over the one-time freedom of the one-time poet. As for life among the incestuous, it hardly matters if a consumer truly *understands* a producer: we are, are we not, all brothers and sisters under the skin and have to pretend to stick together!?

A word also on competitiveness. "Mankind cannot stand very much reality," a poet once intimated, and I would add that it cannot stand very much writing. Bored to death on the one hand by the interminable repetitions of the MFA clones of their MFA teachers and, on the other, by the unreadable so-called writ-ing of the reigning avant-gardists, the last general reader left, faced in addition with this lemming-like overpopulation, has a desperate need of selection. This leads straight into the terminus of competitiveness: the winner-take-all syndrome, another familiar "late-capitalist" life-enhancing marvel. The award system is the crowning glory of this syndrome. It is deleterious not because it is unjust (nothing human is perfect) but because it inflicts an apparently consensual body of opinion on a public not usually aware of its options. The moneybags, playing it even more safely than the universities, select a group of allegedly trustworthy canonizers and mainstream writers conveniently gathered in a number of "Academies"—a group in whom the public can be induced to trust since they are already, are they not, "so trustworthy"—and regularly disburse large sums . . . almost always into the pockets of the already fortunate. The consensus established by this system is an appalling fraud but it is supported by a host of established colleges, universities, institutions, foundations, magazines, and publishing houses so large that it is never questioned. As I pointed out during Octavio's 80th birthday celebrations, the name of "poet" is now so poverty-stricken that it has been abolished. What you now have is the "poet-who-has-had-more-than-three-poems-published-in-recognized-peer-judged-magazines"; the "published-poet"; the "noted-poet"; the "esteemed-poet"; the "recognized-poet"; the "famous-poet"; the "feted-poet"; the "awarded-poet"; the "much-awarded poet"—and who knows whether the State of Kansas, *inter alia,* will not come up with the "saved-poet" or the "much-redeemed-poet" by the time we have all finished? Without lacking in respect, I would point out that even our esteemed hosts here did not describe Mr. Paz, the subject of our celebration, in the first version of their program through anything else but a list of his awards. (This has now been corrected.) In short, there is devaluation of the poet here as the poet disappears behind the award. The award is frantically crying out for an attention no longer granted to the poet: society *pretends* to value poetry by throwing sops to Cerberus, Pegasus, or whatever. All the moneys involved would be far more useful if given in support of adequacy in poetry publishing or of an organization like "Poets in need" devoted to helping sick, poor, or otherwise handicapped poets. If the system is kept, one modification at least could be introduced: by separating "honor" from "monetary reward": let those who need honoring be honored and only those who need money be "rewarded."

It is immensely hard for the true innovator to remain and survive outside the pale. In effect, he or she may be seriously said to face extinction: the law that there are no mute, inglorious Miltons has for some time been stifled under the weight of over-production. In the triumph of quantity over quality, it is now axiomatic that the indifferent and the sheer lousy can and do stifle the interesting and the good. An additional factor in the last couple of years or so: rather like what happens with ecumenical efforts among churches when the world seems little inclined to be religious, there is, in spite of envy and rivalry, an ever-increasing banding together of producers, a great deal of fraternization among individuals and groups recently antagonistic, for valid theoretical reasons, to one another. This, by the process of co-opting freelancers into establishment institutions, is leading to a blurring of the last few lines subsisting between differing schools of writing. We thus approach at ever-gathering speed that state so beloved of the New Age in which "everything is happily, even deliriously, everything": and all is for the best in the best of worlds. I have noticed yet another development: the *New York Times* reported, last August 12th, that those who made money after the sixties and would now like to flesh out their youthful dreams can attend poetry-writing camps in environmentally choice surroundings, with healthy diets and no doubt much yoga, meditation, and hand-holding counseling to boot. Democracy is undoubtedly the only valid form of government but, when "everybody is a poet" in a society which does not want poets, it certainly has massive drawbacks.

Is it any wonder that, added to the deliquescence of any sense of responsibility whatsoever in most parts of the publishing world, including allegedly progressive publishing, the deteriorations I speak of have led to a mass migration of so-called major publishers away from poetry? This perhaps will be the crowning factor in my oncoming revelation, namely, the proposition that Anglo (I use a New Mexican term but of course imply "Caucasian") elitist poetry, as we know it in these United Mistakes, is either dead or dying. If you take the figures of the Pound–H.D.–Williams lineage; adding, let us say, the likes of Crane, Stevens, Eliot, Oppen, and other Objectivists; if you continue with the New Americans as anthologically defined between Donald Allen in the sixties and Eliot Weinberger in the nineties, you have a basic picture of our beauteous graveyard as we approach the so-called Millennium. Doubtless, there will always be names to add and there can be similar lists in other countries and other languages. It is also true that different cultures may escape this dilemma for a host of reasons.

There is nothing new, of course, in the claim that one of the arts, or all of them, are dying: witness, for instance, Lévi-Strauss's ability to foresee the possibility of a world without art. Or there is Arthur Danto's persuasive argument in his "The Philosophical Disenfranchisement of Art" that art has, as it were, entered a post-historical era and disappeared up its own philosophy. *Para acabar,* it is merely that, after a great deal of life creeping toward death, there *is,* finally, death. As Lorca said, "*tambien se muere el mar.*"

So where, or out of what or whom, does the future arise? Where is the creative energy of the first part of the next millennium to come from? An idea out of Octavio's *Otra Voz* has always struck me as valuable. It is that we must look for the survival of *true* poetry not in the horizontal deployment of an ever-shrinking population of readers at any given historical moment but in a vertical time-depth: poetry surviving as a diachronic passage of culture from one generation of readers to another. For me, this time depth is without limit: it reaches back to whatever we can envisage as the beginning of all and any time, encompassing the poetry voiced by any human from that beginning onward, including obviously the immense population of the dead. For me, however, there *would* be a horizontal dimension too, this one stressing not the verticality of any one culture, but the horizontal passage of the torch from one culture to another or one set of cultures to another.

My sense then is that the future of poetry will probably arise, for the English language, out of the indigenous Anglophone so-called Third World which is still closer to the foundations I spoke of at the start than most of us are. From there and also from the so-called Minorities in this and other Anglophone First World countries who, it may be argued, are or can be in many ways, whether deliberately or not, closer to indigenous thought than we are. These "Minorities" in this country have produced many of the poetries I have called "Liberation Poetries" stemming in large part from the Civil Rights Movements of the 1960s—but they are still far from completely integrated into what we label as American Poetry.

Two problems here. The first is that the more indigenous of our worlds are rapidly being homogenized by such forces as economic imperialism and globalization so that the environments that poetry prizes may well be shorter-lived than we might hope. They may yet be defeated by corporate greed, the manipulations of the financial markets, consumerism, the stripping of environmental assets, the atrocities of genetic engineering, HIV/AIDS, the massive digital divide. The second problem is that many, perhaps most, of the poets and writers from there that we value, from an Anglo perspective, have made their names by using the same methods and poetics as the Anglo elite poetries. Here and there, one can pick out a few names that differ. Kamau Brathwaite, for instance, who, if Aimé Césaire were not to be chosen, was the true candidate for the Caribbean Nobel Award some years ago, is an experimenter and bridger of gaps who may represent the future of poetry as I see it here.

To end on a slightly more upbeat note, let me propose a couple more points about our art. I have wondered for years what makes so many young people hunger for the poetic career when the latter offers, except for a very, presumably happy, few, no rewards of any kind: no money, no lovers, no status, no fame, no Mercedes-Benzes, in short none of the goodies our consumerdom hankers for. I used to think that a poet was a god, later that the average poet was a dog; now I believe our average poet, if it can survive, is lucky to be something like a liver fluke progressing through the guts of a sheep. I have finally concluded that the drug of choice here may be the *Prinzip Hoffnung,* that famous particle of *Hope* without which no human being can live or be creative for very long. But Hope by itself is not enough. It needs to be conjugated with *Will*—the wayward possibility of any new, unexpected and unexpectable, desire arising and manifesting—so well argued for in Dostoevsky's "Underground Man." In other words, that which, by propelling Hope into action, finally manages to abut upon the shores of the unacknowledged legislatordom of the world.

I recently found the following in Eliot Weinberger's magnificent edition of Jorge Luis Borges's *Selected Non-Fictions:* "But the best immortalities, those in the domain of passion, are still vacant. There is no poet who is the total voice of love, hate or despair. That is: the greatest verses of humanity may still not have been written. This imperfection should raise our hopes."[2] When it seems to me that the treasures of diversification are being hopelessly polluted by the satanic mills of homogenization and when, at the end of this abyssal century, I conclude that the human race is a calamity waiting to be extinguished, it is to such hopes that I turn for the energy needed to get beyond our so-called Millennium, the *famoso* year 2000.

1999

2.   Jorge Luis Borges, *Selected Non-Fictions,* trans. Eliot Weinberger (New York: Viking, 1999), 31.

Section Three
Exile out of Silence into Cunning

Initiation and the Paradox of Power

A Sociological Approach

While initiation is a very rich phenomenon for the history of religion or comparative religion, social anthropology finds it to be an elusive one. It seems to be so much tied to the intimate development of individuals that it is hard to say exactly in what way it is a part of any given social structure or organization. The classic way of handling the matter is to talk of *rites de passage,* which are especially characteristic of simple societies. At certain selected moments in the life-cycle, society puts all members of a particular age through an initiatic process. Sociological stress is usually laid on those things the age-group learns which will make them better members of their society, and the function of initiation is related to this socializing process. This seems to me to miss out certain very important factors. In the first place, the achievement of maturity in any individual or group is a continuous process whose study is sacrificed to the discontinuity of sociological convenience. Yet

This essay was part of a presentation at the Gnosticism Conference of the International Association for the Study of Religion, Messina, 1964. For more on Burmese Buddhism, see the "Sages and Kings" section in Nathaniel Tarn, *Views from the Weaving Mountain: Selected Essays in Poetics & Anthropology* (Albuquerque: University of New Mexico Press, 1991). I have kept this text here because of its discussion of the self–other, self–self, and non-reciprocity triad, which plays a role in my model of poetic production: *vide* the triad "the *Vocal,*" "the *Silence,*" and "the *Choral.*"

many initiations teach an individual that social recognition at particular moments is unremarkable when compared with the ceaseless process of self-improvement. More important still, it would seem that the sufferings and abstinences which are imposed on initiatic candidates have a function which is not merely that of making them better members of society. They are ambiguous, it seems to me, in that they are also teaching the individual to rely upon himself when society, as it must inevitably do at times, fails him.

It is one of the weaknesses of sociology—the reverse side, of course, of its strength—that it rarely includes within itself the means of studying anyone's escape from society. It is not sufficient, however, to leave such matters to psychology, for they, in turn, react back upon the texture of society and culture in very marked ways. One can, if one wishes, say that, in initiation, society *also* teaches its members how to do without it and talk of a function of initiation in the promotion of self-reliance. I prefer myself to look a little further afield.

Great progress has been made in recent years by the French anthropological school under Lévi-Strauss in the theory of reciprocity. Briefly, the idea is that society is created and maintained through a complex network of exchanges, mainly of goods, women, and language, between men, so that everyone is so dependent upon someone else for his vital needs that no escape from social life is possible. Age-old taboos, such as those against incest or the consumption of totemic foods, can be reduced to simple terms by saying that the hoarding of one's own group's goods or women damages social life by short-circuiting it: obviously independent strands of wool lying side by side are a very different matter from these same strands knit into a textile. Nor need we be primitives or peasants to know that any desire on our part to "get away from it all" is immediately frustrated by the vision of our complex and irremediable entanglement in networks of family, friendship, business, and so forth.

I want to argue that the importance of initiation, in its broadest aspect, lies in that it offers a way out of reciprocity. The stress, in initiation, is always laid upon self-improvement, self-enhancement, self-completion: it is always something that is being *added* to the initiate and, if anything is subtracted from him or her by abstinences or sufferings, it is only as a first stage so that something greater, more important, may ultimately be gained. In the last resort no initiation known to us leaves an individual less powerful than s/he was before. If, in the initiations of simple societies, the stress is usually laid on gaining socially valuable powers, this is not necessarily so in the higher forms of initiation where total power, total knowledge, or any other form of completeness will enable the successful candidate to be entirely him/herself, living in, perhaps, but not dependent upon, society.

In his book on *Kingship,* Hocart, adopting a diffusionist approach, proposes that various forms of improvement are modeled on kingship.[1] Rituals connected with marriage, the establishment of officials, and initiation itself, he argues, must all have been based on the coronation of kings. But I have argued elsewhere that the human capacity for symbolization is limited by its obligation to utilize the brute matter of life as we know it. When we look at these rites we must conclude that it is not the initiate who is like a king but rather a king who is like an initiate. The image or symbol of the complete power which characterizes the initiate is taken from the human field where it can be found: that is, in the kingship, the supreme power on earth, or even in the god-head, the supreme elsewhere. I cannot develop this here but may point to the fact that it is the king who normally commits what we might call "crimes against reciprocity": it is he who has more goods and women than anyone else and it is he, where incest is committed, who usually commits it. It is also he whose person is so sacred that it is hedged around by all sorts of privacies often pushed to great lengths so that the sacred king cannot touch the earth, communicate directly with lesser beings, and so forth. The reason for all this is, normally, that the king must be outside society to a certain extent in that he has to serve as a link between it and parasocial forces. Thus everything happens as if the king is self-reciprocating: he renders a cult to himself, he marries his own blood, his goods are so taboo that no one inferior can touch them; he is imprisoned in a kind of self-sufficient solitude of which we get echoes as late as in Shakespeare and which is the most exalted characteristic of the ideal initiate. It should be clear, I hope, that I am not arguing with Hocart on a matter of historical priority, but rather on a logical one. Moreover, it should be clear to everyone that the initiate and the king, or chief, or priest, in most simple societies are, in any case, one and the same person.

Some years ago, Paul Lévy wrote a study of Buddhism as an initiatic system, and I have recently had an opportunity to look at some of these problems in the context of a field study of Burmese Buddhism done in 1958 and 1959.[2] Lévy concentrated on ordination into the *Sangha,* the order of monks, as an initiatic rite; I attempted to see the whole complex continuum of Burmese religion, including what is popularly known as "animism," in the light of initiatic theory. Now it seems to me that the overwhelming Buddhist concern with self-improvement makes of this religion a crucial field of research for our concerns. Long ago Prince Siddhartha had the choice of becoming either a king or a Buddha, and the implications of his choice still find echoes in modern Buddhist countries.

---

1 Arthur Maurice Hocart, *Kingship* (Oxford: Oxford University Press, 1927).
2 Paul Lévy, *Is Buddhism a Mystery Religion?* (London: Athlone Press, 1957).

A sociologist in Southeast Asia has considerable problems in locating the social context of Buddhism. Basically, things have progressed very little beyond the simple *Sangha-dāyaka* relationship where the representatives of the religion are fed and kept by laymen in a more or less one-to-one relationship. Everyone, right up to and including the king, is a *dāyaka,* a donor: that is, an inferior to the monk. The *Sangha* is not a church; monks associate together on a voluntary basis for a number of purposes, but the order can in no sense be called a corporate body, with its own treasures, possessions, rights and regulations, etc. Individuals go in and come out of the Burmese *Sangha* more or less as they please. The *Sangha* is not a sine qua non of any ritual beyond the simple feeding and upkeep; it is nice to have monks around, but it is not necessary. Monks are not priests with a vital part to play in man-god relationships. In such a context the normal weapons of sociology seem curiously inadequate, and it is certainly difficult to say what the monks *are for,* what is their social function.

If, instead of concentrating on reciprocity alone, we concentrate on the tension between reciprocity and anti-reciprocity, however, we find a much richer situation. The influence of Buddhism has been such in Burma that it is not impossible to think of the Burmese as a man whose main idea is to achieve autonomy, whose main ideal is to leave society behind him. Both psychologists and political scientists have recently illustrated this theme, an extremely important one which must not be hidden by the superficial trappings of so-called modern democracy in Burma. We reach the conclusion that the monk is there to serve as a *model* of non-reciprocity: he is the person who, within disciplinary (*Vinaya*) limits, always receives and never gives.

Now it has been said that Buddhism is such a non-worldly religion that it cannot exist without other forms of religion, such as "animism," spirit-cults, etc., to deal with the urgent matters confronting man in this world. This is true to some extent, though the very long symbiosis of Buddhism and local religions genuinely precludes one from being able to say what is Buddhist and what is not in the prevailing mixture. I have therefore preferred to avoid the view which sees different parts of Burmese religious life as discontinuous and to attempt an overall view of the phenomena found in the field.

We are all familiar with the Buddhist stress on self-enhancement, differing only from other initiatic systems in that, at the very apex of the process involved, the self itself explodes into non-self, or rather something which is no longer either self or non-self. We are perhaps less familiar with a stress of great sociological importance, namely, that placed upon the different levels of awareness of the doctrine characteristic of the people who approach it at different times and in different places. This is not an all-or-nothing system, one in which all individuals are equally outside salvation until, upon joining a church, they acquire the means of salvation. In the latter case, we have a kind of discontinuous, once-and-for-all initiation which various rituals may from time to time confirm; in the case of Buddhism, we have a continuous initiation in which the process of self-improvement goes forward (and backward, of course) not only in one lifetime but also over several. Readings from the canonical texts give me the impression that, virtually from the beginning, Buddhism was regarded as a teaching to which various people would come in various frames of mind. Thus it is not true that an "animist" cannot be a Buddhist; he is merely a Buddhist with incomplete or imperfect knowledge of the doctrine. The notion of perfecting one's knowledge of the doctrine is, of course, found in all religions and is not exclusively Buddhist. But we only have to look, in the West, at the Heaven–Hell or the God–Satan dichotomies to see that, for practical purposes involving the mass of men, we have here a very real difference indeed.

The primary instrument of Buddhist self-enhancement is, of course, meditation. Essentially, in southern Buddhism, this is a process of looking at the world and concluding, after examining all its aspects, that it is not worth the having. One after the other various forms of attachment are sloughed off together with the reciprocal action which they imply. One of the main revelations of this examination is that these various attachments which, because of their variability, seem to be organized in some kind of hierarchy of desirable and undesirable are, in reality, not diverse but, since they all spring from one root, identical and exactly as valuable (or not) as any other. Eventually, in some mainly northern schools of Buddhism, the meditator may discover that all these attachments are the mere shadow-play of mind, thus drawing into "himself" all the different aspects of the world and leaving only the task of putting an end to "himself." We thus have three stages: the first, while still in society, we may call self–other reciprocity; the second, after entrance into meditation, self–self reciprocity; the third wipes out reciprocity altogether, and can be termed non-reciprocity.

Now in the Burmese system, no less than in others, there is temptation. The meditator is warned that, along the very arduous and lengthy way, s/he will encounter experiences which, far from quitting her/him of attachment, will in fact add momentarily to those attachments. This is because there are two branches of mental development, *Samatha*, the way of Tranquility, and *Vipassanā*, the way of Insight, which should be pursued side by side. The attainment of *Samatha* can lead to imbalances, and the meditator may be tempted by the powers that *Samatha* offers as if they were of special value. These powers are straightforwardly magical and include invisibility, locomotion under the earth and in the sky, changing form, entering another body, and so forth. The Buddhist texts are aware of these possibilities, but they can be no more than a false goal.

In keeping with the theory that a lower level of sophistication will always tend to materialize things which the higher level accepts as merely symbolic, a theory to which Mircea Eliade has made the most notable contributions, the average Burmese, in his religious quest, will remain very largely at the level of self–self reciprocity and consider the acquisition of the powers I have mentioned as the highest good. This means, ultimately, that for the mass of people it is not levels of sophistication or comprehension of the doctrine that determine the religious hierarchy, but levels of power. I have pointed out elsewhere that that which does most to confuse and mask the essential difference between the two is that, on the one hand, we remain within an initiatic process all the time with upward progress through hierarchical levels of attainment, and, on the other hand, both ways demand that certain goods and enjoyments should be abstained from so that the greater progress may be made. The *difference* is that the lower person will consider abstinence as a means of acquiring more power; only the higher person, the world-renouncer, will understand that abstention is an aim in itself, "that at the highest point of development the sum of power gained will automatically turn back into the comprehension that will destroy it." At the same time it is important to notice that this does not mean a lack of self-awareness on the part of the person who finds him/herself to have an inferior knowledge of the doctrine. One will often hear in Burma that such and such a meditational practice or such and such an abstinence is too difficult and, furthermore, that to claim it falsely would lead to madness since magical power strikes back at the sorcerer's apprentice. The general acceptance of the whole Buddhist frame of reference means that everyone recognizes that the *Sangha* is at the very top of the scale, at least symbolically, and I often have the impression that the *dāyaka* supports the monk so that he shall do what he, as layman, shackled by reciprocity, cannot do. In the end, as everywhere else in the sociology of religion, we return to the fact that while religious effort tends toward a state of non-reciprocity in its initiatic forms, realism here as elsewhere determines the limits to which theoretical absolute freedom is bound by relative freedom in practice. But the loose structure of Burmese religion and society does permit a wide latitude of claims made by a person on one particular rung of the ladder to those beneath him or her, and the field is very much open to a plurality of small sects each dependent on a charismatic leader and each as short-lived as that leader.

Whether or not other disciplines have achieved a more balanced view of initiation, social anthropology has continued to regard initiation as something sporadically connected with the education of youthful members of society into the ways of their society and working in the direction of socialization. Basically, this is not very different from education, and it seems to miss everything that is particularly religious about the phenomenon in question. But looking at a case in which the *whole religion* seems to be an initiatic system, I have wanted to modify the current assumption that once we have dealt with *rites de passage* we have done with the topic of initiation. A sociologist can, I suppose, insist that Burmese religion, whatever we may call it, does in fact fit in with Burmese society and that, if the Burmese desire is to escape from society, then their religion certainly trains them for that. It still remains to show how we can, in every case, suppose that initiation trains one to be a fully functioning member of society when the value of society and functioning therein is questioned by at least one system we know of. One other anthropologist, Louis Dumont, working with higher religions, seems to have come to similar conclusions.[3]

One final point. It is not too farfetched to say that the overriding preoccupation of the social anthropologist today is with social control: that is who, in any given society, has the say over whom. Most of our studies deal with subordination and super-ordination of individuals or groups in relation to each other, and there has been serious discussion recently (in the Lévi-Straussian articles on dualism and triadism) as to whether social equality is ever possible at all in any form of society. The various forms of initiation reviewed here seem to echo the basic concern with power which is characteristic of all social life. It may be that by stressing self-enhancement and by tending toward the abolition of reciprocity and dependence, initiation creates for the human spirit a place in which the question of power is no longer posed. Certainly the Burmese progress is one from an "animist" stage of being possessed by spirits, through one in which one possesses spirits and controls ever more important and powerful ones, to a final "Buddhist" stage in which the necessity of being possessed or possessing is no longer a valid question. For the true paradox of power is, surely, that when everything is yours nothing is any longer yours; when you have become everything, a complete totality, nothing can be above or below anything else. Whether this is pure escapism or whether it is something which responds very deeply to a basic problem of human existence, it is certainly not for our disciplines to judge. But that does not mean that they can afford to disregard it altogether.

1965

---

3 Louis Dumont, "Le renoncement dans les religions de l'Inde," in his *Homo Hierarchicus* (Paris: Gallimard, 1964).

The Heraldic Vision

Some Cognitive Models for Comparative Aesthetics

*Then proceeding from the individual to the aggregate of Indi-
viduals & disregarding all chronology except that of mind I
should perfect them (my students) i) in the history of Savage
Tribes. ii) of semi-barbarous nations. iii) of nations emerging
from semi-barbarism. iv) of civilized states. v) of luxurious
states. vi) of revolutionary states. vii) of Colonies.—During
these studies I should intermix the knowledge of languages and
instruct my scholars in Belles Lettres and the principles of composition.*

—S. T. Coleridge, c. 1795[1]

1. Poetry and Anthropology

1.1) I begin with a disclaimer. This is as tentative as possible a paper for more than
one reason. I am laying out a grid over territory without being sure of either grid
or territory. Beginning with something apparently simple, a hunch about heraldry,
I have been drawn into the flyways of contemporary interdisciplinary thought.
This thought is moving at such speed that it requires total attention to navigation:
I am a pilot, however, and not a navigator. My comfort, if there is any, springs

---

1 J. Cornwell, *Coleridge, Poet and Revolutionary, 1772–1804* (London: Routledge Kegan Paul, 1973),
   137, and cf. 159, 193, 226, 356. Since work on heraldry has not progressed further, I keep here the
   original tentative nature of these notes.

from the fact that my fears regarding this *periplous* mimic so well the *periplous* itself. The journey takes us eventually through the cloud-covered Scylla and Charybdis of closed and open poetries: the fears center on whether I now have enough data to begin this paper at all, or whether I will ever have enough to end it. We have connected reflections rather than a closely linked text: the problem of which disciplinary "language" or "languages" (if any) in which to talk being fundamental to the attempt.

1.2) I have long been interested in the reasons why such a strong confluence of the anthropological sciences and the arts, specifically poetry, has been characteristic of our time. To document this would require a survey of, first, general relations between aesthetics and the social sciences; second, the interest of modernist poets in contemporary anthropologists like Frazer and Harrison, followed by similar post-modernist interests down to the ethnopoetic preoccupations of many of us today.[2] Such a survey might well begin with a catalogue of those poets and social scientists who have been trained, or have had practice, in each other's disciplines. I cannot do this now, but I believe that a number of agreeable surprises would emerge.[3]

1.3) While the confrontation of poets and other artists with the archaic and the primitive differs in detail as we pass from the likes of Pound and Eliot, through Dada, Surrealism, Cubism, Futurism, and others such, down to our own "ethnopoets," the charter for such a confrontation is best expressed right now in Jerome Rothenberg's preface to *Technicians of the Sacred*.[4] Another way of formulating such a charter would involve recourse to a highly formalized discipline such as "poetics," a field of discourse straddling, or at least touching on, linguistics, stylistics, semantics, and semiology. One view of poetry allowed by such a discipline, a view informed by the sciences of communication, would take the art as a cognitive system characterized by the presence of distinctive features, oppositions, and transformations, standing among other cognitive systems. I wish to concentrate on the cognitive here without *in the least* denying other functions such as the expressive.

2   For a historical view, a very partial list of authors reads as follows: Herodotus, Lucretius, Montaigne, Hobbes, Vico, Rousseau, and Coleridge. We would deal with concepts like "savage," "barbarian," "natural," etc. For Vico, see M. H. Abrams, *The Mirror and the Lamp* (New York: Norton, 1958), 78–284, 105–6, 120, noting, incidentally, Coleridge's nuanced attitude to primitivism (120); and G. Tagliacozzo, ed., *Giambatista Vico: An International Symposium* (Baltimore: Johns Hopkins University Press, 1969).

3   For one beginning, see my "From Anthropologist to Informant: An Interview with Gary Snyder," *Alcheringa* 4 (Fall 1972): 104–13.

4   Jerome Rothenberg, *Technicians of the Sacred* (New York: Doubleday, 1968). For an early view on Surrealism and anthropology, see "André Breton, Anthropology, and the Limits of Culture" in this volume. On early anthropology, I have recently found M. Peckham, *Victorian Revolutionaries* (New York: Braziller, 1970), very useful.

But object-language and metalanguage inhibit each other. A poet, years ago, put it concisely to linguists as follows: "Thank God poets do all this by instinct and don't need to learn all these rules!" In addition, it is unfortunately true that thinking of considerable importance, in Structuralism to give but one instance, is *also* now a bandwagon to which seeming access can be had without too much trouble by a gullible public.[5] In view of all this, let me be clear that, here, I am talking to poets, as my own kind and as, Wordsworth *dixit,* the most readily available of human beings. Though like bowerbirds in their art, they may appear too often to be like magpies and cuckoos in their philosophy. Academic scientists and humanists, on the other hand, so rarely take time out from their disciplines that they often, like the dodo, cannot be talked to at all. I shall therefore be as colloquial as possible.

2. The Aesthetics of Classification

2.1) A poet, then, could be interested in anthropology as the discipline dealing, amongst others, with societies which have a heavy investment in "techniques of the sacred" for the reasons outlined by Rothenberg. He proposes a confluence between their poets and ours on the basis of analogies involving orality (preliterate/postliterate); imagism (prelogical/postlogical); formal minimalization/participational maximalization; intermedia-ness; somaticism; shamanism; etc. What interests *me* most, however, is somewhat different and runs thus: (a) the extent to which both poetry and anthropology deal with the process of classification, (b) the extent to which the anthropological study of classification might lead to valuable understandings in poetics and aesthetics, and (c) the relevance of (a) and (b) to contemporary debates among poets on the origin, nature, and function of poetry. By "classifying," I mean something like the activity of arranging, organizing, or ordering, according to various criteria such as structure or origin, of phenomena into groups whose totality forms a system. I am more concerned at present with structure than origin, but not exclusively. On this occasion, I will talk of the aesthetic pleasure which I believe to be universally obtainable from the act of classification. I will also dwell on that act as part of an exploration of art objects (seen both as wholes and as sums of parts), both at the level of the object

5   The market abounds in books on Structuralism of very unequal value. Due to the deep distrust of real interdisciplinary work in many parts of the academy, specialists in one discipline can foist their "summaries" on colleagues who are not prepared to read the primary texts. A recent book in the art field (I abstain from naming it) has short introductions to Lévi-Strauss, Saussure, Piaget, and Chomsky which are so garbled as to be unreadable. This hardly inspires confidence in the rest of the work.

itself and at the level of the classifying mind in its production and consumption of objects.

2.2) I choose to begin with the simple promptings that led to this paper. I happen to be writing the third volume of a prose work provisionally entitled *Atlantis: An Autoanthropology*. This is an attempt to objectivize a structure baptized "Nathaniel Tarn" and uses "autobiographical" events only insofar as they seem to relate to the elucidation of that structure. Keys to that structure usually come in the form of preferential choices in a range of passions, interests, and hobbies, all of which seem to me to be characterized by one fundamental trait. I shall be calling this trait "heraldic," and the total of these preoccupations the "heraldic vision."

This seems to have begun with the recollection of a childhood experience. I am looking at a beloved or favorite object, let us say a pencil or a toy motorcar. Whatever its actual color, I imagine it in a different color, and then another, and then another. I have a yellow pencil, say, and I imagine the pencil is blue, or red, or green. I may well go on to blue with red stripes, green stripes, and so forth. This fantasy causes me very great pleasure, I might almost say a form of bliss. I seem to be what cognitive psychology calls a "color-child" and I now become interested, incidentally, in what happens to children who do not entirely make the usual passage from "color-child" to "form-child." Reflecting on all this at the time of writing, I note that I am enjoying a proliferation of objects in decorative terms, a pleasing but, as far as I can see, non-functional classificatoriness. I have in fact a paradigm of pencils in mind which is almost as real as the yellow pencil itself.

This has to do with a kind of species-related totality. In view of what I have to say later about a wider kind of totality, let me also record this. Around the age of eleven or so, I imagine a collection of modeler's kits which would allow me possession of a private, concrete "natural history." There are to be wooden or plastic models of sheep, dogs, camels, bears . . . in fact: all animals, all birds, all fish, perhaps all plants, etc. The collection is to be housed in a special room with thousands of drawers and closets. It is pleasant to note that such fantasies have now been embodied: some such kits can now be bought in stores.[6]

6   I am not sure, at the time of writing, whether, in the case of pencils and toys, there were preferences among colors or not. I imagine there were. Nor can I remember the age, but I believe I was older than 4–5, probably twice older. I believe I imagined the kits before I knew about ship and plane kits, but I may very well be wrong. I assume I was, by kit time, at least in part a form-child.

I am very indebted to Dr. Tom Trabasso, who kindly listened to these lucubrations and put me onto R. G. Suchman and T. Trabasso, "Color and Form Preference in Young Children," *Journal of Experimental Child Psychology* 3 (1966): 177–87; and R. G. Suchman, "Cultural Differences in Children's Color and Form Preferences," *Journal of Social Psychology* 70:3–10 Many questions stay in my mind as to the subsequent careers of people in whom the color-child remains alive (our culture intended). See also note 13 (below).

Remembering this was prompted by a consideration, while working on the *Atlantis,* of the nature and origin in me of another passion. I began to think of possible links between the ways in which I enjoy beauty. I have always enjoyed, and still enjoy, watching birds. The birds I probably enjoy watching most fall under Family *Parulidae,* the wood warblers. There are some fifty-three of these in North America alone. Asking myself what I love about watching them, I answer that the body, in a visual sense, is virtually always the same while the range of color and pattern within the basic body-form is different.[7] I find this as blissful now as I found my pencil fantasies blissful as a child.

I go on from this in a number of directions, including philately, uniforms and liveries, badges of identification, certain forms of packaging, etc. Heraldic systems continue potent until this day: they even change across the board sometimes, as when all airline companies change their plane-liveries at more or less the same moment.[8] I'll take two more examples.

It has seemed to me, for instance, that a strong liking for, almost to the point of "collecting," islands may be connected to this theme. I seem to envisage islands as fairly constant in form and variable in content, i.e., I imagine or fantasize something round, with bays, beaches, hills, streams, perhaps a central mountain, located in various parts. But, while islands do have interesting ecological characteristics, while there may well be much actual topographical overlap (on the model, say, of North, South, East, West *Bay*), while demographic "islands" related to social stratification are often formed within a mainland context, something new is occurring here. My imagination or fantasy is strongly at work in this instance, since many islands (witness Britain) are not round at all. It is almost as if my fantasy were approximating "archetypal" behavior: "my" islands resemble the kind of cosmic models archaic World views generate, together with the sacred cities that often embody or parallel these models.[9]

---

7 I am aware of the division into some seventeen genera, but the visual implications seem to me negligible at this point. This may need refinement. Interest in birds goes back at least to age nine in my childhood; in flowers, to early infancy. For changing classifications, see, *inter alia,* D. A. Sibley, *The Sibley Guide to Birds* (New York: Knopf, 2000).

8 Banks, schools, churches, municipalities, and armies still continue to rely on some form of heraldry, especially in some European countries, though the fact that the U.S. prefers "seals" to shields should mislead no one. Transportation liveries (airlines, train companies, automobile makes, etc.) still excite many hobbyists, as well as a variety of uniforms from those of armed forces to sport teams. Much commercial packaging contains heraldic elements which need study: the approach would not be quite the same as Roland Barthes's in *Mythologies* (Paris: Seuil, 1957), but that is an important text. In philately, I have become interested in the recent trend to "thematic" collecting.

9 For Mesoamerican studies, see, e.g., E. P. Benson, ed., *Mesoamerican Sites & World Views* (Washington, DC: Dumbarton Oaks, 1981). In Asiatic studies, see the monumental work of P. Mus, *Barabudur* (Hanoi: Ecole Française d'Extrême-Orient, 1935); and P. Wheatley, *The Pivot of the Four*

It has also occurred to me, to take my final example, that the way in which I perceive the bodies of the opposite sex may verge on the "heraldic." Primary and secondary sexual characteristics seem to me an almost boundless field in which the interplay of what the good Lord sends our way and what we might fantasize as our ideal bedmate or -mates can exercise the erotic imagination (of males, of course, I would not wish to presume . . .). That classification into "families," "sub-families," "genera," and "species" may occur in this domain also goes without saying.

2.3) The root metaphor I propose to account for the common characteristics of these instances is that of "heraldry." I stress the word *metaphor*. As a *historical* phenomenon, heraldry originated in medieval times, predominantly in Europe and Japan, where men of a certain class distinguished each other individually and by family through the use of badges or emblems transferable onto banners, arms, armor, clothes, servants' liveries, etc. The characteristic design (in the European case) involved a basic form gradually standardized as a shield, but easily adaptable to other objects. This shield remained fairly constant in catalogues and compendia: the contents, of course, had to vary in order to function at all. My knowledge of heraldry is limited at this time, but it does seem that simple shields came first (plain monocolored), followed by simple geometrical divisions (horizontal, vertical, diagonal, etc.) and then a whole array of other forms: zoomorphs being perhaps most popular. Faced with the need to develop this system by the spread of chivalry and tempted by the large number of decorative purposes that shields could be put to, heraldry flourished into an art field of great variety and beauty.[10]

What we seem to have, then, here (and in related fields such as flags, seals, tartans, and the like) is (a) a fairly simple form, the shield, controlling (b) a fairly wide field of content elements whose permutations continue to generate an almost infinite, or sometimes truly infinite, number of possible devices or shields.

2.4) A pause for some clarification. We are familiar, from semiotics, with the notion that a surprisingly large array of variants can be generated in a sign system on the basis of very few variables. But semiotics may be over-metalinguistic for

---

Quarters (Ithaca, NY: Cornell University Press, 1971). The writings of Jung and Campbell are so replete with such materials that there is no point in citing particular loci. Mandalas would, of course, have to enter here: on this, see G. Tucci, *The Theory and Practice of the Mandala* (London: Rider Press, 1961).

10   See C. A. von Volborth, *Heraldry of the World* (New York: Macmillan, 1974); and L. G. Pine, *The Genealogist's Encyclopedia* (New York: Weybright and Talley, 1969). We will doubtless have to deal with eventually i) a system of classification, and ii) an art of heraldry developed, or influenced, by artists—some of the caliber of Dürer. This might provide a situation not too different from that of calligraphic art, as Claude Lévi-Strauss discusses it in *The Raw and the Cooked* (New York: Harper & Row, 1964), 21.

many of us. We are responsible, I believe, for finding an operational base from which the majority of artists probably do start and which they share, to a major extent, with their public. There are grave problems here.

Looking at a bird, say, does not normally cause me to re-question *in toto* the nature of "reality." There is reason to suppose that my sighting, and a companion's sighting, will very largely overlap. The aspect of reality I begin with (even if I am fortunate enough to end up with Blake's universe-in-a-bird) has to do with the bird as recognizably (a) a bird, (b) of a certain family (warbler), (c) of a certain species (Yellow warbler). This is taxonomy: there is a history of taxonomy and now, with Foucault, we even have its "archaeology." My particular interest, however, does not rest there. I am interested in the relation of (c) to (b), that is, I am thrilled by the fact of many species *in relation to each other* so as to form a family.[11] I am also noticing that natural selection has given us a certain number of species, neither less, nor more. It is almost (shades of Kant!) as if a god had said, Let there be so many species, neither more, nor less. It is as if a god had *selected,* from an imaginably infinite *x,* a finite quantity.

Now we classify birds, and much else, on the basis of extant distinguishing and contrasting features: we cut up the "real" out there as some god might have cut it up. A kindred but contrasting need concerns itself with classifying things which do not have existing contrasting features. Take the case of five brands of pretty identical cornflakes. The seller's task is to find an emblem which will persuade the consumer that his cornflakes are different and, additionally if possible (through the accompanying message more than the emblem), the only ones worth buying. This is a kind of "heraldry": medieval soldiers, reading a field of battle, had to know which biologically identical male human was so socially non-identical as to be worth either killing or sparing and defending. That which signed him as such was his coat of arms. A property of this kind of classification is that it spreads and oozes. It *generates* as many contrasted shields as are needed in any situation—while ensuring, always, a lack of overlap—and can, one assumes, always generate more. Here, man is a "god," but his creativity almost seems superior to the divine's in that man's imagination never need stop breeding. I'll come back to this in section 4.2.

2.5) What about my pencils, islands, bodies, etc.? Other sets of problems loom.

a) Some series are "natural" (birds, islands, bodies); others, "cultural" (pencils, stamps, uniforms, cosmological models).

11   See Claude Lévi-Strauss, *The Savage Mind* (Chicago: University of Chicago Press, 1966). Note the non-sociological nature of "family" here. A sociological family could only be composed of warblers of one species!

b) Of the "cultural" series, some are "material" (pencils, stamps, etc.); others, more "ideological" (cosmological models).

c) When fantasy comes into play, new kinds of classification appear to emerge. It is as if they had to do mostly with (i) an imposition of the "cultural" onto the "natural," and/or (ii) an imposition of the "ideological-cultural" onto the "material-cultural." Thus, the "natural" and the "material-cultural" might, in many ways, be similarly treated or overlap.

d) The impositions seem to be connected with a process which involves making objects "same" or "different" (homogenization/heterogenization or identification/discrimination).

e) The area of overlap in (c) may relate to the fact that, whereas all "natural" phenomena are going, upon being perceived, to possess contrasting features, assignment by human intervention of contrasting features to "cultural" phenomena is going to differ according to whether the "cultural" phenomenon be material or ideological. You can represent an airplane, as you can a bird, by a picture isomorphic with the plane or by an arbitrary *sign*. An airline, as a *company*, or an air *force*, qua force, is going to have to be represented only by a sign basically arbitrary, however much a depictive aspect may enter into it (e.g., a pair of "wings"). Thus, "material-cultural" phenomena are going to behave more "naturally." When fantasizing about pencils (or planes), I can multiply the colors (equivalent to all warblers) or I can multiply the one color (equivalent to warblers of one species). My fantasy is transforming a "cultural" into a "natural" object. The process is complex. I can seem to be doing this through using a "natural" feature such as color. But the situation is "culturally" tinged when I imagine (as I did when a child) not pencils in all possible "natural" colors but pencils in those "cultural" colors I knew to be available to pencil-makers. At the other end of the scale, I can take a set of all available airline or air force "logos" and note the extent to which they begin to look "species-like" in the sense that "wings" or an equivalent ("bird," "Pegasus," etc.) will stand a very high chance of inclusion in the design. I cannot exhaust the matter now, but it does seem as if this aspect of the selective function of consciousness suggests that, while everything is *ab initio* "cultural," much of our endeavor comes to look like a transformation, or a "depositing," of the cultural into the natural.

2.6) Let us further complicate the picture for a moment.

a) In the warbler case, I merely recognize a member of a warbler species. It is isomorphic with its description in a field guide to birds. I limit myself to enjoying the variety of species. The same could be said of, say, stamps. I could even "collect" pilots' or flight attendants' wings.

b) In the island case, I recognize that islands are "really" multi-shaped and isomorphic with their description in an atlas. But I fantasize that they are all round with central mountains, etc. Here, I homogenize the "natural" by projecting an ideal-type onto it.

c) In the pencil case, I do not start with "natural" shapes whose variety I recognize, but with a "material-cultural" shape which is, by and large, standard. This very standardization, perhaps, is one cause of my heterogenization by projection in my childhood.

d) In the female body case, I recognize, on the one hand, that women are "really" multi-shaped (though noting that, in biological taxonomy, this has nothing to do with "species"). At this level, I might recognize that no woman is exactly "my type," thus that there is no "standard." On another hand, I might recognize or create a "type" in my head which I project onto women as they appear, thus creating a kind of "species" or "race" within womankind and affirming that there *is* a "standard." Within the "standard" thus made up of my idiosyncratic likes and dislikes, there is probably a core-standard (meeting with which might provide "love-at-first-sight") and various degrees of non-core variability, which might encourage or inhibit decision. The continuous rather than discrete nature of the traits in question makes for fluidity, no doubt, in the decision process. I now have a projection of certain "requirements" while, in another sense, I also have a selection of a range of women among all possible women. There is probably no reason why this should not apply to women imaging/imagining men.

2.7) Note the interplay between homogenization and heterogenization. "Projecting," or collecting, pencils of *one* color would be trivial. Fantasizing that a set of pencils of many colors were actually of one color would be bizarre, or even pathological. The island fantasy escapes pathology because islands are not standardized in the first place. But why do I tend to standardize them by homogenization? Because I have to get them, as it were, *down* to a certain level of co-existence into a "collectible" paradigm. This suggests that I am moving my pencils *up*, but by heterogenization, to such a level of paradigmaticity. It also suggests that I am getting women *down* when thinking of a "type," that is, standardizing by homogenization while, simultaneously, *raising* the "type" itself by accepting a certain range of differentials within the total possible range. The result may also be described in terms of a "band" or "frequency width" of paradigmaticity.

Again, I am reminded that my pleasures come from the interplay of shield and shields and that I will interfere with reality "heraldically" by adjusting it to this requirement of pleasure.

Clearly, much depends on the level at which one chooses to signify and thereby project/select the interesting characteristics: collecting the "same" stamp, for instance, occurs often, but it occurs at the level of micro-differentiation and not homogenization.[12] As soon as we touch on imagination and fantasy, we have to deal with complexities of "archetypes," "prototypes," "preformations," "ideal-types," and so on at one end of the scale, and with "idiolects," "canons," and "lexicons" at the more individual end. I am left, at present, with some very tentative terms such as "real," "projective," and "selective" heraldry which continue to require further refinement.[13]

2.8) A possible "heraldry" not mentioned as yet: that of *personae* or masks (in poetics) or roles (in sociology and psychology), where the ego would be the shield, its masks the shields, might constitute a bridge toward the social sciences. We might wish to ask, at some point, whether the question of individual/social should enter into our discussion of parts and wholes: indeed, we would be repeating a

---

12 I am under no illusions as to Freudian reactions to the topic of collection. But there are other questions. The formation of paradigms of any sort would seem to imply collection. On the surface, collection implies a consumer, but, in the form of *collage,* does it not also imply a producer, especially in our day? Is collection one basic form of the artistic process? If so, would this be true of random-procedure levels in composition as well? How significant is random-procedure really, and what is its exact relation to mimesis in the widest sense of co-relating "natural" and "cultural" orders? What about the *objet trouvé* in Surrealism and the surrealist ambivalence about whether anything is ever truly random: *le hasard objectif*? Is it not true that, for surrealists, there is always a wider sphere within which the elements of metaphor from the most disparate universes of discourse (e.g., Lautréamont's sowing machine and umbrella) cease to be perceived as separate and contradictory? See André Breton, *Manifestoes of Surrealism* (Ann Arbor: University of Michigan Press, 1969); and André Breton, *L'amour fou* (Paris, 1937); also a badly neglected classic on surrealist myths, Michel Carrouges, *Les Machines Célibataires* (Paris: Arcanes, 1954).

13 I have been keeping such words as "projective" and "selective" quite loose here in the conviction that I am not well qualified in the psychological approaches which would help. It is clear that Gestalt psychology must have its say here, possibly through such work as R. Arnheim's *Art and Visual Perception* (Berkeley: University of California Press, 1974) in aesthetics. I confess to a deplorable ignorance at this time of Piaget. My debt to Dr. Trabasso (see note 6, above) extends to his putting me in touch with the work of E. H. Rosch and K. Nelson; see E. H. Rosch, "Natural Categories," *Cognitive Psychology* 4 (1973): 238–50; and K. Nelson, "Concept, Word and Sentence," *Psychological Review* 81 (1974): 267–85. Telescoping unforgivably, I am prompted to want to know more about views in which cultural categories seem to be less arbitrary than had been thought and Euclidian space comes to us initially structured. This must have implications for the respective roles of "nature" and "culture" in classification. I would wish to know more about the implications for a "heraldic vision" of Rosch's analog, as opposed to digital models. Nelson's thesis that concept develops out of experience of a single instance, that perceptual analysis (detotalization?) is derivative (often in terms of color and size) from a conceptual core-meaning whose essence is function, seems to allow a translation in which "function" would come before "decoration." In terms of "heraldry," this might read, "Shield for defense comes before shields for beauty": see section 2.8. D. E. Berlyne, *Conflict, Arousal and Curiosity* (New York: McGraw-Hill, 1960); D. E. Berlyne, *Aesthetics and Psychobiology* (New York: Appleton-Century, 1971); and D. E. Berlyne, *Studies in the New Experimental Aesthetics* (Washington, DC: Hemisphere, 1974), would be material, for instance, to the question of saying neither too much nor too little in a poem: the problem of "stimulus complexity" (see section 4.3. of this paper).

Durkheimian journey were we to do so. I note, in passing, such things as the fact that I never seemed to fantasize about functions in my pencil case (by giving the pencils different colored leads, for example). I note too that the question of function must be gone into for "heraldry" in general insofar as there does seem to be a problem in developmental psychology regarding the exact relation between function and decoration. If we imagine two men roaming the forest, do they fight on meeting because they want to and have swords and shields, or because their shields are of a different color? Such a naïve question reminds us that shields seem to identify individuals *before* they identify groups and lineages: or is this an illusion? Such a ragbag of references to anthropology implies no more than further questions at some later date. For the time being, let me pass to the problem of shield/shields or whole/parts in recent anthropological research.

A major area of attention paid to classificatory procedures has been in the anthropological work on so-called primitive classification of Durkheim, Mauss, and Lévi-Strauss. These procedures are associated, in tribal contexts, with "Totemism."[14] Simplifying grossly, "Totemism" has to do with selection among natural objects (often but not exclusively zoological or botanical) by a tribal group such that the differences perceived between the objects selected will be reflected back on the group in order to establish different sub-groups within it. The difference between eagle and crow, for instance, will be used to establish a difference between *biologically identical* sub-groups now *sociologically non-identical* as Eaglepeople and Crow-people. This allows the division of the group into sub-groups for all sorts of purposes, including, eventually, the division of labor. Natural species, then, are not just "good for eating," as anthropology held before Lévi-Strauss, but they are also "good for thinking." Classification of the universe around men, both natural and cultural as well as material and ideological, is necessary to the very function of society.

Provisionally, however, I point out that, whether we take the "totemic" symbol as *emblematic* (with Durkheim) or as *archival* (with Lévi-Strauss), it is not required of anthropological theory that the symbols be "good for beauty" in addition to being good for eating and thinking. Now, even if I were dealing only with one poetic

14 See Claude Lévi-Strauss, *Totemism* (Boston: Beacon Press, 1973); Lévi-Strauss, *The Savage Mind;* and Lévi-Strauss, *The Raw and the Cooked.* I must reserve for another occasion any attempt to consider Lévi-Strauss's specific statements on the arts. His treatment of "nature" and "culture" in each of the arts obviously requires special attention; cf. M. Foucault, *The Order of Things* (New York: Vintage, 1973), xix–xxi. See also E. Durkheim, *The Elementary Forms of the Religious Life* (New York: Free Press, 1968); and E. Durkheim and M. Mauss, *Primitive Classification* (Chicago: University of Chicago Press, 1963).

imagination, my own idiosyncratic one, I would hope to be suggesting that there is a primary aesthetic component to the act of classification, both in the production and consumption aspects of the "heraldic vision," which cannot be reduced to any form of function other than the aesthetic. This hypothesis, and I would not like to think of it as more than that at present, may have implications for the study of art.

3. Classification and Totalization: The Heraldic Vision in Blake

3.1) I now want to give this discussion some badly needed content by looking into the "heraldic vision" as I perceive it at work in Blake.

First, however, I refer to an important mechanism identified by Lévi-Strauss in his discussion of the classificatory aspects of "Myth" and "Totemism."[15] A classificatory system of the "totemic" type establishes, by means of a series of species abstracted from the known world, a group of referential categories such that each species, together with much that pertains to it, will form a category until the exhaustion or saturation of that world. Further, these categories will form a system. The "totemic" symbol acts within the grid so formed as a transformational operator capable of being moved between extreme poles of universalization/generalization and individualization/particularization. The movement would seem to be most often expressed as a process of totalization or detotalization (putting together and taking to pieces) of the totemic operator.

Let it be so that the whole world for Tribe X is divided up between three subgroups known as Bear-people, Seal-people, and Eagle-people. Many items from the environment, habitat, food, habits, etc., of the bear, the seal, and the eagle will fall into the category constituted by each animal—so much so sometimes that the whole known world will be divided up between the three. The three creatures will also be taken to pieces: head of bear, head of seal, head of eagle, etc., all the way through the anatomy. Each zoomorph could, then, for various purposes be seen as a run from, say, all bears/certain kinds of bears/certain colors of bears/a local group of bears/the food, habitat, etc. Same with seal and eagle. Totalization would then tend to involve any movement to the generalization pole, while detotalization tends to move toward the particularization pole. Processually, to use a term in *this* context from the anthropologist Victor Turner, detotalization might be the taking to pieces of a system for dialectical purposes, normally with some form of

15 Lévi-Strauss, *The Savage Mind,* 146–49, 151–54, 169, 175–76, 178, 250–62. On the "totemic operator," see especially the diagram at 152.

re-totalization in view.[16] This seems to me to be paradigmatic of artistic creation. But let's get to Blake.

3.2) What, then, is the content of such great Prophecies as *The Four Zoas* and *Jerusalem*? What Northrop Frye has identified as the essential Romantic myth might be read as follows.[17] An entity, Albion, exists in a state which seems like repose. It is not clear whether Albion is equal to, or coterminous with, the universe (view one), or whether he is smaller or lesser than the universe (view two). A perturbation, not unlike the Fall in Genesis, occurs in Albion as a result of which he is menaced with disintegration or actually disintegrates. Follows a long conflict or set of conflicts which are the matter of a poetry with as high a degree of redundancy as one finds in any major art. Whether certain divine forces remain outside of Albion (view two) or whether they are internal to him (view one), goody forces eventually prevail over baddy forces, integration over disintegration. Albion falls into parts but returns in the end to totality.

This echoes totalization and detotalization in Lévi-Strauss. In effect, the disintegration of Albion, the Cosmic Man, is not unakin to a society (or, more precisely, its "ideal" image, which I'll here call *ecclesia*) breaking up into its component parts and then uniting again. We remember our school day images: the breaking up of Israel and the Diaspora, or the division of the map between White, Red, Yellow, and Black "races" or various empires. (Again, as in the case of "real heraldry," we work from the total to the part, from society, here, to totem as it were: let's note in passing that this, for *art*, may imply an inversion of what happens in Lévi-Strauss, for *Totemism*). Albion breaks up into Albion$^{1,2,3,4\cdots n}$ serving, if you like, as "totems" to sub-groups named after them (Israel → tribes of Israel): the sons and daughters of Albion in their manifold complexity. This is a model for other detotalizations—tribes but also counties, cities, cathedrals, and universities of Britain; revolutionary nations of Blake's time, etc.—and generates the matrix in which the "Human Composite" can be apprehended diachronically. Blake follows a process, familiar from primitive classification, of dividing up the world among the lineages of Albion so that we get embarrassingly detailed lists in the Prophecies whose function, when totalized, is to produce a reduced model of the cosmos.[18] Here I should note that one of Lévi-Strauss's most convincing arguments relating to the visual arts (in *The*

16   On Victor Turner's contributions, see section 5.2 of this paper.

17   N. Frye, *A Study of English Romanticism* (New York: Random House, 1968), ch. 1.

18   Blake is, of course, highly aware of the systematic nature of his enterprise in his sense that he must create his system in order not to be enslaved by another's. The Prophecies that I am dealing with are mainly *The Four Zoas, Milton,* and *Jerusalem*. For detailed lists of the type I discussed here, see

Savage Mind, chapter 1) specifies the role of the reduced model in the definition
of aesthetic experience.

3.3) The term I oppose in my own usage to the Edenic *"ecclesia"* is *sparagmos:* a
rendering, tearing, or mangling applicable, as I learn, to the dismemberment of fer-
tility gods as well as to the Crucified Christ.[19] I probably got it from Frye,[20] though
my usage is, I believe, different. *Sparagmos* here is detotalization. Now, there is every
reason to believe that Blake saw the *sparagmos* of Albion as occurring over and
over again, either within a cosmic Fall and Redemption (if we take the view
Albion = Cosmos) or not (if we take the view Albion < Cosmos). This constant re-
currence would follow from the notion that each reader of the Prophecies is himself
or herself Albion, as well as their writer, Blake himself: indeed, that all men and
women are potential Albions.[21] From this point of view, it becomes immaterial to
discuss whether *sparagmos* comes before *ecclesia* or the reverse: as far as the ideology

---

David Erdman's *The Poetry and Prose of William Blake* (Garden City, NY: Anchor-Doubleday,
1965), 158–59, 181, 206–8, 223–25. But this is an initial suggestion (the process is ubiquitous in
Blake), and I have made no attempt to catalogue all the lists. For charts of category ascription, see
S. F. Damon, *A Blake Dictionary* (New York: Dutton, 1971), 212.

   An excellent study of Balzacian cosmic models is M. Butor, "Balzac et la réalité," in his
Répertoire I (Paris: Editions de Minuit, 1960). My "The Created Creator and the Agony of Time:
Balzac's *La Peau de Chagrin,*" is in manuscript.

19   Re theological considerations, it would be interesting to open a digression here starting with
Coleridge on the Greek gods and going on to consider why there has been such a persistence of
classical pantheons in the thematics of poetry down to this day. For now, I would guess that some
form of polytheism (rather perhaps than pantheism) is necessary to the kind of "vision" I am postulating here, a societal one in that the gods of a polytheistic situation are, *de facto,* a *society.* The
poem no longer viewed as machine, or plant, but as society. Recent poets have tended to bring
other pantheons into their work: I guess that Maya and Buddhist pantheons (they seem to pre-
dominate) are fulfilling the same function as the Greco-Romans do as late as Pound and Eliot. G.
Davenport's Pound studies like "Persephone's Ezra," in *New Approaches to Ezra Pound,* ed. Eva
Hesse (Berkeley: University of California Press, 1969), show quite clearly that at least two sub-
groups in Pound's "society," the goodies and the baddies, are represented by two different sets of
gods standing for different social values, and there are probably more than two.

20   N. Frye, *The Anatomy of Criticism* (New York: Atheneum, 1965), 148, 192–93, 222.

21   I shall want to look at 1) being torn apart, and 2) falling apart. There may be little difference. *The
Bacchae* may be a good place to start. The very degree of redundancy in the Prophecies is one aspect among many of Blake's generalized view of the basic scenario. We might also decide that the
uncertainty about Albion = Cosmos / Albion < Cosmos may be one of the ways in which Blake
deliberately sets up tensions within the text in order to leave open a very difficult question. One
formulation of "view two" could run as follows: Albion is an emanation of the Cosmos, but not
the only one—since, for every individual, every nation, every cosmos, there is an "Albion" in the
same sense in which there is a Buddha in Buddhism for each such class. Should "view one" prevail, Albion would probably have to be equated with the Absolute, Eternal Reality, the Unwob-
bling Pivot, Atman, *Nirvāṇa,* and other such. The radical contradiction here at one level is
resolvable at another level: see section 5 of this paper.

behind the poem, or the process the poem is trying to promote, is concerned, this is chicken-and-egg-land. What *is* very important, however, concerns the fact that the *formal* constraint on this ideological matter tends to operate in one direction and not in its reverse. The form of a prophecy given by Blake will in effect turn out to follow the sequence *ecclesia-sparagmos-ecclesia* (*nova*) (or initial total, detotalization, retotalization) rather than either (a) *sparagmos-ecclesia-sparagmos* or (b) an endless chain which could only exist in virtuality. An art object, both then and now, can only exhibit a certain cut in reality, a certain portion of it, and we do have to look at what we actually have in hand.[22] This is far from meaning, of course, that Blake does not do his best at most times to mask this constraint: I'll pick up on this in a moment.

I would argue from this that *closure* (initial total) is a sine qua non of the art object in its initial moment or "genesis" (in Zen terms: its *original* face) and that most such objects will work or be worked back toward closure as a *terminal* retotalization as well. This argument may be unsympathetic to partisans of a totally "open" poetry. Would they be more likely to accept a *dialectical* view in which, working out of initial closure, detotalization would stand for the processual, "open" element in poetics? This question takes us into our next section.

4. Structure and Process: The Contemporary Debate

4.1) We come out here onto the fertile delta of contemporary poetic debate. I am not far from thinking that the closed-open dialectic just suggested is, in fact, the root transform of a whole series of problems including, among others, whole/part, content/form, space/time (or synchrony/diachrony), visual/verbal, written/oral. At a higher level of abstraction, we might have a parallel run of pairs such as culture/nature, discontinuity/continuity, paradigm/syntagm, metaphor/metonymy. A long hard look is needed at each of these pairs: by their very nature they resist such regimentation.[23] But let's give them a trial flight.

---

22 As it passes from process back into structure, the poem would immediately open up again into paradigmatic scope. Taking Dante's *Commedia* at this moment would then involve, at least: (a) Dante's trip as pilgrim, from which he does not return until the moment we read the last line of *Paradiso;* (b) Dante's trip as scriptor, from which he has returned the moment we approach the poem; (c) Dante's rehearsal of his trip at the time of his death, upon which he has not yet set out; (d) Dante's no longer being among us; and (e) the application of all this to Everyman. This can be refined. Admittedly, such considerations have not been foreign to Dante scholarship. I am indebted here, of course, to the theory of narrative from Propp on down.

23 I might be tempted to place another pair, "Structuralism/serialism," among the "higher level of abstraction" pairs here listed if I could be sure of understanding Lévi-Strauss's discussion in *The Raw and the Cooked*, 23–26.

4.2) The great issues of our episteme revolve around the issues at stake between Structuralism on the one hand and Phenomenology on the other.[24] The criticism frequently leveled at Structuralism (it would be more correct to speak of Structuralisms or structuralist methods, and the same may be true of Phenomenologies) is that it detracts from the value of human time by denying its sequential character, the conditions of its *freedom,* by organizing it for us, very variously of course, in a predominantly *spatial* manner. "Organization," here, may well be, or mean, imprisonment. The reply to such criticism, if I understand it correctly, generally involves the claim that, in order to perceive time at all, and certainly in order to *present* it, discontinuities have to be introduced into the sequence which will eventually lead to some form of spatial presentation. As Foucault puts it, sequential arrangements are foreign to representation, hence his stress on such pairs as taxonomia and genesis, rhetoric and grammar, etc.[25] As Gombrich and Goodman insist, there is no innocent eye: "The eye comes always ancient to its work, obsessed by its own past. . . ."[26] "History," as Lévi-Strauss puts it, is always "history for" a particular human purpose or viewpoint and, as such, can never be seized in its sequential purity.[27]

My own training happens to have been in Structuralism rather than in "Process" philosophy or Phenomenology. Structuralism and the "heraldic vision" share many elements: what is chicken and what is egg here I will not debate just now. Let me see how I fare in trying to accommodate both viewpoints. It is not more than a trial.

Telescoping Albion and the Divine Imagination, as Blake, I believe, gives us license to do, let Albion stand for the state of a poet's mind at the outset of a cre-

24 Thanks for a discussion with William V. Spanos at Binghamton in early 1975 and for a subsequent reading of his criticism, especially "Literary Criticism and the Spatialization of Time," *Journal of Aesthetics and Art Criticism* 29, no. 1 (Fall 1970): 87–104. Some aspects of this confrontation may be an extension of a crucial confrontation in the first half of the century, that between Surrealism and Marxism. For a 1964, much too conservative, formulation of some of these issues in terms of private/public poetries in relation to scientific thinking, see Nathaniel Tarn, "Poetry and Communication," in Nathaniel Tarn, *Views from the Weaving Mountain* (Albuquerque: University of New Mexico Press, 1991).

25 Foucault, *The Order of Things,* 70, 82, 84–85, 113, 132–38.

26 E. Gombrich, *Art and Illusion* (New York: Pantheon, 1960). The quotation is from N. Goodman, *Languages of Art* (New York: Bobbs-Merrill), 7. I have not paid enough attention here to art historians and aestheticians. Arnheim and Gombrich spring to mind; there are many others. Spanos indicates W. R. Worringer, *Abstraction and Empathy* (New York: International University Press, 1967), as an important master. S. Nodelman's extremely useful piece, "Structural Analysis in Art and Anthropology," in *Structuralism,* ed. J. Ehrmann (New Haven, CT: Yale University Press, 1966), calls attention to the *strukturforschung* school of such scholars as Riegl and von Kaschnitz-Weinberg: unfortunately, not too much of this seems available in translation.

27 Lévi-Strauss, *The Savage Mind,* 257.

ative act. Wherever Los stands in the chain Albion^{1-n}, let him be Los if you will. The poet's mind will contain a world-model which might be partly or wholly unconscious (the sum of the life to date, the sum of the poems). I see that model, when first found in the mental thicket, as *closed* in upon itself, *whole*, rich with *content*, *spaced* out as a garden (*hortus conclusus*), *visual* in that it teems with images, engraved upon the thicket, i.e., primarily *written*.[28] It will do no harm to invoke organicism, to speak of a seed or field of seeds. The field of seeds is a field of *metaphors*, a *paradigm* of possible adventures in nomination; the inscribed code is bursting to get out and express itself. We start, let us be clear, with culture and not with nature. There is no "origin" of art any more than there is origin of language: Adam is a fiction invented because a story appears to have to begin somewhere, because culture has to imitate nature in giving an art object an origin, a genesis, a birth. Actually, there may never be origins in nature either, except in appearance.

Starting from our initial total or world-model, we next see the generation of process. The *part* thrusts itself out of the whole in the manner of a shoot or of a sparagmatic Fall. It manifests itself, out of content, as *form*, espousing the sequentiality of *time, verbal* in seeking out its form, *oral* in the very biology of its manifestation. It is, in a word, projective. For Blake, this processual aspect has been brilliantly described by George Quasha in terms of poetic torsion (1970). Charles Olson, of course, has given us its charter for our present (1966).[29] Our model calls for a localization of metaphor in the initial seed: once the discourse is embarked upon, the process must be resolutely syntagmatic and metonymic, constraining or reducing the order of similarity to that of contiguity by the sheer power of imaginative voice. The motto of this stage of the creation is perhaps *Je Maintiendrai*:

28 On the primacy of the written, Jacques Derrida's vast output is obviously material. It is clear that an artist, especially if he be "processual" in his feelings, might reject the suggestion that he starts out with any kind of "world-model" as he begins to write his poem. As I have pointed out, the illusion that, while process occurs, there is nothing else but process—i.e., there is nothing else, past, present, and future, but liberty and freedom—is the illusion which is *necessary* to the act of the poem, the performance of it, its making. Nevertheless, I believe that the poet is constrained by structure both at the outset and at the termination of her/his creative act. The initial constraint may well be unconscious; there may even be repression for very pertinent reasons. To a reader of Lévi-Strauss, this question also opens out onto the problematic ratio of unconscious/conscious components in his view of classification.

29 G. Quasha, "Orc as a Fiery Paradigm of Poetics Torsion," in *Visionary Forms Dramatic,* ed. David Erdman (Princeton, NJ: Princeton University Press, 1970); and C. Olson, "Projective Verse," in *Selected Writings* (New York: New Directions, 1966). In a valuable conversation (February 25, 1976) on open/closed, structural/processual, influence/"transmission," Quasha proposed ceasing to equate "open-form" poetry with open-endedness and looking at what escapes from the middle of a poem.

these things will stick together, by god, though I have to pay for it with the world.[30]

Re-totalization carries Albion back to Eden in the form of a "fruit." But how does the "fruit," following on from the "flower," become the "seed" of a new art object? The possibility for me is that the artist, representing in her/his moment of achievement culture as the run of all existing and virtual art objects, seeks to introduce her/his retotalization into nature as if it were a natural object, an idea not unakin perhaps to the Marxist view that human history must eventually dissolve back into natural history. This *pretence* changes "fruit" into "seed" by transforming a completion into a beginning, a retotalization into an initial world-model ready for process again. The significance of an Adam, or Albion, lies in the pretence on the part of art that its objects have a natural origin, that art imitates life or, indeed, *is* life. In reality, of course, we know that life not only imitates art; it is a product of art.

4.3) I return to my theme by asking how the poem seeks out its processual way within detotalization. Operating between the initial total and the retotalization, the poem works as if it were passing from a "real heraldry," through a "projective heraldry," to a "selective heraldry." I am aware myself, when writing about an object, of a strong urge to catalogue its elements, to exhaust its description, to saturate the representational field with a fully responsible isomorphic portrait of the object. Let's suppose I treat of a beloved body as a "heraldic object." I am tempted to say, "The hair is . . . the eyes are . . . the lips are . . . etc." (this happens in Renaissance *blazon* poems). I am aware, as I do this, of a debilitating aspect to my activity. This arises, I think, from the fact that, in this detotalization, I am striving to distinguish these elements from those of all other possible bodies belonging to the same "heraldry." In order to do so, however, I have to refer *back* to my initial total: what I know of the "real heraldry" of the female body. This backward look—like the look to Eurydice—kills the object. The way *forward* implies selection for maximal artistic stress by rigorous attention to the elements in their *particularity*, a *particularity* which *opens* the elements to other paradigms in the oncoming metaphorical process of the re-totalization. This move forward is exhilarating rather than debilitating, moving through projection to "selective heraldry" and the establishment of the personal paradigm of femininity. *Now* Eurydice is

30   Reading some notes made in 1970 after writing this, I find, "The poetic function projects the principle of equivalence from the axis of selection (e.g., metaphor) into the axis of combination" (i.e., metonymy). See R. Jakobson, "Linguistics and Poetics," in *Style in Language,* ed. Thomas A Sebeok (Boston: MIT Press, 1960), 358. On structure as that through which it is possible to pass from the seen to the spoken, see Foucault, *The Order of Things,* 134–35.

above ground in the full view of day; *now* I can look at her and face the new structure. She can now be deposited into nature so that she becomes the new lover from whom I, or another poet, male or female, may move forward again.[31]

Note that the poem here is in no way different from a sexual act seen in and for itself, as well as in its aspect as an act in a chain of acts. We have been asking, after all, not only for an aesthetic of the individual art-object but also for an aesthetic of the run of all existing or virtual art objects. The lovers start as structures for each other. As the act progresses, they sparagmatize vis-à-vis each other into a kaleidoscope of bodily parts. After climax, they fall gradually back into themselves and into the unity of their faces, but it is a condition of ever-renewing love that these faces be not the faces they were before: a *re*-totalization has occurred which will carry each of them into the next sexual moment.

Three other notations. First: the property of process is to cause one to believe, while it is moving forward, that nothing but process exists, and this may be fed in no small measure by the pretence that art is life. Yet process is moving inexorably back toward re-totalization, toward structure. This too could be taken as an aspect of "living" if death were also: but death is the last thing we want to look at. However this may be, I report here another fact of my experience which is that, at the height of the creative act, I experience the wonderful feeling that nothing I can possibly utter is or could be *non*-poetic. I attain, in other words, total virtuality at the apex of the processual function. I find, however, that it is precisely *then*, in that golden moment, that I become aware that the flow has stopped, may indeed have stopped days before. We are back in that which has been done, in structure. But we have noted the extraordinary "naturalness" of the processual experience.[32]

Second: in regard to the "shield" and its variants, I would argue that the heterocosmic view of the art-object (that which makes us refer to world-models and their elements) arises from the fact that we establish, "heraldically," a metaphor of pantocratic power in the poetic process. Contradictions between the many and the one, the whole and its parts, are resolved by men into "heraldic" systems in order that they might partake of the pleasure of *knowing* what the one form *is* which is behind a plethora of contents. We give ourselves godhood in the deadly serious games of art by miming the pleasure we *think* a god enjoys in *his* total knowledge

31   Another take: Orpheus "looks back" at regret for Eurydice and can pay no attention to the Bacchantes. They tear him to pieces and throw him into a river (process). A "selected" Orpheus, composed of head and lyre, will land on Lesbos, originating future shrines from which the god will speak again as oracle.

32   I hope to develop a model of "litanical," "idyllic," and "elegiac" (later lyric/idyll/elegy) as an outcome of this.

of his creation. Our religions may be no more than projections from the aesthetic pleasure we derive from the "heraldic vision" in our arts.

Third: there is an aspect of *sparagmos* we have not yet considered and that has to do with the flying apart of culture we seem to be experiencing in our time. Much of our major poetry has tried to deal with this in a conservative sense, the sense of "these fragments I have shored against my ruins." It is perhaps for this reason that it seems to be the *form* that mimes the cultural *sparagmos,* whereas the *content* continues to proclaim a desire for the whole.[33] Does this desire continue in the more progressive, radical processual poets of the new "metapoetries"?[34] Do their works "return to structure" or not? What is the present status of the aesthetic of the fragment, the aesthetic of *unendlichkeit*? What is the role of Rothenberg's criteria of multi-medianess and maximal participation in this debate? The love of, and miming of, *origins* and *genesis* in our search for the "primitive" I may have accounted for. The set of this paper has not allowed the same attention to some of Rothenberg's other criteria.

5. The Veil of the Goddess

5.1) I must press on. What we now have to consider is a crucial determination of the role of time and space in the poetic imagination. I have tried to review, albeit with a bias, the respective positions of Structuralism and Phenomenology. There may, however, be another option, one which has always had a great appeal for the poetic imagination. This option may be termed Hermeticism, or, as I prefer to call it, with a sociological echo in mind, "Initiation." I would not be the first to perceive a kinship between this and some aspects of Structuralism.[35] It has caused antagonism toward "Initiation" on the part of certain literary critics, especially those who stress the importance of historicity.

It would be simple indeed to say that "Initiation" radically spatializes time in the sense that the repetitiveness of Albion's detotalization and retotalization is equivalent to circularity. Circularity, as Poulet has amply demonstrated, is archetypal spatialization.[36] But I have tried to show that *re*-totalization is never identical with totalization: the "fruit" in culture, if not in nature (and who is to tell,

---

33   See, for instance, Davenport, "Persephone's Ezra," 173.
34   See George Quasha, "Metapoetry: The Poetry of Changes," in *Open Poetry*, ed. Ron Gross and George Quasha (New York: Simon & Schuster, 1973).
35   G. H. Hartmann, "Structuralism: The Anglo-American Adventure," in Ehrmann, *Structuralism*, 160; and Spanos, "Literary Criticism and the Spatialization of Time," 97.
36   Georges Poulet, *Studies in Human Time* (Baltimore: Johns Hopkins University Press, 1966).

with mutation possible?), is always at a step removed from the "seed." The truth is that there are two Hermeticisms, one in which, yes, human nature really is eternally the same, human problems likewise, and there is nothing new under the sun; another in which some form of accommodation with History becomes possible by postulating an *evolutionary* factor in human consciousness and problematics. The writings of Owen Barfield spring to mind here and cause us perhaps to look at re-evaluations of the relative weight which Western and Eastern initiatic systems should have among ourselves as poets today.[37] In any event, it would seem possible for the poetic imagination to escape from the stark alternative of i) a point of view from which History is impossible and ii) another from which nothing but History is possible. Perhaps we have a *both/and* situation rather than the depressingly familiar *either/or;* perhaps we have, too, a possibility of coming to terms with *both* the closed and the open factors in our arts as Makers.

5.2) Before I try to draw the implications of this, let me insert here the recognition of a new direction in anthropology that poets ought to welcome. Symbolic anthropology, in the hands of Victor Turner for example, calls for close attention to the "unacknowledged legislators of mankind" as "possessed by spirits of change before changes become visible in public arenas."[38] It is especially pleasing to see how often Turner invokes Blake. Turner's notions of "structure" and "*communitas*" move in the direction, unthinkable a few years ago, of bringing within the sociological consciousness, if not the conditions of a balancing asociality, at least those of a creatively oriented anti-sociality—or, as he phrases it, "liminality."[39] Coming to his work after the main formulation of this paper, I have found with excitement marked correspondences between Turner and myself on a variety of questions.[40]

---

37   Owen Barfield, *Saving the Appearances* (New York: Harcourt Brace, 1965); and Owen Barfield, *Unancestral Voice* (Middletown, CT: Wesleyan University Press, 1965).

38   Victor Turner, *Dramas, Fields and Metaphors* (Ithaca, NY: Cornell University Press, 1974), 17–18, 28.

39   Ibid., 47, 52, 268–69, 298.

40   Ibid. on "temporal" and "atemporal" structures and "the cybernetic effects of cognitive and normative structural models," 35–36; on "Metaphor," 24–25; on a sociological view of "*sparagmos,*" 234; on the "Edenic" quality of "*communitas,*" 237; and on the relation between nature/*communitas* and culture/structure, 252–53, 256–57. On symbolism in general, see *Forms of Symbolic Action,* ed. Robert F. Spencer (Seattle: University of Washington Press, 1969), 8–9. On the problem of the anti-social and the asocial (while recognizing that, methodologically, Turner might refuse such a view), I still prefer the model set out in "Initiation and the Paradox of Power" in this volume, and "Primitive Secret Societies," in Tarn, *Views from the Weaving Mountain.* The corresponding arguments in Turner would be found in Spencer, *Forms of Symbolic Action,* 5; and Turner, *Dramas, Fields and Metaphors,* 238–41, 259, 275–76, 287, 292. I have not yet pondered properly Turner's material on color symbolism. The arguments in Victor Turner, *The Forest of Symbols* (Ithaca, NY: Cornell University Press, 1967), especially 88–91, obviously require

There is no doubt that, in conjunction with structuralist anthropology, an Anglo-American symbolic and/or cognitive anthropology alive to both Structuralism and Phenomenology is developing rapidly with exciting interdisciplinary implications for cognitive psychology, linguistics, and aesthetics. I hope to continue looking in this field to such names as Leach, Geertz, Douglas, Fernandez, Tedlock, Hall, Hymes, Munn, Gossen, and Crapanzano among many others, without forgetting such teachers as Griaule, Firth, and Redfield.[41] If I may put in a personal note here, I find it ironic that anthropology was beginning to take this direction just as I was giving it up in despair of it ever doing so! Whatever my "prophetic" powers may be, this says little for my predictive ones!

5.3) I go back to the matter of 5.2. Poetry in our time is required to be *closed* in that it is now, after the demise or near demise of formal religion, one of the chief depositories of our culture's traditions. I don't know whether shamans need erudition, but priests probably do, and the names of Pound, Eliot, H.D., Rukeyser, Zukofsky, Olson, Duncan, Dahlen, Guest, Blackburn, Economou, Mac Low, Schwerner, Irby, Kelly, Dorn, Johnson, and Waldman, among many others, hardly warrant a view that poetry and scholarship belong to different worlds. Poetry, with us, is also required to be *open*, however, in the accepted sense that no tradition can *be* tradition at all unless it is always making itself new. Here already, there is no closure without openness, nor openness without closure, and while, processually, we must always be "open on the forward side" (in David Antin's words)[42] in order to believe in our operation at all, the danger of bathos alone would prevent us from saying that we go the way of all flesh like all flesh all the time.

Time and Space are both dimensions of all experience which can be and are shaped by the mind both individually and socially. There is unlikely to be pure space or pure time in our experience, but there can be transformations in which space and time might be apprehended by the mind, indeed the whole being, as reduced to zero, whether by the greatest magnification, on the one hand, or

---

this. Turner's discussion of orectic/normative referential polarization in symbols—in the general context of a statement such as Gehlen's that "man is by nature a cultural creature"—seem to me to bear strong relationship to what I say here regarding the role of any art object in the production of another; see Spencer, *Forms of Symbolic Action*, 9, 17, 23.

It is part of the imbalance of this paper that anthropologists critical of a lack of historicity receive less attention: see Stanley Diamond, Eric Wolf, and the authors included in *Rethinking Anthropology*, ed. D. Hymes (New York: Pantheon, 1972), among many others.

41 For a complete bibliography, see the original version of this paper in *Alcheringa* n.s. 2, no.2 (Fall 1976): 39–41.

42 See his major work in David Antin, "Modernism and Postmodernism: Approaching the Present in American Poetry," *Boundary 2* 1, no. 1 (1972): 98–133.

the greatest reduction, on the other, according to the model (*via positiva* or *via negativa*) employed. The spatialization of time is then but one such transformation, and I would suspect that a temporalization of space might well coexist with it: indeed, this may be one possible reading of the art of music. These transformations will usually serve a function: they will be "for" in the sense of geography "for" or history "for."

But again, not necessarily. In regard to "Initiation," I would add that, as we move from the world of input and output, or from the world of self–other reciprocity, through the world of self–self reciprocity, toward the world of non-reciprocity, everything happens as if the categories of space and time as normally known to us cease to be relevant. The passage from reciprocity to non-reciprocity is total, immediate, and, in the final moment, irreversible. To the best of our knowledge, the rules of the world of reciprocity govern us until that moment. After it, if we are to take informants' exegeses seriously, they cease to be binding. Here the accepted borders of the sociological would be transcended. For what occurs when the mountains which have been mountains, and then have not been mountains, become mountains again (Zen saying) is strictly defined as nonreciprocal. It *is* interesting, however, that a new nonreciprocal "sociology" arises immediately on the symbolic level, characterized by the absolute coterminousness of whole and parts and the summation of all time and all space. Thus the assembly of Buddhas and Bodhisattvas in the Mahāyāna, the great white rose of Dante's *Paradiso*, Blake's "Great Harvest and Vintage of the Nations," among others. I read this transform, at any level on which we might require a metaphysics, as equivalent to the deposition of the art-object by culture into nature, so that a new and as yet unheard of culture might be chartered with a genesis.

5.4) The concept of a "heraldic vision" might appeal to poets because the average view of human time produces something slower than the scientific view of time. Even if culture is on the move with ever-accelerating speed, something in the human condition appears to require a continued defense of "human universals." These universals *pretend* that the human condition is timeless, that human happiness/unhappiness have never really varied much, that knowledge and beauty serve as consolations for the near-impossibility of our condition, that the world of the senses is steady, that the sun will come up tomorrow as it came up yesterday and today, and that it will be recognizable as the sun. What matter if these views are in one way or another patently untrue, false, mythical, and inauthentic? If they have *always* been so? Our dilemma lies in the fact that we only have to say they are to feel a terrible anxiety: it is also true! we want to shout: it is not only untrue, it is also true!

There would seem to be something permanently *archaic* then in man's requirements (including the aesthetics of cognition) which expresses itself through the poet as guarantor of these universals. It has been pointed out that the *archetypal* and the *primal* (structure) are different from the *archaic* and the *primitive* (event). The archetypal and the primal *pretend* at an origin or genesis: it is the condition of their efficacy that they cannot believe their pretence. The most beautiful contradiction in art is that it will be authentic to itself only by being inauthentic to nature. *Ars longa vita brevis,* but art must pretend to be brief if life is going to tolerate it at all. We live forever and die forever exactly in the same moment.[43]

5.5) In describing a waterfall, Coleridge, that great precursor, spoke of the eternally similar form and the endless variety of content: "the continual *change* of the *Matter,* the perpetual *Sameness* of the *Form.*"[44] Coming upon this recently, how could I not recognize the essential precondition of the "heraldic vision"?[45]

Insofar as the widest universe has always been there from the beginning, insofar as we do not ever discover but only *re*-discover, we adhere to the primal and the archetypal, that is, to closure. Insofar as, by our poetic acts alone, in that one *scandal* of the creative process, we have our only becoming, we move forward out of the primitive and archaic into history to "make it new." That the existential contradiction is *absolute* here is implied and accepted by what I've said before.

---

43 5.4 obviously requires refinement. I would certainly like to consider all this in the light of Barthes's view in *Mythologies,* that bourgeois culture's fundamental inauthenticity springs from its transformation of "culture" into "nature" precisely *in order to avoid* change. Nature, involving "human nature," if seen as invariant, inhibits any desire or motivation for social change. From his point of view as a Marxist at that date, Barthes criticizes this. My own view, inspired by the impossibility of Baudelaire's "*N'importe où pourvu que ce soit hors de ce monde,*" to which I would add "*pourvu que ce soit hors de cette langue,*" as well as its eternal desirability, seems to be moving in the direction of a radically schizoid thesis regarding art and nature only capable of being resolved at the level of what I here call "initiation." As men, we experience genesis, living, and dying. As artists, we create what we are compelled to see as a deathless order. The order must pretend to be subjected to genesis, however, in order that we can *tolerate* the discrepancy between ourselves and our creations. That is, while Barthes's "inauthenticity" may be deplorable from a political point of view (and I would so deplore it even in myself), it may be a basic human requirement on some other level. The "beautiful contradictions" continue to puzzle us, sometimes ludically, sometimes intolerably. The view that modern literature is a return to a pre-classical episteme is found at large in Barthes: my most recent reading of it is in Foucault, *The Order of Things,* 43–44, 81, 89, 96, 118–20, and especially 103. I bring this up in connection with our consideration of the archaic and the archetypal.

44 See E. L. Griggs, ed., *Letters of S. T. Coleridge* (London: Oxford University Press, 1956–71), 2:853–54; and K. Coburn, ed., *The Notebooks,* vol. 2 (London: Routledge Kegan Paul, 1961), item 2832.

45 Goethe would occasion similar reverence. For two suggestions, see C. W. Hendel, "Introduction," in E. Cassirer, *The Philosophy of Symbolic Forms* (New Haven, CT: Yale University Press, 1955); and Arnheim, *Art and Visual Perception,* 73.

Whether the widening of the universe of discourse, the process of poetic discovery, will ever re-totalize us into Eden or not, it is *forever* too early to say. Here the full beauty of *homo ludens,* the player, trickster, or joker, stands at the gate whipping us on sometimes, gently dancing with us at others. As we move toward whatever awaits us, into whatever freedoms, it remains a fundamental poetic task to keep alive the ideas of unity, of the shield, the emblem of that wholeness, initiatic or not, which we wish for ourselves and for others. My notion is that it *is* ultimately initiatic and that it would square with a cosmic heraldry which provides, universally, the basic model of human security. The "Human Composite" in Blake is the image of this: I am a good enough Durkheimian to accept that we are all one man. For the rest, the tribe has always been there, fellow tribesmen, and it is also true that the tribe has only just begun. There is that mysterious call, at the end of *Faust,* to the eternal *Shekhinah.* Let us now convene each other to the eternal narrative and commentary on the eternal *Shekhinah.*

1967

Archaeology, Elegy, Architecture

A Poet's Program for Lyric

To Michel Deguy, Hans Ten Berge, Roberto Sanesi:
poets, critics, friends.

1) I want to look with you today at the conditions for existence of the poem, especially the lyrical poem, in three of its most important states. First, as POEM, a unit which has a first line, or beginning, and a last line, or end, and appears to enjoy an independent existence in the world of poems among other poems. Second, as this unit, POEM, now considered in its aspect as one member of a chain of poems, also with an apparent beginning and end, the chain being the totality of poems written in a lifetime by a poet, something I shall call OPUS. If the poet in question be dead, OPUS is closed; if s/he be alive, OPUS is still open-ended. One problem then is the nature and extent of OPUS's meaningfulness to the poet at the moment of writing POEM. Third, this unit OPUS may be said to have a place in another unit, vast this time, which might be defined, with Robert Duncan, as the "Symposium of the Whole," but which I shall here specify as the totality of all poems written thus far as well as yet to be written, the possibility of poetry if you prefer, and call PAGE. With PAGE, since humanity is not yet extinct, we are also likely to remain for

---

This piece was designed as an oral presentation and was first given at the University of California, Santa Barbara, on November 8, 1978. A modification might have to be introduced in future as a result of more recent achievements by *poet*-critics.

the foreseeable future with an open-ended situation. Beyond PAGE, the ability to say anything meaningful recedes; though just to push the envelope's edge, I might conjure the possibilities of PAGE as TEXT and SOUND in a direction I can only call political, and even, perhaps, push the excursion as far as SILENCE, if this can be done without too much metaphysics.

Readers of contemporary criticism will be aware, at this outset, of the fact that such remarks about POEMS, OPUS, and PAGE appear on the surface to continue granting an authoritative priority to the person and function of AUTHOR. Structuralists and post-structuralists, however, acting on suggestions in Nietzsche, Marx, and Freud, have spoken at length of the dissolution of the subject and, in this context, of the meanness and inadequacy of the notion of AUTHOR. The very linearity of any discourse, its having beginnings, middles, and ends, is also questioned and falters before a vision of texts as composing a far larger field of venture, something like an advancing tide or a widespread geological layer, in which qualities such as adjacency, complementarity, and correlation would replace linearity as the essential features of any discourse.

To do more than allude to this would be to pre-empt the whole remaining space of this lecture. Let me, however, show awareness of the problem and desire to return to it, by advancing three remarks. First, my novice's involvement in the debate should be revealed in the strategies used to discuss the triad POEM, OPUS, PAGE. Second, such involvement will not mitigate my suspicion that, even if s/he is to be the *last* of all authors, the lyric poet should remain an author irreducibly for very weighty aesthetic and political reasons. Which is because, third: I cannot escape another suspicion that, for all the talk of decentralization and deconstruction in present-day criticism, and for all the claims, on the part of a Michel Foucault for instance, to replace "author" by "teacher" or some such expression, the poet, when facing criticism, is still facing an authoritarian structure of no mean dimensions. Critics still sit as judges over us; they still pull one poet down in order to push another up; they still sell one lineage at the expense of another to advance their theories and canons; they are still subject to their own political imperatives in that authoritarian publication determines their very survival or not. Not only are they, for the most part, and there are honorable exceptions, rarely aware of the slave in their own basement—the living writer as opposed to the safely dead one; it is also that they continue to do all this while talking of joining us in our enterprise. For what we face these days is a situation in which critics are interested in *usurping* the function of poets (the commentary is not secondary to the poem but adjacent to it in shared primacy and can even share a nature with the poem), while poets, on their side, are less and less equipping themselves to battle with critics when, from time to time, they realize the need to advance their fading eruditions against them. If this piece defends the notion that the *poet*'s poetics still have a role to play in contemporary thought, I shall be satisfied. It is necessary to try to make peace between poets and critics so that they can both, in the future, venture their standards against far greater enemies.

2) If they can be said to have started somewhere, these reflections may have been initiated by a recent walk through the ruins of Teotihuacán, Mexico, some twenty-five years after my initial visit to that most awesome of ancient American cities. "Wow," I thought, "how they have built up this place!" No sooner thought than laughed at, of course. But what did emerge was the peculiar status of archaeology in repeating an original architecture. These buildings had once existed (quite, or not quite, in the way the archeologists had reconstructed them, or, let's say, had refracted them into our present times); they had been buried (an invisible past), and they had been restored, thus constituting perhaps a visible present, as well, in the influence they would have on that present, as an invisible future.

Now, the situation of POEM, as we look at it here, may share in the status of visible present, with roots in the invisible past. As it gets itself written and inscribes itself into OPUS, POEM may be looked at first as a unit in an ARCHAEOLOGY of the past, principally when it joins the other POEMS which have been spoken or written before it. Second: the same POEM may be a unit in what I tentatively call an ARCHAEOLOGY of the future, meaning by this what we can say of the role of this POEM in the ongoing constitution of OPUS. Finally, it may lead us toward ARCHITECTURE as a principle ahead of all possible ARCHAEOLOGIES, a point I also think of, in the code I'm using here, as the transformation of PAGE into TEXT and/or SOUND.

Thus, I want to examine the backward-looking and forward-looking dimensions of POEM. I shall call the backward-looking glance ELEGY and the forward-looking glance LYRIC, seeing these two terms not so much as descriptive of particular *kinds* of poems but rather as analytical of directional modes in all short poems which have the lyrical thrust as their original being or intent, the intent, in short, of biologically induced SONG.

A glance at other sources. We should undoubtedly familiarize ourselves with the uses of the term ARCHAEOLOGY in the contemporary criticism I alluded to. Taking their cues from a number of modern thinkers (Freud looms large in this case, with his excavation of the patient's psyche, his concern with the debris and monuments of an original, now, in pathology, misdirected desire), present critical ARCHAEOLOGIES are guiding paradigms in the trend toward the de-linearization of discourse. It might be said of this now, however, that philosophical ARCHAEOLOGIES, like the philosophical ANTHROPOLOGIES which preceded them, are remarkable for the way in which they elude the very realia which scientific archaeology attempts to record. Enough, perhaps, if I state that, despite all attempts to avoid linearity and sequence, a poem does continue, in important senses, to have a first line in exactly the same way as a site continues to have a first hearth, a first residential place, a first resource-management feature or set of such. As for the *ruins,* which are the prized object of monumental archaeology, and which are not dislodged in any way by the minutiae that "dirt" or "settlement pattern" archaeologies adopt as their objects, they also have a concreteness sympathetic to poets which will not succumb to the curious etherializations practiced upon them by contemporary philosopher-critics. There is unmistakable excitement among the latter as they appropriate the terminology of a pilot-science, but, beyond that excitement and the application of a few elementary notions, such as stratification, we should not be over-impressed as poets, or archaeologists for that matter, by the critics' entry into this paradigm.

What then of ruins as ruins? Here, we have, in the history of culture, a recognizable relationship between the poet and what one historian, Rose Macaulay, has called "The Pleasure of Ruins." The most important element of her study for my purpose is probably that in which she records the historicity of ruin-appreciation: mankind came to enjoy ruins in the same dateable way in which it came to enjoy beaches or mountains, albeit with different time-scales. While ruins were enjoyed for long-enduring reasons from the known beginnings of western culture (Macaulay refers, amongst other things, to the peculiarly vengeful rage with which Hebrew prophets, for instance, revel in the ruin of enemy cities), it does seem as if the Romantic period is the great moment at which mankind goes a-gadding among ruins, those of Greece and Rome first and foremost, but with others not far ahead. If it is also the moment when it goes gadding toward natural miracles such as the Alps, we may have the question of the coterminousness of nature-gazing and ruin-gazing as a research topic before us. If, further, we have a possible relationship between ruin-gazing and a kind of prefiguration of what the industrial revolution was to do to landscape, we have yet another. When we turn to the actual erection of false ruins in gentlemanly gardens, we have, it seems to me, the possibility of a kind of magical action against that industrial revolution. Among *late* nineteenth-century painters of ruins, we find the astonishing spectacle of some representing known monuments, such as the Louvre, the Bank of England, or Buckingham Palace, as ruins! Are these fantasies, occurring when they do, prefiguring an ARCHAEOLOGY of the future all the way up to the bombs of World War II and our own environment-murdering present, with political implications of a more incisive kind than the mere Ozimandian *"Look on my works, ye Mighty, and despair*"? Another topic of research: the real and imaginary cities in the poems of Baudelaire's time and after, especially perhaps Rimbaud's *Villes*?

Which brings us to the age-old association between ARCHAEOLOGY and ELEGY and the recognition that ruins, as well as the whole paradigm of tombs, bones, jewels, minerals, and other fallen entities in them, are often diacritical of the presence of an ELEGIAC mode, of the act of looking backward which characterizes ELEGY. Joachim du Bellay, in his *Antiquités de Rome,* with his extraordinary internalization of the eternal city picked to pieces by successive generations of vandals into invisibility, can be one of our mentors here in our glance at ELEGY.

I bracket all reference to *"Grave Elegeia . . . walking with long step and short"* as she appears out of Ovid's *Amores* and shortcut metrical considerations by letting Coleridge stand here by himself, in his translation from Schiller:

> In the hexameter rises the fountain's silvery column
> In the pentameter aye falling in melody back

This underlines the lyrical thrust of the hexameter, pulled back, each time in the distich, by the elegiac backward fall of the pentameter. I prefer to keep it rather than the notion that ELEGY as nostalgia was a relatively late perversion of a metrical device in much the same way as I prefer to forget the suggestion, when we look soon at Orpheus, that this hero originally came out of the underworld *with* his bride in order to retain the tragedy of Eurydice's loss following the backward-looking glance of the hero.

Coleridge also furnishes us with another precious clue:

> Elegy is the form of poetry natural to the reflective mind. It *may* treat of any subject, but it must treat of no subject *for itself;* but always and exclusively with reference to the poet himself. As he will feel regret for the past or desire for the future, so sorrow and love become the principal themes of elegy.

A genre-criticism which I find unrewarding does inform us that there are two kinds of ideas about ELEGY; and mention of Schiller indicates a tardy discovery on my part of this poet's crucial role in the definitions—so tardy, in fact, that I had written all of this before inserting this very comment about him.

> A superficial idea about ELEGY, first, might run as follows: Rome was once here. It is no longer (Wailing).

and will give us the simple and undisguised lament for all goodies lost. Another, deeper, view sees ELEGY as philosophical poetry *par excellence,* meditational in tone, processual as it comes, revelational as it moves from a constricting, sorrowing darkness to the ultimate comfort of self-enlightenment. In reality there is no major difference except in level between the wail of despair at loss and the consideration of what loss is about. We *may* know a lot more about primal loss since Freud than was known in the times of the Lake poets—yet Coleridge's stress on "reference to the poet himself" and his coupling of love and sorrow tell us much of what we need to recognize in order to continue. If man looks at ruins and becomes ARCHAEOLOGIST, it is because he operates in a field circumscribed by loss of an original and perhaps irrecuperable "other" (an "other" even though it might, narcissistically, be himself) as well as sensing that, even if only for a while, he continues to be alive where all else is dead. He continues, that is, as observer of the ruin he will eventually be also. *But,* and here you have a space I shall call, again with a direct debt to Schiller (mediated too long by Northrop Frye), IDYLL within POEM— all importantly he is a ruin *not yet.* For in that desire for the future which Coleridge twins with sorrow for the past, the poet can always love again, save her/himself again, recover from disaster. S/he can sing, can thrust forward yet again, even if, in doing so, s/he walks Janus-like, with one face looking behind, another looking before. I shall argue, then, that the *whole* of what I call POEM here is *at all times* simultaneously looking-back and looking-forward. The modes of that looking, however, will be different at different stages in the making of POEM.

One last remark. You all know, I'm sure, of the ancient myth of our culture, or cultures, whereby we exist in a latter day, a fallen age, the age of iron. Many people today know its Hindu form of *Kali-yuga,* but it is in Hesiod also. In myth, this iron age was preceded by an age of gold, one of silver, one of bronze. Warning us perhaps against too sharp a distinction between irrecuperable GENESIS and historical beginnings, myth and archaeology meet very interestingly when we realize that the sequence bronze–iron is a scientific archaeological recognition: we have the real world here, where we have a refracted, fantasy world in the sequence of gold and silver. This continuity between a fantasy world and an experiential world will play some part in what I next have to say.

3) My remaining matter I divide into three parts: a consideration of Orpheus, a look at some previous things I have had to say about POEM, OPUS, and PAGE (recapitulation, looking back, or CRITICAL ELEGY if you wish); and, finally, some exemplars from Rilke and Neruda.

I doubt there will be consternation if I take Orpheus as a guiding myth for LYRIC. The subject may well better suit a whole series of poems, but this is a CRITICAL POEM rather than anything else. Once again, then, the story of Orpheus. It will be the usual one except for one twist. In order to offer a model which can deal with LYRIC in general as well as individual lyrics, I am going to tell not of one Orpheus but of *three.*

One Orpheus, I shall call the Ist, is born in "The Divine," perhaps the son of Apollo. We have it that, insofar as he sang in a language intelligible to *all* creatures, he partook of the golden age. Herder locates our realization that there never was a golden age in the late eighteenth century discrediting of the idea of one original language. This divine Orpheus, however, disregards Herder, coming to us, as he does, from the fantasy world, trailing Wordsworthian clouds of glory: his singing power. He enters my model, partially depicted in the diagram, from the upper left-hand corner at point 4.

Our Orpheus IInd enters the diagram sideways like a crab and on the surface level of our daily existence at point 6. This Orpheus IInd is a rather *nebbish* creature, a kind of shadow of the other two, a person of great potential which came to nothing. This Orpheus could have been a poet but his doors of perception were closed very early, either in his birth trauma, or by his parents, or by his society. I pre-empt what there is to say about this Orpheus on the right-hand side of the diagram, where you will meet him again later at point 7, by hazarding the guess that, after the death of his wife, he remarries someone whose name is never "Eurydice," but then, it was a long time ago, in another country, and besides, all these wenches are dead. I am not scornful of this shadow Orpheus, however much of a non-poet he turns out to be, for, look, he passes right through IDYLL, at point 2, and awaits a whole future sociology, if only he swears to remain, for now, a *real* reader, a *non-poet*, rather than become what we know only too well, the incestuous *poet*-reader of poetry.

Our last Orpheus, Orpheus IIIrd, is the one whose life you know in such intimate detail. His birth and early life are occulted by the divinity of Orpheus Ist so

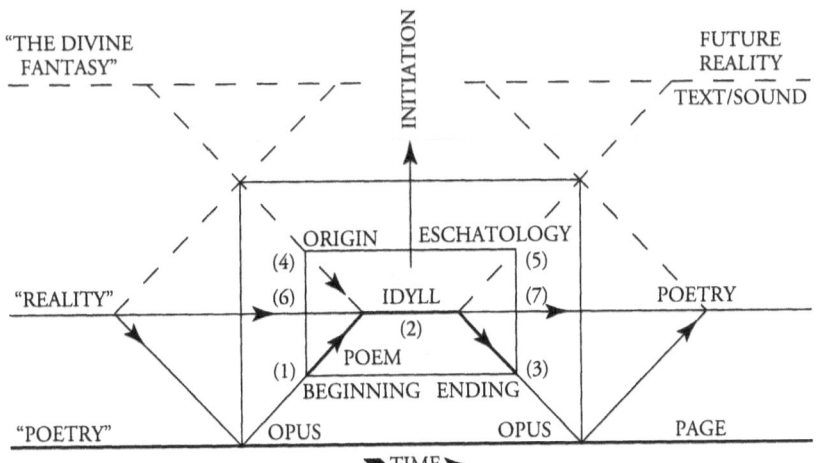

that he comes onto our stage, at point 1, as Orpheus "already-begun." We know of him that he married a wife, Eurydice, and that his summoning of Hymen, god of marriage, to his nuptials did him little good, was in fact ominous to the nth degree. Eurydice is bitten by a snake, dies, and ruins into Hades. Orpheus is all loss and lament. He turns ARCHAEOLOGIST, goes down into the abyss of all worlds where, commenting on the powers of Eros to Pluto and Persephone and hinting at their own subjection to Eros in days gone by, he is granted permission to take his wife back up. One condition, the poet's "Catch-22": he must not look back until they are up and out.

Recall that alleged original version whereby the pair did get out safely. Let it be so that Eurydice is a form of Persephone, who was also taken down to ruin by King Pluto. But since the fields should be green at least half the year, it was fixed up, by two brother gods mind you, *not by men,* that Pluto and Zeus should share her. Of this objective requirement that Persephone be with us half the year, note that she is not *fetched* by any living being. Subjective ELEGY, on the other hand, sends Orpheus down for Eurydice: it is an individual piece of salvage archaeology, not a collective one. *Objective* poetry, if it ever exists, will be *collective* or it will not be at all, but objective poetry will never know an ELEGIAC mode.

When Orpheus Ist comes down from "The Divine," he has no memory of Eurydice, he may indeed never have been married: it is as if life were the lesser part of death, so steeped is he in divinity. This is perhaps the Orpheus we shall encounter in Rilke. Orpheus IIIrd, whom we may meet with in Neruda, acts as if life is the greater part of death and begins immediately to climb into POEM. He *does* remember Eurydice, for as an Orpheus "already-begun," he may have gone for her many, many times; he is also conscious of the position of POEM within OPUS: the sum of all those former times. He moves upward, leading Eurydice out of ruined Hades, thrust by LYRIC toward the light. This energizing self-potentiation, to use Spitzer's term in his discussion of the "orgasmic" aspects of Diderot's style, is in essence forward-looking. But it contains an ELEGIAC looking-back, which is the question Orpheus asks himself as he remembers Eurydice. Is it she? Is it she? he asks himself—it was so dark down there in Hades—taking her to pieces and putting her back together again, numbering to himself those traits that make her different from all other women, make her stand out against woman *as such,* so that he might, by these essential, crucial selections and particularities, know whether it is she or not. In much the same way, centuries later, Dante (that male Eurydice fetched by his Beatrice from the depths of Hades, consigned there by Lucia, Lady of Enlightenment); in much the same way, Dante's unspoken question is answered—though in reverse, since we are here dealing with Dante-*Eurydice's* questions about Beatrice-Orpheus—by the *Guardame ben, Ben son, ben son Beat-rice,* the loveliest moment in the *Comedy.*

And let it be said here that we must hear much more from Eurydice hencefor-ward where a woman poet will ask herself whether she is a female Orpheus asking questions of a male Eurydice, or the old Eurydice looking very differently at Or-pheus than he sees her looking at him—but this I shall hear from the woman poet and not from myself, except to the extent that I am also woman. . . .

And Orpheus IIIrd, here, must reach a moment in his questioning which I must identify as the crest of POEM, that moment at which the insistent question of the identification of Eurydice leads to the looking-back, the activation of that internal process, pivoting on the requirement of going further-forward in certainty—for otherwise, with anyone else, it is not worth going forward—that moment in which he must be so sure of OPUS that he will risk both their deaths on the wager.

And Orpheus looks back at Eurydice. He looks back at her looking-forward to him, and, in that moment, the whole of their married life is enacted. It is, of course, a repetition, a repetition of their previous life on earth, of which we know nothing except that it was ominous. Indeed, it may be possible to see this as their *only* life, their only IDYLL (in which, therefore, everything must be done or left undone), by generating another story of the pair, one in which they had *never* been married on earth and in which Orpheus had gone for a wife among the dead because that is the only place where wives are found. Nor shall I overlook yet another story of an only marriage: one in which Eurydice had never died. The snake was only a night-mare, an allegory of unrecordable loss and gain, the pair's attitude to which would one day lift despair into happiness or down happiness ever into despair, according to their view of the thing, their sense of the heights and depths of IDYLL.

We are at IDYLL, remember, and, like love in the movies, it cannot last. Eury-dice faints back into ruin, or turns gently back into ruin; there are various possible versions. Orpheus continues on.

Our Orpheus IInd, you remember, remarried and dropped out. Orpheus Ist had hardly dropped in. Orpheus IIIrd finishes POEM, a POEM which has to have a last line after a first one, which has to die as it was once born. The look-forward is still there, in the ongoing life of the poem; the looking-back functions simultane-ously, though at this time we may suppose that the ruins Orpheus mulls over are not so much those of Hades as those he has himself made of his life by his pri-mary disobedience. And at last Orpheus comes out with his POEM, with its death upon it, about to become the seed of future poems. "If the seed do not die . . ."

But, in our story, it is not Orpheus Ist who comes out into the light. Or-pheus IIIrd, with his dying POEM, *has* breathed in the light and then gone back down into Hades from point 3, looking *again,* as he knew he would, and despite all prohibitions, for the Eurydice. He is wiser now: every time he remembers her a little better, though there are always questions, always backward-lookings which will send her down again after too brief an IDYLL. He acquires some wisdom, some fingertip *craft* perhaps, which puts the shine more and more on his OPUS.

Who then comes out at the top of the light? It is our Orpheus Ist at point 5. He mourns Eurydice constantly (not "real life") and cannot in any way turn his attention to other women, but *note,* it is not he who goes back down again. It is rumored at times that he makes love to boys instead, even being credited with the introduction of male homosexuality into his neck of the woods. Angered at this, other women, the Bacchantes, tear him apart in a great, archetypal *sparagmos,* perhaps an echo of the *sparagmos* he inflicted on Eurydice before the moment of IDYLL, perhaps a vengeance. Whatever the case may be, the Bacchantes throw his limbs into the river and they float down to the sea. It is the river of time, the river of the fantasy of perpetual process, the river in which one is *eternally* floating it would seem, a fate fit for the divine Orpheus Ist. And when he reaches a shore and is re-totalized, it is not a complete Orpheus that we have; it is a selected, an "essential Orpheus" packaged and available forever at a couple of dollars as long as inflation is kept down. What has been selected is two elements: the head and the lyre. Here Orpheus Ist *prophecies* for the rest of time: here he shrines and divines in ESCHATOLOGY rather than POEMS. Is it incidental if the place he lands up at is Lesbos, the place of the love of women for women? I just note this fantasy end, responsive to the earlier male-to-male structure, lest we get lost in all the possibilities.

At point 3, then, POEM into OPUS; at point 5, a fantasy. Meanwhile, life for the poet has been lived and we have, in Mallarmé's words "*l'explication orphique de la terre.*" At points 1–3, in the distinction proposed by Edward Said, we have a beginning (and an end) rather than an origin or genesis and . . . perhaps . . . a last judgment.

So: two inverted cups in a diagram: the point of contact being IDYLL, the marriage. We know now why Orpheus had to go back for Eurydice: that search *enables* everything else, allows us to tell stories, allows poems to be born like children of the couple. What may be important is the mesh between a beginning story and an origin story. *Why* is it important? It may be that there is a third element in the matter of making a start on any poem or on any story. Alongside POEM and OPUS, it would be called PAGE. Alongside BEGINNING and ORIGIN, it would figure as what I have elsewhere called INITIATION.

4) In a previous CRITICAL POEM, "The Heraldic Vision,"[1] I was concerned with an aesthetic of classification wherein the poem was considered as a world-model. I started there to look around for *two* aesthetics, suggesting that at least two were required: an aesthetic of the individual art object, and one of all possible art objects. Translated here: an aesthetic of POEM and an aesthetic of PAGE. Much said, however, seemed to call for a third, mediating aesthetic—here called the aesthetic of OPUS. What was it that suggested the usefulness of OPUS?

Entering the current debate among poets about the relative roles in the poem of structure or "closure" and process or "openness," I suggested that both were constitutively involved. My model was one in which a poem emerged out of an initial TOTAL: a structure composed of the totality of the life led until then by the poet as precipitated in her/his poems. The poem was written as process but ended once again in structure, ready to enter the OPUS as a basis for other, future poems. Process was looked at as a DETOTALIZATION and the final structure as a RETOTAL-IZATION: there are echoes of this in the Orpheus story. The apex of process, my IDYLL, was characterized by the poet's experience of her/his voice as *interminable* and her/his state of being as poetry-producing without *any* non-poetic residue whatsoever. IDYLL, however, was by its very nature short-lived, even though experienced for a moment as everlasting. The ecstasy of "Dostoevskian" epilepsy or the "*Rinasce! Rinasce!*" of *La Traviata* are of the same vintage.

I added, although almost subliminally, that IDYLL was the moment at which the poet experienced a timeless and spaceless continuum, also accessible through a phenomenon known to certain traditions as INITIATION. By timeless and spaceless, we can mean a state of no time, no space (*via negativa*), or one of all time, all space (*via positiva*). The function of INITIATION provides an alternative for the poetic imagination whereby it need not be trapped in either (a) the view that history is insignificant, or (b) the view that nothing but history is significant. The meaning of coming to terms with both structure and process in poetry requires, on the one hand, that certain basic human securities be felt to exist at the level of structure; on the other hand, that creative insecurity or adventurousness be looked for at the level of process, so that life might have, overall, a forward-looking and acting orientation. Even though the securities of structure might imply "bad faith" or "inauthenticity," something stubbornly undeniable in the poetic condition spoke to the human condition at large requiring these apparent contradictions.

Looking back at past production and, simultaneously, forward to future production, like Orpheus, the poet, at the time of POEM, and more especially at the

1   In this volume.

time of IDYLL, lives two realities at the same moment. On the one hand, s/he lives beginnings and ends, knowing that each poem is going to be compounded of the ruins of all previous poems and, in turn, *become* the ruins on which future poems are built. On the other hand, s/he can accept OPUS as a prefiguration of PAGE. OPUS, bounded as it is by the biography, then becomes one poem in the collectivity of PAGE, a collectivity whose origins and ends are lost in evolutionary time, thus being, in terms of any *praxis,* literally unthinkable. It is here that the poet's work best exemplifies *hope:* unthinkable hope.

If, then, we link POEM with BEGINNING/END and PAGE with IDYLL/INITIATION, the link of OPUS with ORIGIN/ESCHATOLOGY becomes structurally clear. At the same time, the illusoriness of ORIGIN (though for me it is a vital illusion, vital to the existence of poetry and constitutive of it) becomes all the more poignant. This poignancy is expressed in the three possible versions of the Orphic scenario. At one and the same time, Orpheus descends into his adventure from ORIGIN and reascends to it again afterwards (I call this return an ESCHATOLOGY) *and* he rises from a BEGINNING toward the adventure, redescending into an ENDING/CLOSURE after it. A descent which, in its turn, is but a repetition of the previous descents after Eurydice. Finally, he forgets about Eurydice, marries someone else, and confirms his status outside of poetry.

In "The Heraldic Vision," I described IDYLL as an event in which the *conscious* realization of intemporality, of Eluard's *poésie ininterrompue,* arising out of the *unconscious* mere living of it, came exactly at the moment when POEM began on its way from process back into structure and the "death" of POEM was near. One could also talk of Baudelaire's concept of *rhapsody,* a kind of fear of overload, of terror at the world being too immense to be accounted for by the fragile enthusiasm of POEM—whence the corresponding onset of manic depression. *Rhapsody* is close to *Rapture.* In semiotic terms there is a fear that some phenomena will not find rules of expression, or, alternatively, that there will be a plethora of rules such that the occasion of dealing with them will be interminable. Again the terror of overload. As a last example, "rhapsody" may be expressed as the fear of the great white light said to meet the dying person in the *Bardo Thodol,* or Tibetan Book of the Dead, read here as the fear of sinking individuality and discontinuity into the collective continuity which Buddhism calls the *deathless* or *Nirvāna.* Clearly, we could also translate some of this into the terms used by Harold Bloom in his *Anxiety of Influence,* were it not that the authoritarian nature of that critical project is revolting to the poet as fundamentally divisive of the republic of letters. What seems clear then is that IDYLL, however difficult it is to stand, and stay standing, within it, let alone to pass through it, is a potential *gate,* to use a Blakean term, that moment in the day which Satan cannot find. But whether we enter or not is a matter which, alas, hardly depends on each one of us alone.

To close this section, a reflection on PAGE might serve to lead us into Rainer Maria Rilke. PAGE, as the ultimate destination of poetry, reflects for me first the Mallarméan white page before which this particular poet was, you remember, so terror-struck. In this guise, PAGE presents itself as a terrible Pascalian silence. A complementary notion might be that of a *black* page: a page so laden with repeatedly inscribed letters and words that the writing had also become invisible. Think of certain Paleolithic superscriptions. The implication of the black page could be fatigue, Frank Kermode's sense of an ending, a sense of *"La chair est triste, hélas, et j'ai lu tous les livres."* Perhaps an echo from Saussure is suggestive: if continuity is to be preserved, the page will have to be turned when completely covered so that a new white page can be faced. It is like the weary moon turning to us its dark side while it rests in the invisible, then turning round again: virgin, hesitant, white. Or the sun going under the earth at night and coming up in the morning. In any event, the color of ambition here seems hopeful, the color of achievement not so— it is deathly as far as our model's correspondences go. In fact, however, this is a defect of our particular dark time: PAGE remains always the same, awaiting our history, the way in which we will write it down, deathward or lifeward, as we can or choose to write it. For PAGE is also *pagina* in Latin, a trellis to which a row of vines is fixed, hence, by metaphor, a column of writing, the vine being also a *texture* which will block out the light if left unpruned. Thence PAGE, if we write lifeward, becomes at long last TEXT. And here, in the partial diagram, "REALITY," unlikely as it may seem, becomes REALITY.

5) Before reaching Rilke. "Orphically," INITIATION may best be gotten at by remembering what the descent to Hades could have been originally. In classical myth, the hero descends in order to know the boundless environing PAGE of physical death. He goes to those who have lived *before* in order to know what will befall him and mankind *afterward*, in order, in a sense, to prophecy. The timeless omnipresence of death is a negative mode of INITIATION (it is also possible to think of the death all around us as eternal life). According then to how a poet saw us as proceeding from life or from death, so might his poems have that much of a different final destination.

The great *Duino* poems of Rilke bear the title of *Duino Elegies* though they do not seem to contain an ARCHAEOLOGY, nor, *prima facie*, a set of ruins. Their history as we know it exhibits more than most a poet's sense of OPUS. While the various stanzas of any given poem appear to have fallen on Rilke like storms, he seems from the start to have awaited them knowing the basic *gestalt* he wanted for his

POEM and OPUS. In particular, we remember being told that the tenth was intended as the last one from the start, so that when an eleventh presented itself, it was used in place of what was then the fifth, while this fifth was relegated to another collection. I'm sure we could cite many examples of that kind of pre-cognition which is the surface manifestation of a deep overall sense of OPUS.

Another reason we should be fascinated with the *Duinos* here lies in the bifurcation inherent in the role played by Orpheus. Rilke claims to have been concentrating on the *Elegies* and to have been "given," within the same time period, the *Sonnets to Orpheus*. It has also been observed, by Rilke and others, that the *Sonnets* were positive, forward-looking praise poems primarily, while the *Duinos* were full of "lament" and thus considered by Rilke as in some way reprehensible. What I find moving here is that it may be the *Duinos* which contain the true essence of Rilke's "Orphism" rather than the *Sonnets*. I wish to concentrate on this.

First, however, a quick look at a separate lyric of Rilke's, the poem *Orpheus, Eurydice, Hermes*. Rilke here picks out from myth a third figure, Hermes, guide of souls, to appear with the two we normally expect. Why? The main point Rilke wishes to make in this poem is that Eurydice is already so dead that not even the most faithful, daring husband can rescue her. Beautifully, he pictures how:

> *Sie war schon aufgelöst wie langes Haar* / She was already loosened like long hair, / and given far and wide like fallen rain, / and dealt out like manifold supply. *Sie war schon Wurzel* / She was already root.[2]

Note, first, that Orpheus could hardly have handled her himself, when she was so sparagmatized, without being involved physically in turning round whether he wanted to or not. But, more importantly, look at the crucial moment of the poem:

> And when abruptly, / the god had halted her and, with an anguished / outcry, spoke out the words: He has turned round! / she took in nothing, and said softly: Who? / But in the distance, dark in the bright exit, / someone or other stood, whose countenance / was indistinguishable . . .

Eurydice is so overwhelmingly involved in her death that there is no way whatsoever she can fulfill the first function of a spouse, which is surely to recognize the partner. Hermes, then, is necessary *so that* there may be someone to announce that "he," the husband, has turned round; *so that* the wife may murmur,

---

2 Rainer Maria Rilke, *Duino Elegies*, trans. J. B. Leishman and Stephen Spender, 3rd ed. (rev.) (London: The Hogarth Press, 1948). I have stayed with the translations I matured with.

"Who?" and *so that* we may be attuned to her point of view, Orpheus being un-recognizable and dark in the bright exit. The signs are somehow inverted now: it is Eurydice who is alive and Orpheus who is dead, and the poem retraces her steps back home leaving the hero's fate in silence.

Now, if there is one guiding idea in Rilke, it is that our existence is truncated when we fail to recognize death as a constitutive aspect of life. Death is the other side of life, momentarily invisible, a failure to come to terms with which cripples us. While Rilke does not acknowledge it clearly, I believe that, to him, death was fuller than life and that, if anyone needed a fetcher, it was Orpheus, the not-yet-dead, and not Eurydice. To my mind, the *Duinos* thus represent a triumph of a very high order in Rilke, documenting a hard-won, very momentary adjustment in the balance between life and death, a triumph of the possibility of IDYLL—in the ninth and tenth, especially—after a long conflict in which it had, or the belief in it had, been refused. We know from the rest of his work how he believed him-self to have been bypassed in regard to the possibility of human relationships: an-imals, yes; angels, yes; between them, nothing.

This inversion of an expected order in the signs for life and death, which I would read, in the terms I use here, as a descent from an ORIGIN (at point 4) to an ENDING (at point 3) via a painfully accepted IDYLL, leads to inversion in other signs as well. I leave aside the refusal-of-IDYLL theme for another time. What takes place at the end of the *Duinos* is a leading of Orpheus by Eurydice, a leading in-volving passage through a ruined landscape, so that, to our amazement, a project which had not seemed to admit of an ARCHAEOLOGY turns out to exhibit one at its end rather than its beginning.

In the ninth *Elegy*, the passage beginning *"Ein Mal / jedes, nur ein Mal"* ("Just once / everything, only for once) and continuing as

> *Aber dieses /ein Mal gewesen zu sein, wenn*
> *auch nur ein Mal: / irdisch gewesen zu sein, scheint nicht widerrufbar*
> But this / having been once, though only
> once, / having been once on earth—can it ever be cancelled?

leads to the affirmations that "we keep pressing on and trying to perform it" and "we, perhaps, (are) here just for saying" through a series of acceptances of POEM, OPUS, and, finally, IDYLL itself at

> *Erde, du liebe, ich will*
> Earth, you darling, I will!

a strangely truncated hymn to earth rather than woman (Eurydice as earth?) with the hint of RHAPSODY at the very end of the ninth, almost as if he did not want to deal with it at this moment in "Supernumerous existence wells up in my heart," the ninth's closing lines.

The tenth *Elegy* opens like Bruckner's *Te Deum* or Strauss's *Last Songs,* with a tremendous burst of praise—but then almost immediately turns back to lament. We are led to a "City of Pain," a bitterly ironic satire on religion's fake "deathlessness." True life-acceptance, for Rilke, must accept death as half of itself, perhaps the better half, fully, and uncamouflaged behind inauthentic systems of punishment and reward. But it is only, ultimately, by including life in death, rather than including death in life, that Rilke averts the peril of life's distortion by orthodox religion. Just back of the city of religion, a youthful hero encounters another reality, is drawn further, and seems to fall in love with a female who turns out to be a youthful "Lament." The sequel has a strangely staccato, indecisive effect. First the youth ". . . leaves her, turns back, / looks around, nods. . . . What's the use? She's just a / Lament," the poem tells us.

Then, an elder Lament talks to the youth and begins to take him through a city of ruins: mountain mines, "polished original pain," "drossy petrified rage from some old volcano" (the geological model coming before the archeological), and then "the temple columns, the ruins of towers . . . the graves . . . the sepulchral stone." All this while, it is hard to tell if she is taking him *down* or *backward* or merely *further on: "Doch ter Tote muß fort:* But the dead must go on." We sense that there is going to be one last turn in the proceedings. The elder Lament (we need further thought on this passage from a young Lament to an original Mother figure) shows the youth a stream, saying, "Among men / it's a carrying stream," which I hear as an echo of the stream which carried the dismembered Orpheus. Then, suddenly, they stand at the foot of a range. Amazingly, it is a climb that now begins, that of a young man alone: "Alone, he climbs to the mountain of primal pain."

What have we here? Is it, as I think, Orpheus following Eurydice, Orpheus Eurydicized as it were? Does the Eurydice turn into a *mother* and the Orpheus into a *boy* because they are no longer in this poem, the tenth, but *already at the beginning of the eleventh,* Eurydice now the mother of the girl she will be in the eleventh and Orpheus young again, beginning over again? But we know that the eleventh does not exist, except as the new fifth, a poem to be looked at in this light on another occasion. Is Rilke with all his might attempting to preserve the upward-thrust of LYRIC? Is it that Orpheus no longer needs Eurydice, now that he is dead in his turn? And yet he climbs and seeks to POEM, placing the sense of OPUS ahead of him rather than behind him. But, at the last, he can only fall into an antinomy with the dead pointing *up* at things which themselves point *down:*

catkins hanging from a tree, rain *falling* in spring. And the final lines preserve this upward/downward movement:

> And we, who have always thought / of happiness climbing, would feel / the
> emotion that almost startles / when happiness falls

with a semblance of resolution only in that ambivalent "happiness *falls.*" It is in this sense, mainly, that I see Rilke ending at point 3 rather than at point 5.

Many questions—to which the answers will, I think, lie in the motionlessness which he has imparted to his life-principle, the negativity of life to him, despite all his struggles. This is a problem where the personal set of the poet and his political set shade into each other in ways hard to unravel. I may come back to this again.

It is also possible that we are trying here to *force* an issue. I mean that the contradiction set up by enunciating together "it is falling / it is rising" is resolvable in one sense by noting simply that, in our gravitational world, what rises usually must fall. While the reverse is not necessarily true, it remains that a height is also, in its very nature, a depth. It is often such realia of our phenomenal world that bring the poet up to a *situation-limite,* a wall beyond which one cannot go but which, in itself, generates some fruitful imagery. That it is still the case that a poet consciously or unconsciously *chooses* to place her/himself in relation to such a wall is illustrated, however, by some remarkable developments in a masterwork of Pablo Neruda: *Las Alturas de Macchu Picchu.* These *Heights of Macchu Picchu* are the crown of a long poem celebrating the American continents after Neruda's return from the war in Spain. The poem manifestly and openly concerns an archaeological topic on its surface as well as in its depths. That it is also ELEGY will not take us long to find out.

The extraordinary thing about *Macchu Picchu,* as I see it here, is that it presents us with two elegiac models, a conventional one I'll outline first and another, much less conventional.

A conventional model depends, I hope it's clear by now, on a landscape which comprises three strata: a level earth we walk on; an underworld, be it Hades or not; an overworld, be it Heaven or not. This landscape is found here. We move from an underworld stress, in parts I–III, to one on the surface level of a horizontal contemporaneity in parts IV–V (with an apparent block against rising within V itself) and then to a sudden ascent above ground in part VI. To illustrate: we have, in I, the "world like a buried tower" (an initial archeological index) and the words "sinking . . . lower . . . plunged . . . unfathomed waves . . . I sank," etc., illustrative of the underworld action. In IV, there is an ambivalence in the expression "wrecks and heights" at line 4, another suggesting an upward thrust but including a leveling width at line 9 ("the awesome spiral way") and finally the horizontality of the exploration "river by river, city by city, one bed after another" of the circumference of human life. Part V remains uncertain, speaking of "particles of death which cannot be reborn" and detailing again a plunging movement into human wounds which echoes part I but also prepares us for the poet's brotherhood with the builders of Machu Picchu later on. Then suddenly, in VI: "*Entonces en la escala de la tierra he subido / entre la atroz maraña de las selvas perdidas / hasta ti, Macchu Picchu*" ("Then up the ladder of the earth I climbed / through the barbed jungle's thickets / until I reached you, Macchu Picchu").

The conventional model is also found, in another instance, in an Orphic scenario: whether in what appears to be a truly Eurydicean form, the "*Sube conmigo, amor americano*" ("Come up with me, American love") of part VIII (here, though no woman is named, it is hard to forget Neruda's unquenchable erotic poetry), or in substitute forms, induced perhaps by a political allegiance already sounding in the qualifier *americano,* such as the city itself or the slave that is buried underneath it.

But Andean ecology is such that another model is soon revealed which seems to take over from, and prime over, the conventional one and results, not so much in an ascent, an IDYLL plateau, and a descent, as in a constant oscillation up/down, down/up, *both* taking place *above* the level surface of our world.

There are a number of factors at work here. First, the concrete reality of the Andean chain, especially as experienced in narrow Chile, underlines a fact about ascentional imagery already pointed out: a mountain is also an abyss. In the extraordinary environment of Chile, we get the picture of ever-flowing waters both ascending from the Pacific coast to Machu Picchu, that "high reef of the human dawn" (notice that very Lévi-Straussian high *reef*), and then cascading down from immeasurable heights back to the ocean again.

More importantly, Machu Picchu has another astonishing and, archaeologically, most untypical aspect. While it is true that our own Classical World and its successors show us ruins on heights all the way from the Parthenon at Athens to the Mounts of St. Michael in Celtdom, it is rare that anyone reaches his past so high in the sky as the Inca does, out of Cuzco, to his fortresses towering above the river Urubamba on the long winding (I was going to say Hadean) road to the "ultimate" city. Our imagination of relics indicates that we *down* into ever deeper strata for them, even if we work under temples, ziggurats, pyramids which are quite eminently situated. The thrust of the ARCHAEOLOGICAL is, in other words, downward, or even regressive, even as the ARCHITECTURAL is upward and progressive. (We should remember, however, that mistaken sense of buildup at Teotihuacán I spoke of at the start.)

Thus Neruda's choice of a distant past, situated at the summit rather than the foot of a high peak, may be one factor in the extraordinary oscillation we find in the later sections of the poem, apparently caused by a tension between the archaeological imagination and the real object it is, in this case, exercised upon. A related tension is introduced into the realm of time and space. We do, I think, tend to think of the movement *up* as being *forward* in time; the movement *down* as primarily *backward,* whatever the reality on the landscape's ground and in poem-making. At Machu Picchu, even if one does not go down to the future, one certainly goes up to the past. And, as a matter of fact, one does go down to the future too: witness Neruda's calling up of the buried slave who will arise to birth as his own brother.

How politically fortunate for the poet the contingency of his project came to be! With his past on high, and our natural association of the summit with progress, the poem can, at one and the same time, be both ELEGY *and* a hymn to future and to progress.

Now, whether we have, in Neruda's *prima facie lay* world, any echo of the refractions noted in the Orpheus scenario and in Rilke is problematical. It is curious to note that the downward inclination of part I coexists with an opening to the whole poem which reads, "From air to air, like an empty net, / dredging through streets and ambient atmosphere, I came . . ." almost as if, simultaneously with the initial oceanic descent, there were an echo of a fall from celestial Origin rather than a rise from a Beginning. But it is a distant echo: Neruda is firmly planted in ambient human life; there is no over-investment on his part in ORIGIN. Whether the same holds true for ESCHATOLOGY is less certain.

That we have echoes of a possible IDYLLIC moment in the static litany of part IX (there is much to be added about links between LITANY, REPETITION, and IDYLL); that his IDYLLIC moment, if it is such, seems echoed, in the last part (XII), by the lines "out of the depths spin this long night to me / as if I rode at anchor here with you" with its constant up/down beat in such expressions as "like a torrent of sunbursts / an Amazon of buried jaguars"; and that the poem ends, in this same part XII, with a resurrectional theme reminiscent of the "*Sube conmigo, amor Americano*" in the opening "Arise to birth with me, my brother": all of this suggests that the poem might be going from a point 1 to a point 5 in structural opposition to Rilke's.

The slaves cannot resurrect, but the poet can speak for their dead mouths. The persistence of fantasy, characteristic of point 5, is, in the lines just quoted about riding at anchor, followed by "And leave me cry: hours, days, years, / blind ages, stellar centuries," where the radical future, as imagined by Neruda, reminds me of nothing so much as the head and lyre of Orpheus enshrined at Lesbos. Perhaps, in this respect, Neruda is a transitional Marxist poet, still attached to much of the imagery of the Spanish side of his inheritance, especially the Catholic, and therefore plugging his vision of OPUS rather conventionally into the collectivity of PAGE.

Two examples of refraction, in Rilke at the beginning, in Neruda at the end, illustrating perhaps something about the way in which the death/life, backward/forward equations, when weighted this way or that, condition the fate of LYRIC in POEM, OPUS, and PAGE. I hope to have made the point that Coleridge's regret for the past *and* his desire for the future are both involved in ELEGY and sanction its claims as one of the most philosophically inclined modes in all poetry.

A few more words on the political aspect of the matter before ending. We have seen PAGE as always open toward the future, OPUS as open during a life, and POEM as a closure fitting into an open, but which is, in addition, open in the middle, through the gate of IDYLL. And we have drawn some conclusions from all this.

I now suggest that it may be in what appears to be the weakest member of the chain, this POEM crowned with IDYLL, that the most powerful leverage to the future is found. It seems as if IDYLL as process can work miracles, can lift an insulted "reality," so damaged it has become unreal, to its former power, can transform art into a deathless order by lifting it into PAGE, *provided* that it believes in itself sufficiently not to fall back from the great white light of a collective *hope*. What happens within IDYLL as a recuperation of the immediate present, a present more and more distanced from us by the insult to our "reality," is a program in the *now* for what passing time also achieves in OPUS. For, as OPUS goes forward, the poet acquiring confidence and craft, it may be that each successive IDYLL reinforces that leverage, or the chance of its being effective.

But as long as this partnership of present and future is held in check by the inability of the individual to transcend her/himself and accede to the collective, until which time poetry will remain subjective and never objective, we shall continue to live simultaneously in an unreal world, only apparently "real," and a fantasy world miming totality and wholeness but for all practical purposes nonexistent. And that long too, poetry will remain the lowest, not the highest, of human activities, oppressed as it is today when it has turned into a commodity so incestuously peddled that it has no genuine currency outside the internal trade of poets themselves.

Poetry suffocates under a mass of language which more and more challenges authorial status as well as its own. The present which POEM tries to celebrate is ever more usurped by an artificial future which our social unreality imposes upon it as the computers of Big Capital demand of ever more of us that we live ahead of ourselves, instead of in the now. The very ally on which poets should depend most, that critical activity which should aid the birth of POEM, has never been so close to usurping the function of poetry as it is now and the authoritarian structure of criticism becomes ever more blind to the slave in its own house: not the dead poet, mummified and packaged, but the living poet who should be its contemporary and partner. The net result is to weaken OPUS as the principle of continuity, to question the very existence of the poetic vocation as an ongoing project, thus throwing the poet back into POEM as, each time, the *single* venture this breath s/he draws here and now may allow the poet to complete.

Apparently cut off from the continuity of OPUS and the gradual path of access to the collectivity as well as to the realization of art as a deathless order, the only defense of poetry is to behave as if POEM were the norm and as if art were subject to the same birth and death as nature in its own objects. Succumbing to the weakness of not being able to triumph through IDYLL because of her/his oppressed condition, is it any wonder if the poet today seems to make scandalous claims for POEM which bear so little relation to what appear to be the facts?

And yet the stubborn belief persists in the poet that POEM is the prefiguration of work correctly understood in a society correctly institutionalized; that beauty, in Schiller's magnificent formulation, "is freedom in appearance," and that the poet is the prototype of the truest humanity. For, if the object of all this effort were ever to be achieved, the original, long-prepared home returned to, and mankind's long exile from itself be over, then OPUS and PAGE could be free at last to reveal the deathlessness of the order of art as the *work* of mankind, in the same way as history would be the *nature* of mankind, both the fruit and the seed of those poems which had been deposited as information into it. But nothing can be accepted short of that end of exile and, until it has been already begun by the collective, it will not be seen to exist. As long as this is the case and as a matter of method, poetry must continue to be the irreducible enemy of consensus and not its friend, accepting the hostility of the unreal world into which it is born and fighting it with its own unreality.

It is from this situation, in our Orphic myth, that Orpheus Ist, our *true* poet laboring in the Hades of the modern world, is generated as a refraction of Orpheus IIIrd. If our prefigured future were ever to materialize, and our story would accede to myth again, Orpheus Ist would disappear into Orpheus the IIIrd, for he would no longer be required. And Orpheus the IIIrd would himself then merge into Orpheus the IInd, our long-neglected *nebbish*, when, as in all good fairy stories, the ugly duckling would turn out to be a swan and all mankind would have become poets.

Among the "philosophic proofs" of his new science, Vico, alongside mythologies, heroic phrases, etymologies, mental vocabulary, and the like, lists "The great fragments of antiquity, hitherto useless to science because they lay begrimed, broken and scattered" which will "shed great light when cleared, pieced together and restored." It is an astonishing eruption into the truth that ARCHAEOLOGY and language are knit so closely together. As Edward Said has pointed out, "[I]t is burial that for Vico gives rise to history," another hint from that extraordinary ancient at the role of traditional memory in ARCHAEOLOGY.

But should a future reality occur, at any time forward of ourselves, the ARCHAEOLOGY, both of past and future, will no longer be required in that there would no longer be any need to recognize Eurydice in the dark when she had stepped out so completely into the light. Then those basic human securities demanded in us by the primeval and archetypal in our natures would no longer be demanded, since they would be there in the common texture of everyday existence, available to everyone in their daily work. Nor would the adventurousness of the primitive and the archaic in us be required, for there would be enough adventure in the quotidian to keep everyone happy. It is at this point that ARCHITECTURE might begin and that PAGE would at last emerge into TEXT and SOUND, leaving behind once and for all the quiet of burial. One says "might begin" because of none of this is there any guarantee; no contract has been signed toward utopia, no compact entered into. Everything is in the effort, the push, and of this the life and work of LYRIC are the most adequate model we have at our disposal.

1981

The Choral Voice

A Diptych re Anthropology and Poetry

Amid the seeming confusion of our mysterious world, individuals are so nicely adjusted to a system, and systems to one another, and to a whole, that, by stepping aside for a moment, a man exposes himself to a fearful risk of losing his place forever.

—Nathaniel Hawthorne

Language lies on the borderline between oneself and the other. The word in language is half someone else's.

—Mikhail Bakhtin

1) I became an anthropologist in the early fifties through all sorts of misapprehensions. Born and raised French until World War II, I had studied English and history at Cambridge and saw myself primarily as a poet. Unhappy with postwar England and persuaded that my true language was French, I had returned to Paris in 1948. Uncertain how to choose an occupation, I sampled Parisian culture to the full: the most exciting newspaper I have ever known, *Combat*, was an excellent daily guide through the plethora. It carried news of what was being done by French anthropologists, especially those at work in Africa and Oceania.

One day, a movie, *Rendez-vous de Juillet*, led me to the Musée de l'Homme at the Trocadéro. I trembled for two or three days, then enrolled in the courses. By 1951, I was at the University of Chicago; by 1952, in Guatemala for a first bout of fieldwork; by 1953, at the London School of Economics for postgraduate work; by

1958, in Southeast Asia for a second fieldwork project; by 1960, beginning a seven-year stint teaching at London University.

Stanley Diamond asked for this. It says something about me that, whenever I am asked to write such a memoir, it happens that I am far from my notebooks and diaries. I realize this sentence says two things. What I had meant to say was "I have a passion for being elsewhere." What I add is "My records are so exhaustive that they exhaust me. I prefer to remember without recourse to them."

In Paris, freshman anthropology could be summed up as the Marcel Griaule outfit. Griaule saturated his first-year people in Dogon material. While only relatively interested in Africa, this to me meant romance, exoticism, travel. While social structure and social organization must have been mentioned, I managed to elude them in favor of belief and ritual systems. Soon, I knew Dogon ethnography by heart, and it was a shock to me, later, when I found out the extent to which British social anthropologists initially disbelieved in it.

Aside from the exotic nature of the Dogon symbolic system in its cosmology and sacred history, what attracted me from the beginning were the esoteric aspects of the system, the studious ordering of masses of detail, the puzzling out of where to put an almost countless number of elements so that they would form a whole. For me there had always been a close link between beauty and classification.[1] This appears to be linked to an ontological insecurity about the *where* and *when* of things (one I have always associated with inefficient training in the exact sciences and mathematics as a child), the *how* also, but less so. Travel? *Periplous:* making sure that the shape of the map is what the land says it is. Being able to *look:* as one can, for large distances, flying over desert, tundra, or ice.[2] Symbolic systems? The magnificence of *fit:* yes, *a, b, c,* in these places, fit; *m* fits; *t, u,* and *v* fit: my god! This alphabet really *works!* I can leave it for a day or two, come back: it *still* works. Amazement. Pleasure. Thankfulness. Beauty. The willingness to accept countless hours of field and desk work to reach that. Also the exhaustion at the thought of beginning again for a second time, in Burma say, so that, ideally, perhaps, there should only have been *one* field for life. . . . I have always wondered how this could have been fitted in with Charles Olson's concerns at that time: in his *A Bibliography on America for Ed Dorn.* I met Olson too late and in the wrong circumstances.[3]

---

1 "The Heraldic Vision," in this volume.
2 Hence no doubt the attraction to Alaska or New Mexico or Far Western China where geography can be *verified,* especially from small aircraft, as nowhere else on earth.
3 Charles Olson, *A Bibliography on America for Ed Dorn* (San Francisco: Four Seasons Foundation, 1964), Writing 1.

It was easy moving from Griaule to Lévi-Strauss. In those years, he was lecturing in abundant detail on Amerindian symbolics, harvesting the treasures for *Mythologiques*. The same passion for *fit* was at work, almost more a question of the viable than the true, the Sherlock Holmesian attention to detail, the totalizing obsession. In a work of French research, no dog is ever left sleeping, no stone unturned. With less intensity, but with loving scholarship, Paul Lévy taught Southeast Asian systems: the Paul Mus legacy of folk-Buddhist interrelationships, and this was the area I thought would be mine.[4]

That there was much else in anthropology came home to me at Chicago. Yes, I could be the first to lecture for Fred Eggan on Lévi-Strauss's kinship theory (distressed at having to get away from religion but relishing the details); I could report on Griaule or Maurice Leenhardt to fellow students or write back to Paris about the new physical anthropology. But the Chicago faculty grossly overestimated my Paris training: there was all the *rest* of anthropology to learn, the whole Anglo-American side of it, and all this had to be done in one year for the Ph.D.

I learned that the discipline was mainly interested in the "science of society," how human groups of various sizes were structured and organized, and that, all too often, such an interest meant primarily attention to the minutiae of economics and politics. A delaying factor in my awakening was work with Robert Redfield. It was possible to go on feeling like a poet with Redfield. He was someone who could say and mean, "You are going to do fieldwork in a place so beautiful that you will thank me every morning when you open the window."

I found a niche for myself within his concept of "World view," one of the categories he had thought up (with help from Dilthey et al.) to deal with the comparison of total cultures. Within it, I felt I could continue to study religion, albeit by perverting somewhat the project he had designed for me.[5] In later years, I perverted another research project (not Redfieldian): the study of relations between the *Sangha* (order of Buddhist monks) and politics in Burma. Or rather, I bust a gut trying to do both this (to satisfy a grant) *and* carry out systematic work on Messianic Buddhism, an almost unknown field in Theravāda Buddhism and a crazy symbolic system if ever I saw one. I also insisted on following French tradition insofar as possible by mastering the *Orientalism* involved and not just the ethnography.

---

4 The reference is to Paul Mus, *Barabudur* (Hanoi: École Française d'Extrême Orient, 1935), still one of the major works of twentieth-century scholarship.

5 See Nathaniel Tarn, "The Literate and the Literary: The Anthropological Discourse of Robert Redfield," in Nathaniel Tarn, *Views from the Weaving Mountain* (Albuquerque: University of New Mexico Press, 1991).

The pigeons finally came home to roost in Britain. After the Maya fieldwork, it made no sense, for many reasons, to go back to France. Writing in French had failed. I settled in at the London School of Economics. It was awkward talking about an unfamiliar subject like Guatemala instead of Africa or India: my papers were always too long because I had to give twice the ethnography that other students provided. But the overwhelming problem was British social anthropology. After the exciting forties, BSA had settled into a routine. To simplify a great deal (and without disrespect to my esteemed teachers), most things seemed to be reduced to *social control* and the question how leaders imposed themselves on the led. The details of symbolic systems (hence distrust of anyone like Griaule or, for different reasons, Lévi-Strauss) were pure *ethnography* and did not accede to science. Overwhelming interest in religion meant little: an anthropologist should be ready to move from problem to problem as the urge to understand *society* or formulate scientifically valid *social laws* required. Fascination with a particular area also meant little: human problems were above geography. While I eventually managed to do my own research and teaching at the School of Oriental and African Studies, an areally defined school of the University, the countless theoretical courses taught, the seminars and conferences in methodology attended, seemed to erode the basis of my attention. On return from Burma, I had finally begun to write poems I could then respect and had found a "literary world" in which I could function as a poet. Dropping out of anthropology in 1967, I left the academy for publishing, though I returned to it in 1970 through English, romance languages, and comparative literature.[6]

2) *Gelassenheit:* letting be, or letting being be, a term from Heidegger which, though incorrectly from the point of view of etymology, *I* also hear as *lassitude.* Early on, in a poem from my first book *Old Savage/Young City,* I distinguish between the righteous justicer and he who lets be. How to deal with justice-to-the-observed when it is shown to involve control-of-the-observed? To have each thing in the world in its right place, treated, known, and recognized as it should be, is, surely, a viable version of justice as well as a worthy political objective? *Yet* it has unerringly contributed to localizing much for the purpose of *destruction* (genocide) or, at best, *theft and plagiarism* (ethnocide). The study of such and such a people contributes to its being pinpointed on a map: its goods are exploited, its land stolen, its ecology destroyed: it is raped. The area is opened for tourism or even amenities-migration, the perversion of arts and crafts, the debilitation of its

---

6   "Toward Any Geography / Toward Any America Whatsoever," in this volume; Jed Rasula and Mile Erwin,"An Interview with Nathaniel Tarn," *Boundary 2* 4, no. 1 (1975); 1–33; and "Child as Father to Man in the American Uni-Verse," in this volume.

people, their reduction to servility and economic slavery. The leprosy has spread relentlessly and continuously. He who would see anything or anyone "pure," "untouched," "unviolated" (and this is *always* relative) is in competition with half his kind, trying to reach a "beauty spot" before too many others do. The goodwill of science is powerless against this: at best, all one can ever do seems to be remedial for a while. Anthropology cannot avoid blame among her sister sciences. Compared to ecology for instance, and granted that ecology *interferes* almost by definition, what have anthropologists *done* for their "subjects"?

It may also be the case—I am struck by a recent reading of James Hillman on "oppositionalism"—that our favorite strategies of classification relate above all to possession, control, appropriation, governance rather than to the knowledge of the *thing as is*.[7] The conscious, intellectual mind into which one has poured such huge energies is a tyrant of his own life and the lives of others. I have myself refrained from giving these mental efforts a status more important than that of "*game*." The career-involvement of most will not allow of that.

Years ago, I interviewed Gary Snyder about such matters in a piece entitled "From Anthropologist to Informant."[8] The title, chosen by Snyder if I recall correctly, implies that you cease interrogating others when you yourself begin to have something to say. I have gotten to the point of wondering now if you do not desist whether you have anything to say *or not*. I have often felt, over the years, that I would have preferred to be an archaeologist because objects of material culture speak but do not *answer*. Or a geologist. Not a zoologist, I think, because it seems to me that animals do speak and do answer.

In thinking about a more amenable anthropology, I would wish for a negative enablement. Toward getting rid of most observer interference, I would argue for ever more exhaustive, purely descriptive *ethnography* with minimal "interpretation." The same would go for history—"ethnohistory" being principally what can be known from the period between a people's archaeological past and its ethnographic present. I would stress a good deal of ethnobiology as a way of contributing to a pool of human knowledge about ecology. Despite its importance for our knowledge of social control, precisely *because* of its importance, I would downplay everything that had contributed to our knowledge of social, economic, and political organization, particularly in regard to macrosociology. I know that whole philosophies of society *depend* on such knowledge and analyze reality from the standpoint of its categories. But I know of few or no powers in the world that have

7   James Hillman, *The Dream and the Underworld* (New York: Harper & Row, 1979), esp. 74–85.
8   Nathaniel Tarn, "From Anthropologist to Informant: A Field Study of Gary Snyder," in *Alcheringa* 4 (Fall 1972): 104–13.

used such knowledge wisely in regard to the usual objects of anthropological study under their rule. The human race is out to *eliminate* the simpler societies in our world: it is as stark as that. If the *whole of* anthropological effort, the *whole profession,* stopped in its tracks and devoted itself uniquely to the cultural preservation and survival of indigenous peoples, it would not be enough. As it is, infinitesimally small fractions of the collective effort find their way into this. Powerlessly, we watch the disappearance of our subject matter, "the lovely tribes falling like shadows" of one of my poems. When I reach this point in my thinking, I would like to do away with anthropology altogether. Its only justification seems to me to be linked historically to a very circumscribed period, one during which certain peoples have been coming to an ability to record a past which their parents had allowed to disintegrate. Anthropologists at that moment have had the technology to record that past, even if under the illusion that it was a present. They should hand the record over and disappear, leaving "their people" to reassume their own fate.

It comes to this. Either the object of study is destroyed. Or it/they have been strong enough to survive as subjects in their own right. They are informants in their own right. *They speak first.* Ultimately, in no walk of life, in no place on this planet or beyond, is there an "Informant" left, in the old sense of the word. I can measure my unfairness—but, *de jure,* if not *de facto,* anthropology no longer exists.

3) For the sake of argument, let's now try out a stance from which no one asks or answers questions. The poet now stands alone, divorced from all her/his previous occupations, those which, a critic can probably demonstrate, so frequently nourished her/his early work. S/he is presumably free now to converse with the creative angel and it alone. The recording angel has stubbornly fought, for years, the tendency of the creative angel to appropriate experience, sink it into the poet's psyche, let it come up transformed and alchemized by that fire which, we hope, still burns in him or her. But the recording angel is now defeated. The poet may feel poor, but there is a richness in that poverty: knowing you rely only on your own means as you descend into the abyss of your own life. You are disinformed both of information and disinformation. Whatever you accomplish or fail to accomplish is yours alone. No one is telling you anything; enquiries are not answered; you have ceased to make any.

Perhaps it is at this *very* point that the *other* will be met and that the poet will come into the possession of his/her own society.[9] The original, unimpeded, unin-

---

9 I believe this to be my first formulation of the *Choral* element in the model of poetic production dealt with at length in other parts of this volume. The *Vocal* element will eventually differentiate between individual singer and choral singer.

terrupted voice is many, not one, for the more itself it is, the deeper it reaches into its own inner nature, the more, beautiful paradox, does it come upon the truth of all being while also becoming the not-itself. The voice is not reached by going to others; it is met by going to one's own deepest self and discovering how un-self-ish it can be. To "become an informant," in the final sense, is to let a voice speak which is not the property of any one person—or only such in the liberality of allowing all voice to speak within it. To be an anthropologist in the final sense is no longer a bringing of many voices, the surface of other voices, to the collective singing place and exhibiting these voices in an ordered and governed fashion. It is a letting be of voice, in the confidence that the deeper it can go and the more it is free to express itself, the more *collective* it will be heard to be. I am not now talking about the me-me-me generation but about the most profound direction of the poet's life and craft. Whether there is any physical presence of listeners in the singing place, or not, is of no ultimate importance. As long as there is world, the poet continues in the singing place. There is no need for listeners because when a voice is so deep that all speak within it, all are simultaneously listening: no one need come or be brought to the singing place since we all listen to our own voice in each and any one voice. The subject/object of poetry is only voice; the voice is both form and content indissolubly. And *Chorus* from origin, if it rings true.

The singing place we are talking about is "the place where everyone is" because the one universal in human fate, apart from being born into it, is leaving it at the end for such a place. Perhaps we must give ourselves up, regulatively, to the evidence that the only collective we will ever meet is "among the dead." That the *other* should be met on this surface we inhabit seems impossible, given the all-prevailing constraints of fratricidal strife under which every one of our actions or aspirations eventually finds itself. I do not find it absurd to speak of a "republic of the dead" from which all good comes: many of the anthropologist's erstwhile objects of study believe in such a state and in its bounty. They also believe that we should go willingly toward that place in that, willing or not, it is our only destination.

To adopt this stance the poet gives up more than s/he acquires. Acquisition has been added to acquisition; power to power. Now acquisition has toppled over itself into a complete disinvestiture. It is not yet felt as richness. Desperate as s/he loses her/his heroic attributes one by one, desolate as s/he gives up one struggle after another, the poet moves toward the mysterious gates, proclaiming aloud her/his massive "poverty." It is only to be hoped that, unlike Kafka's hero, s/he will be able to let her/himself in. For in "the place where everyone awaits," s/he may be rich.

And praxis? One looks up at the legions of the "republic of the dead," materialized in the volumes on our shelves, and bemoans the overwhelming growth of a cancerous illiteracy which deprives society of the help of this republic. The poetry of scholarship once savored, an exhaustive attention paid to a particular, well-loved, and well-polished subject among all subjects—how could one give up the *dialogue* which has been established with these volumes or even with a few living practitioners still present among us for a while? After all this abstinence and abnegation, would one not also be contributing to destruction in allowing this culture to die? Even if it has been a cannibal culture, destructive of all else, has it not preserved all else within its record?

And there is also, within the terms of the singing place, another possibility: that the voices which are fully themselves are brought to that place together with other voices to perform in *Chorus,* rather than in question and answer. If, as it often is, the paradisal assent be considered dull, we can still turn to the greatest among our achievements to ascertain that it need not be so. In *Paradiso,* for instance, there is still question and answer within *Chorus* where a Dante has found ways of dramatizing the absolute perfection of agreement in our republic.

It is a far cry from where we are to such a *Chorus.* We have been plagued by too many *false* revelations of equals or teachers among those we once studied as inferiors. This may be, however, because we have been looking for the wrong things, trying to bring up miracles where there is only another everyday—more beautiful than miracles. The poet as informant can only go toward the former object of study as informant and hope that something new will result from the meeting.

And, of course, s/he might begin with the writing. S/he might try to put the whole *dialogue* in new writing, the field of another kind of voice than those we have heard before. A helpful, in-forming voice, eager to reach and accept the other's voice. Already in *Chorus,* or eager to reach for *Chorus.*

It might get started like that. Anyday, it could begin like that. Anyday, it could begin.

1986

Exile out of Silence into Cunning:

Being Notes on Elsewhere and the Myths of Presence

Exhortation from elsewhere to the guardians of here: What you must grant me now is the same status as an anthropologist grants the "native informant" s/he studies in a "tribal" society. No time to send for vitae, to check references, lists of awards, prizes. You cannot wait for "time to do its work," relevance to be established, place in the "canon," position in "literary history" (or in outer darkness). The young scholar who is to write about, explicate, derive, justify me has not yet gotten into school, passed her/his exams, sweated her/his degree, achieved tenured security, prepared her/his lectures, astonished the populations with news of a neglected mastery. You are going to give me credence; it is me you are going to have to believe. Right now.

"Elsewhere" implies a here you are relating to. To that extent, elsewhere is exile. Then: exile is, for the vast majority, perhaps for everyone, exile *from*. There is a thing, person, place (not oneself, other) to be parted from, and this is exile. Exile is absence from a "presence," the loss of a once established good, an "origin," the distancing from anything which, in our persistent longing, assumes the colors of paradise.

In *this* informant's exegesis, however, exile is not *from*. Exile plainly *is*. Exile is the thing, person, place, at the *archē*, the presence, the established root, the *paradiso*. To be exiled *from*, if that can even be thought, is to be separated from the exile that *is*. It is difficult and dangerous to be exiled from exile: you have to start a whole career in the world, assume a history. You have to make up elsewhere for a great deal you never had at root. By subjective extension, this is the problem of the whole race: that it has assumed a history. (Even the "primitives," even the "archaics.") It is departure from this root of exile which ignites all our troubles. We imagine we have been exiled from a time-and-place which, somehow, was not exile. It might be our one and only "original sin." If such a thing can still be in any way considered . . .

> *Instruction (as before):* Assume correct biographical factors and socio-economic background to justify this stance. (Further details to qualified enquiries only.)

In the classical sense, what is being-here for a poet? A *lyric* poet, committed to the populous craft of song? Say it is voice. Not in the surrogate sense of "voice" as organ of "unique personality" but in the production of noise from vocal cords and larynx, probably tied to mentation as such. The origin of voice? Apart from the physical machinery, we know as little of how voice arises or wherefrom as we know about how thought arises and enters mind, and wherefrom. In the form of *archē/logos/*origin/presence, voice then, agreed, at best: myth or illusion. When the poet is "being-here," voice seems real enough, speaking the poem. At *archē/logos/*origin/presence reality is hard or impossible to grasp. There is no "here" for an aborigine: everywhere is infected *ab initio* by "there" or "elsewhere." The aboriginal thing, person, place itself is already elsewhere. It is hard to know what can be "real" when the depths are so unplumbed, unplumbable. Hard to know what architecture can stand and endure when archaeology is so lacking in foundations. Or how to proceed to *architexture,* the emergence of text out of thought and voice. Were we to place writing at the beginning of our notes, rather than voice, another exile might manifest itself: text out there with voice under erasure for the time being, text primordial in an already elsewhere, message in the margins to a sick or dying page.

It might also be that *archē,* by definition, can neither arise nor subside. Especially if it is already exile. If *archē* cannot *move,* origin cannot become presence, presence cannot give out voice: that syntagm cannot be enacted. But then, it is equally true that it is very hard to find a foundation for voice, poem, text. These are on the loose, at the surface, hanging out on a highly problematic film over an equally problematic abyss.

When we depart from exile, we fall elsewhere, everywhere into place. If we know little about the source of voice, we know that voice, in place, assumes spatial and temporal colors, accents of history, overtones and undertones of the *Lebenwelt.*

Place, consider further, is the *nature* of a temporal and spatial situation or circumstance (weather, climate, geology, fauna, flora, et al.). Awesome, *place* is interpreted by voice as god/power/guardian; these form hierarchies in the cosmos thus made manifest: villages, towns, regions, countries, continents, planets, galaxies. Each one of these comes about as voice—to be attended to by all other voices, voices which color each other, stain off on each other, each being a voice fallen into place. Now, when voice is fallen into place: is it spoken by the poet? Is the poet still with it throughout this long, complex fall? Or has the poet been left behind somewhere on this exhausting journey, so that s/he is now in exile from voice—or voice in exile from the poet? Since everything is in exile everywhere, try saying that voice is no longer spoken by poet but by *self. Self* is voice fallen into place.

Let *self* in turn be a collection of stances, attitudes, orientations, passions which we believe ourselves to be constituted by. Dialogue opens between self and place, self and self, place and place. Each self is moving through a world of places, *nature,* and other selves, *culture,* indissolubly intertwined: we simplify here because there has long been no "pure" nature and there has never been "pure" culture. In this cosmos, there are myriads of voices, interacting with other voices; myriads of selves interacting with other selves; voices and selves working off each other: *"je est (toujours) un autre / [un autre est (toujours) je]."* So much is this so that self rarely speaks from a single "I": I is always, to some lesser or greater extent, already complex, multiplex when it becomes architect. Thus we live in the world, write writings, enact careers, achieve fame or oblivion. Usually oblivion.

> *Instruction (as before):* Consider the ultimatum. As time has progressed the future has shocked us—so many shocks that future falters. Every thing is present and our "being here" is almost exiled from time. The transmogrification of poetry from a "vocation" to a "profession" has moved at absolute speed. To be a poet today is to be defined, especially in America which defines so much else, in terms, not even of a self, but of a *curriculum vitae* of publications, teaching positions, awards, prizes, and grants. It is not the poem which is production but what the poem brings in: not in cash, alas, but in the softer currency of poet-as-culture-maker, poet-as-status. It is more important that poetry should be theoretically produceable than that it should be produced. Status stands in for self standing in for poet. This is the absolute abyss of exile, this and the massive fabrication of further statuses in the writing schools of the continent. Academic monopolies and trusts. Disciplinary cartels. Teacher teaching taught teaching more taught. Inbreeding. Incest. Poet reads poet, publishes poet, finances poet to provide cannon fodder for the academy. Even an ounce of something like the *original* surrealist revolution would have covered the faces of these decoys with

unmentionables. *Any* of such, out of *any* margin, while awaiting the one and only, real, genuine, unique revolution. This addressed to poets against the vice of co-optation. At this point of threat, reverse the model, as with all mental games, a healthy procedural device.

Look at it another way. In the absence of information as to its origins, voice has often been understood as a product, not of the envelope, but of *inside* or *outside* the poet. When coming from the outside, it has been envisaged as arriving from afar, possibly from a diagonal, from above. When coming from the inside, however, it is often thought of as sourcing up from deep down, perhaps from the deepest. Since we are dealing with myth, a certain amount of reciprocity, even reversal, between the terms may be permissible. Thus, the *above* of the outside (from which one "falls") and the *below* of the inside (from which one "rises") might be the identical point of departure—if you envisage an *all-around* to wherever-you-happen-to-be.

Now look at current available *dicta* as to voice and silence. It had seemed for some time that voice arose out of, and doubtless returned to, silence. Academic critics have seen the poem as aspiring to the condition of light, music, silence without much about where it might aspire *from*. Voice, in this view, very much inside/below. For the sake of argument, call the arising the field of the *vocal* in which we have already witnessed the interplay of self and self. The social world of the poem is based on reciprocity: once self is, it allows of *other;* once *other* is, it implies self. We have freeplay of *parole,* charm of unending invention; inexhaustible *process* of the *newly-said:* unending process depending precisely on belief in the newly-said as *poésie ininterrompue / poésie ininterrompable.* Here, in the time-space of the vocal, all is subjective. Anything beyond the sovereign self-voice is illusion to be kept out of mind. Painfully, sovereign voice struggles against the grain or current to enunciate the newly-said as the price of a tradition of the new it belongs to. This despite the fact that it knows it lives in a collective, with a myriad of voices striving for the same goal, either ahead of it or behind it in understanding and in skillful means.

How much of this has been questioned? A whole *army* of soldiers striving to be *generals,* and only a few of them making it? How much is the statistical probability of saying the *newly-said* attended to? Isn't the whole structure of our education into writing predicated on the allegation that every student's pack will contain a poet's baton? How do we *stand* these harrowing contradictions (which are but life, of course, as any Darwinist will tell you . . .)?

How much of *silence* has been questioned? Not much. Silence locked in, it seems, on itself. Locked in on nothing? On everything? How can one *say?* ("What we cannot speak about . . ." *und so weiter.*) Certainly, if the sovereign self-voice debates in there silently, like a foetus, that silence of exile should bear interrogation? We can hypothesize that self–self in dialogue closes off the *vocal* and its self–other reciprocity. If the *vocal* is the place of the *poem,* I would advance *silence* as that of *opus:* knowledge the poet has in depth, fore or aft, of all s/he has written and all s/he will write—which, whether s/he knows it or not, already interferes with the nearly said. It is time, we might add, to diversify aesthetics: the single poem is *one* unit of study; what is not yet understood is the poet's abyssal knowledge from birth to death of the *whole works* as it affects the production of any single unit.

> If thou forgettest the right hand of thy cunning, O Jerusalem, let Jerusalem forget me. If thy tongue cleave to the roof of thy mouth, let me not be remembered by thee. . . .

In Blake's Eden, the state above Beulah (that of human marriage), poet marries poem. Marriage, back there in the myth or *archē,* was that state of acceptance of another, a radically other, out of the security of accepting oneself. The poet could accept a non-poet (call her/him "reader") in exogamous union, could also accept the dream of another language, hence the possibility of *translatio.* But if Eden is itself exile *ab initio,* we do not have marriage now but incest. Here is the in-talk, refusal of the reader unless s/he is a poet, refusal of another language (all must be murrican), of *translatio.* Here all is borrowing, from the already written; all is intravocal and intratextual. *Différance* or not, dear scholar, look to endogamy now. Everyone aboard the rocket will be siblings or parallel cousins.

Carry this a little further. In good disputation, no ground is allowed to stand for long as ground if yet another ground is disclosed below it. However indefinite, however intermediate it may in turn prove to be. In the silence of *silence,* it is as if we required another level against which to push *archē* and its paradigm of concepts; we can *imagine,* locked in our *episteme* as we may be, the shadow of the terminal wall. Create this as the *choral* and specify this outer edge of the myth somewhat as follows. Elsewhere of *langue; structure* as that which process optimistically surges out of but inevitably falls back into: William James's "substantive"/"transitive." Argue that the already said is the inevitable fate of voice where poetry cannot be born yet is always born nonetheless: inherent contradiction. Here: not poem, not *opus*—but *page/text:* the total possibilities of poetry, ever been or ever to be, third aesthetic against which *opus* measures itself rather like poem squaring off against poem in sight of *opus.* No time; no space; no reciprocity in that self *is* other as other *is* self exactly—"the sense of the universal equality of things." All is objective in the *choral:* the *vocal* a reciprocal illusion (i.e., even if illusion, *choral* and *vocal* require each other). Elsewhere of the dead, perhaps, or of "tradition": lineage of the living dead as against those who have no place in memory because they had none in social life: in that sense, "ancestors." Collective projected into the past from the conflictual *vocal* and thus allowable. Source also of a future projection, perhaps, into the classless realm of the end of history.

Whatever the games played by academics on the theme of "anxiety of influence," note that it is in their nature to refer back to the past. A poet, for the academic, is in conflict with her/his forebears, not with her/his generational siblings. Hence the fact that the unacknowledged slave kept hidden in the basements of even the most radical critics is invariably the truly contemporary writer. A practitioner, however, knows that the hardest struggle is with these siblings/partners— *whatever* the degree of acceptable intertextuality, it is safe to wager that not one poet would relish being classified as entirely unoriginal. No matter how hard each one of us tries, there are not enough prizes to go round for everyone. In the allegedly objective "republic of letters," it is hard on the spirit to discover here too the cancerous dilemma at the heart of all human situations: acceptance of a given fate versus attempts to tamper with its course. If myth is a necessary illusion attempting to mediate seemingly irreconcilable social conflicts, the *choral* may be more necessary to us than we imagine. And *silence*, the great mediator, may still contain more seeds than we would credit any philosophy with dreaming up for us.

Final instruction: Recognize this as a poet's discussion of an artwork, here the poem, a structure whose center never resides *inside* the structure, it is said, but is to be found *outside* it, referring back to some *logos*, itself the *archē* (or referring back to *archē*), while forward it refers to *telos*. Note Walter Benjamin on the decline of the man of letters vis-à-vis the scholar (he) used to be indistinguishable from.

Alternatively, take a step "out of the philosophy" or out of "logocentrism"—in which case delete the *archē* paradigm. Fortify absolute exile as standing in for exile: not the mark of a particular set of circumstances but the brand of Cain on *all* humans. The poem, in a perpetual play of significations *ad infinitum,* abjures Rousseauist nostalgia and leaps into Nietzschean freeplay: open question onto the future. Delete the backward-looking elegiac function in the constitutive myth of lyric poetry (Orphic); preserve only the lyric thrust into ever-negotiable futures. In any event, process is now interminable, poetry completely uninterruptible, as Eluard would have wished. There will be no return to anything since everything is departure. You will make your home in exile. Everywhere is elsewhere. It is our state of being, what we do, and where we do it, down here.

1989

Regarding the Issue of "New Forms"

Despite the absence of members of the Language Poetry community, in the strict sense, at this gathering, I remain in their neighborhood because I am convinced that works like Charles Bernstein's "Content's Dream" and Ron Silliman's "The New Sentence," to quote but two titles, are the most energetic, brilliant, and challenging critical works to come out of our craft since, let us say, Olson's "Projective Verse" or, back of that, the essays of Ezra Pound.

These books are so demanding, however, that I sometimes wonder how those who are not trained in present-day academic "theory" (Structuralism; Neo-structuralism; Deconstructionism, etc., across the board of linguistics; general aesthetics; the social sciences and especially political science) are going to have the patience, or indeed ability, to engage them.

This may come close to saying that the natural destination of the Language community is the academy, something many of them might claim to detest, although, of course, they do cannily recognize that such battles have to be waged at the sociological centers of intellectual power. For better or for worse, this today

Paper given at a session on "New Forms," Naropa University, Boulder, Colorado, July 16–23, 1989. My original suggestion had been for a conference of "Language Poets" and "New Americans," but this was not possible.

means the academy. Silliman has addressed the M.L.A.; Bernstein has taught at Princeton and is about to teach at Buffalo. I suspect that a great many practitioners of our craft would prefer to stay very clear of these matters. I don't think we should, but I hope it is possible to deal with the subjects involved a little more simply, to de-jargonize them without gutting them altogether.

I come back to the most sacred of all our present sacred cows: L-A-N-G-U-A-G-E. That which is "signified" by language (simplifying here, I'll call this the conceptual aspect referring to a thing designated by a linguistic unit—say "content") takes a less and less privileged place in discussions on art and science to the benefit of that which, in language, primarily effects the signifying, i.e., the "signifier" (which I'll call the acoustic or written element comprising a linguistic unit referring to a thing—say "form").

From Saussure on down the opposition signifier/signified has been incredibly fertile. In certain periods of early Modernism when it has been possible for artists and academics to converse meaningfully, the exploration and exploitation of the signifier (call it the "foregrounding" of the signifier) have been a major impetus in artists' attempts to break away from traditional "closed" forms or to cause those closed forms to explode into "open" ones.

We have had a number of these explosions: Futurism, Vorticism, Dada, Surrealism, Imagism, etc., all the way down to Projective Verse, Open Poetry, Language Poetry, and the like. It is tactically useful to artists, fighting for their own place in the sun, and behaving in this matter very much like sectarians in religion, to pretend to uniqueness or extra characteristics in their respective "isms." There is nothing more fascinating than to see the various European movements crossing national borders one after another, meeting fraternal or rival receptions on their way. Only the other day, I was reading the Russian Khlebnikov's "Futurian" manifestos, with their angry jabs at Italian "Futurists," some years after reading the various French, British, and other receptions of the Italians and their successors. And how often, on the mercifully rare occasions when I've "taught writing," have I had to point out to a student that s/he was unwittingly doing the 2,500th dilution of Surrealism as imported into these States by the Xs, Ys, and Zs it would not be hard to name! I long sometimes to be able to spend a few minutes in the mind of a critic born a couple of hundred years from now when so much of this will have been compared to death and gradually factored out to a few essential twentieth-century contributions! Doubtless the same will apply to much of the stuff we do now: for instance, to that massive garaboo: the question of Modernism versus Postmodernism versus Modernism . . . and so on *ad infinitum*.

To get back to Language. We know from linguistics that the signifier in most situations is arbitrary and that it is the relation between signifier elements that endows a statement with signification. We then have a continuum of possibilities in manipulating signifiers. At one end, we take a set of signifiers and jumble them such that it will not be possible for a receiver to ascribe any signification to this message chain whatsoever in terms of the sender's language—or any other that might legitimately be described as a language by an ideal gathering of speakers from all human languages.

At the other end, let's make a chain of signifiers such that the hearer or reader receives a perfectly straightforward utterance in her/his, or any other, language, something of the order of "Charlie came to lunch today" or "I want to buy Allen Ginsberg's latest book"—further specifying that we mean "our friend Charlie X" and not Charlie Y or Z, or mean A.G. the "famous poet" in case there are any lunatics wandering around being poets and writing as "Allen Ginsberg." Linguistics and Communication Theory tell us that you have to surprise the receiver of a communication if you wish to keep her/his attention. This, in the end, as Diaghilev knew when he said to Cocteau, "*Jeune homme, étonnez-moi,*" is the rock on which *all* art is ultimately built and without which it totally fails to function. In about ninety-five cases out of a hundred, an art object is only to achieve success if it says something the receiver has not seen, heard, or thought before.

It is fairly obvious to most that an utterance destined to last is not going to locate itself at either end of the continuum I've just defined. The first pole has had its tries (the Dadaists, the *Zaum* Futurians in Russia, the *Lettrisme* of the French fifties, a number of Concrete Poets, the beast language of McClure, and much else): it keeps on reappearing, full of hope. Most recently much of it has gone by names like "Disjunctive Poetics."

Of course, there are ways of finding this kind of utterance important. One is to imply that these utterances are reaching some kind of infra, supra, or para level above, below, or beyond the norm of human utterance and that, although it is not possible to "understand" them logically in the normal rational ways we understand things, nevertheless there exists "some level" of comprehension on which we can use and deal with them. A lot of effort was put out in early Modernism to prove that such language went back to an "ur-language" of humanity, a kind of pre-Babel state of primordial purity. Or that its value lay in some occult, secret power akin to that of mantras in religious systems. In such ways, these utterances fall within the categories of primitivism or hermeticism, usually one of these two.

A somewhat less hackneyed claim, and one more contemporary, is to urge that it is very difficult for any signifier whatsoever to reach zero level of communication so that the various orders which we impose on our set of signifiers tease, tempt, and dance with meanings, however transitory, however ephemeral, and give us something of what we could wish for from an utterance . . . if not everything.

It seems clear, however, that very few people have carried the point to extremes. McClure, for example, has no more done his total output in Beast Language than, to shift things considerably, Hugh MacDiarmid has written all his poetry in a Scots reinvented by him and certainly not as available worldwide, or even nationwide, as straight English English.

The truth is that when you look, say, at Khlebnikov's early poems of this type, you are not so much pleased with them as poems—what happens rather is that you acknowledge them as experiments which had to be made at that time for many theoretical reasons. It is good that they are there, but that is about the sum of it: the experiment has been made rather than not made; the "fanscape of possibilities" effect has been demonstrated; language can be totally "wild"; now let's get back to *business*. It would be interesting to find out how many people *re-read* such poetry—unless they are writing, as they say, *off of it*.

The other point to remember is that many things "new" are worth doing when they are truly new. When they are some seventy-five years old or so, their value may be less. This bears saying when we are in the middle of an extraordinary period of denial-of-the-new, fed by theories such as Benjamin's on the "Age of Mechanical Reproduction" or those which claim we cannot have the new because we are perpetually playing with the "already" said, heard, or seen and must subsist in an eternal show of mirrors or simulacra. A period in which all art seems to be in a state of imitation of the past, a state of NEO-something-or-other (Neo Romanticism, Neo Expressionism; Neo Surrealism, etc. etc. etc.); Neo-Neo-Neo vying for the least original, or most banal, of positions in the game of eternal return and repetition. I'll get back to this.

In our current state of culture, it is easier to persuade oneself that art cannot have anything to do with the other pole of signification, the one which produces the banalities of our everyday utterances and conversations. Here, if anywhere, is the place to vary the chain of signifiers in such a way that surprising utterances can result. Almost all our forms of infra-realism, sur-realism, and para-realism emerge from the effort to vary the menu at this end.

Our possibilities, right now, seem to be: 1) You can have decided that the task of the signifier in traditional poetry is, by creating a sonnet or an ode, approximate, in its sphere, to the production of an everyday, i.e., probably "banal," utterance in daily speech. You can open up the poem's form by refusing the elements of, say, rhyme or agreed-on prosody. The whole avant-garde poetic lineage from Mallarmé on down has done this. You can even do this in the cause of bringing back into poetry the kind of "banality" associated with everyday speech—either because of an Eliot's notion of the role of prose in poetry, or because of a Williams's interest in the native speech, or again because of an Olson's interest in the breath units of spoken utterance. In this case you are likely to be de-banalizing by giving some kind of new context to "banality." Importantly, you are breaking the unsurprisingness to which a particular class of utterances has been traditionally subject. It is even possible to create a new art of the "realistic" if the elements of apparent "realism" have been absent from an utterance-form for too long: but this does not make realism into any the less stylized a form of utterance. The considerable work on the "transparency effect of realism" of a Roland Barthes has been largely devoted to this issue.

2) Alternatively, a very broad range of possibilities opens up in the realm of what I have called teasing, tempting, dancing. Almost everything that goes on among those who wish to baffle referentiality without totally doing away with it falls into this category. The ways in which it can be done, almost in terms of a user's manual, have been exhaustively catalogued in the Language Poetry critical books I've mentioned. (And nowhere do the Language poets get closer to New Criticism—as Silliman at one point ruefully admits.)

Clearly I believe the possibilities of what we can do to be ultimately limited in this direction and, indeed, through repetition, to be becoming more and more limited. There are many reasons why we find it painful, if not downright impossible, to admit this.

One is the joy of discovering (and rediscovering over and over) the fact that there appears to be something, Language, which is our very own toy, which we are, as poets, uniquely qualified to play with. The more foregrounding of the signifier, the more language appears to have acquired an independent (some might say Frankensteinian) existence and the more it has seemed NOT to be our job to put signification into Language but to let Language find and make ITS OWN significations. The more, also, it has seemed that we have a completely independent charter for our existence, and that, in a time when poetry seems to be less and less wanted in our society, is surely one of the greatest possible consolations.

The other main reason is a much more subtle one. In closed poetry, the thrust seemed to be to jump from closed structure to closed structure, without—such seemed the force of tradition—much room for process. It appeared to the various Modernists, however, that open poetry left room for unending process, uninterruptible process (Eluard's "*poésie ininterrompue*"), and that, in short, there were NO limits to the possibilities of the NEW. I have tried to show elsewhere that this is an illusion, a necessary illusion, and, as such, probably present in all poetry at all times but that, in the end, the fall is always back to structure.[1]

You may be recognizing here the idea that the restricted nature of formal pre-occupations and associated activities foregrounding the signifier is tragically evident. This despite the presence of marvelous bodies of work, Barthes's is an example, which argue that the whole nature of modern literature foregrounds the signifier in this way. For me, a major sign of the failure of all this is the astonishing speed at which it has become the dominant mode of academic discourse. There is a limited number of topics around which our arguments revolve over and over, as if they were stuck in a tedious groove. One of them is the question of new forms—as if we were never to realize that, however limited they were also, variations in "content," in the signifieds, were LESS limited than variations in form. This is what I want to go on to.

It may be, this is where the Language poets are significant, that the crux of the matter is political. You are familiar with the argument that what has to be guarded against at all costs is the petrification of language into bodies of received, and thereby "oppressive," understandings which perpetuate a status quo inimical to the interests of "progressive" society. The message of the *Linguini* (my name for the Language Poets) is that everyday referentiality must be avoided above all in that it is the residence of oppressive understandings. This is demonstrated (not, of course, for the first time) with much show of logic, indefatigable irony, and force.

The results, however, are debatable on three main counts. First, I have yet to be convinced that the difficult Language works are actually working on the average reader or man-in-the-street as opposed to the already "converted" fellow-poet. Or even reaching him. If they do not, what on earth has this to do with any viable radicalism, that is, with something other than "armchair" (usually academic) radicalism? Second, what is being done 90% of the time is a repetition of what various strata of the avant-garde have been doing since Mallarmé: it is hard to avoid the sense that "*Un coup de dés jamais n'abolira le hasard*" was so brilliant and so hard-won on Mallarmé's part that it already pre-empted for all time the space daily re-occupied by these reruns.

Third, these repetitions are enacted at a time when whatever public poetry may have is less and less enchanted with what the avant-garde produces and is turning away from poetry by the droves. All of this, of course, in the context of a

---

1   See, for instance, "The Heraldic Vision" in this volume.

massive turn away from reading altogether in favor of the media. More seriously: all this continues at precisely the time when whatever social elements remain young, enthusiastic, and altruistic discover that one of the very few remaining paths to pure and true fame—because almost totally unsalaried in conventional terms—is poetry. In other words, a society *under-producing* readers is, at the very same moment, *over-producing* poets, with the massively incestuous and socially short-circuited results I've tried to describe for the last ten years or so.[2]

Where does this lead us? Back into the arms of the sausage-machine writing schools producing poets by the droves who, writing in the exact tracks of their teachers, produce the academic poem, the photocopy of their teacher's poem which is the photocopy of their teacher's? Back to a moment in which, at the beginning of the co-optation of the creative arts by the academy, some launched the firm belief that none of the avant-gardes had *ever* meaningfully achieved anything of value? No, absolutely not.

One place where it might lead us is toward another try at defining the parameters of a concept of "content" more sophisticated than what we have been given this far. I grew up and came into poetry at a time when the doctrine, out of Olson and Creeley, was that "form is never more than an extension of content" with its corollaries—a creed that always puzzled me, believing that there were so few forms available for what seemed always to be a far vaster variety of possible contents. More and more lately, I have been asking myself what exactly IS the content we have at hand.

We believe we know the content of the "academic" poem I mentioned a moment ago. It is the believed-to-be-sensitive trace left in an individual ego, highly sensitized to such traces, by a special, valuable, unique event transferred onto paper in sensitive language which, together with all the other sensitivities, will signal to its readers that "this IS poetry." You know: what people in their minimalistic language today refer to as a *really, REALLY* important statement in really, REALLY important language. Among ourselves, the non-academics, we are by now persuaded that the traces, egos, events put down in the scribblings which their authors have the nerve to baptize by the holy name of "poem" are in fact trivial, monotonously repetitive, and, furthermore, ever more closely associated with the yuppery of the yuppiest class of yuppies that ever yuppified this yuppificated nation.

In order to combat this yuppification—and what are we dealing with here, after all, but the most sedate and unproductive consumers yet produced by our

---

2 See Nathaniel Tarn, "Open Letter Regarding a Proposal for an Order of Silence," in Nathaniel Tarn, *Views from the Weaving Mountain* (Albuquerque: University of New Mexico Press, 1991).

received and therefore oppressive understandings?—the various strata of the
evolving avant-garde have resorted to one major remedy. This is to claim that the
last dregs of the ego, the unqualified, unique, superb, sublime contribution of Romanticism to the arts, have to be evacuated from the art object. A variety of "ob-
jectivisms" results. The latest, in this line of argument, is the *Linguinis'*.

What has been overlooked falls under a number of headings. 1) In the face of
an ever more complex world and an unbearable mass of information amounting
to totalizing INFOGLUT, the self or ego as the one potential discriminating factor each of us owns (including the binding together of discriminated factors into
possible reasons for living) is being extracted more and more from the art object. I
do distinguish between a discriminating self and a non-discriminating (non-)self,
but we'll get to this later.

2) Alternatively, this is worse, it is pretended that this discriminating factor *is*
being extracted—"pretended" because, in truth, the factor *cannot* be extracted.
For the ego is an ever-retreating but never-absent junction through which a signifier can be wedded to a signified (or vice versa), through which signals coming
from things and events can be transmitted into utterance, and it is the *only* possible such junction.

How do we tell that this is a "pretended" evacuation? By watching, for instance, the criticisms in our Language Poetry texts against the primacy, among
their predecessors, of "voice." Voice, it may be argued, is to present poetry what
"style" once was in the past: the way in which you diagnose whether there is, *or
not,* a presence worth hearing and knowing behind words heard or read. You know,
however, that "presence" is a commodity very much under suspicion by these
same theorists so that they would like to get rid of that also.

In terms of sectarian studies, of course, the reason for what is happening is
plain: insofar as a new sect has to differentiate/distance itself from the previous
sect in order to appear worth hearing, it has to challenge the previous sect's mo-
nopoly of attention. Voice, you'll remember, was, with Williams's stress on native
speech, with Olson's stress on breath, or with Ethnopoetics at large, the signature
of the poet worth her/his salt. Consonant with the return of "theory" to *Writing,*
seasoned with sophisticated deconstructionist assassinations of the very notion of
authorial presence, the new community has a lot of trouble with the claims of
"voice."

With the same philosophies in play we have a far reaching de-hierarchization
of all possible propositions: a passion for what I call the "fanscape of possibilities." The basic notion here is that what one finds under one's nose is valuable and
to-be-attended to—not because of any intrinsic interest it may or may not possess

but simply, basically, primordially because it is *there*. This sells well with Neo-Neoism and with the commodity culture to which Neo-Neo is attuned (never mind what you *need:* look at the zillions of products you can buy in order more and more to depend!). It is also very easy then to conceive that what is *there* includes, prioritarily, the procedures and methods with which non-authors "generate" poems in the absence of anything that might remotely resemble the long-popular and respected commodity "inspiration," let alone the more general affliction named "desire."

The political implications are curious. You seem to be destroying the hierarchies of financial capitalism's technocracies by constantly subverting their values and the language expressing such values. You might however be creating conditions in which the absence of hierarchy leaves a power vacuum which can only too easily and rapidly be re-occupied by the rich and hawkish. In the absence of a social class which can receive and act on the highly complex messages of our avant-gardes (and how we all fool ourselves on this one!), do their politics carry? Is there, to use Charles Altieri's term, "consequence"?[3] Yes, one welcomes the hopes and the positive thinking in Language Poetry theory, and it is a good sign that, as Silliman points out, they so preoccupy us. *No*, one does not necessarily have to buy all their claims.

The answer then to those who hold that Language Poetry is, within its own enactment, a form of the basic class struggle (the "whys" are clearer to us than the "hows" in such arguments) seems to be that the most fully conscious and public-minded of poets enact critical political awareness in the poem without having to go through all the acrobatics performed by the reigning avant-garde. More importantly, they enact it without giving up many of the traditional prerogatives of poetry so easily jettisoned by such an avant-garde. This I take to be, to refer to one instance, the formulation of the "analytic lyric" or "lyric contention" upheld by the magazine *Acts*. It is present, often implicitly (notwithstanding the Language Poets' great beef against the New Americans that their poetics are not made explicit), in much other contemporary work held by its authors to be just as political and as formally radical as that of the L.P.s. There remain political problems in both approaches, which appear to throw them back-to-back as requiring a synthesis. But this takes us too far for the time we have here.

It may be that there is a problem with both those who see an art-object as a locus of class struggle and those who see it as revealing intimate options which refine the receiver's perceptions so that they could be better fitted to partake in social

---

3   See the exchanges between Jerome McGann and Charles Altieri, as well as the strong differences of opinion about "accommodation" between McGann and Von Hallberg, in Robert Von Hallberg, ed., *Politics and Poetic Value* (Chicago: University of Chicago Press, 1987).

struggle. The problem area may lie in 1) the professional hazard of taking too exalted or optimistic a view of the art-object's political potential and 2) taking too limited a view of society at a time when reality seems to be overtaking theory and technological development is forcing one world on us far faster than we had dreamed possible, with huge changes imminent in the categories with which we usually define the social.[4]

There is also more to be said about "voice" in order to access a more thorough understanding of the poetic self and the act of poetic production. But this is the subject of another essay: it follows hard upon in this very book.

Ombligo de Tesuque, 6.30.89–8.04.89

POSTSCRIPT; BERLIN, MAY 1990

To our astonishment, in the last six months or so, politics here have been moving so fast it is hard to accommodate our understanding to that movement. Culture cannot keep up. We leave New York with the wreckage of the great ship Pantheon Books and the vision of a self-destruction of American culture: all one can fantasize now is the absolute ruin of corporate publishing; that everything should be brought back again to a beginning. Expanding Small Press clouds move in our heads, vying to drown out our educational statistics which are as tragic as they have ever been, perhaps a great deal more so.

Across the Channel, the British papers continue to behave as if only three poets existed, the same Alvarez set up as American models for his countrymen thirty years ago: Lowell, Berryman, Plath, plus three Brits—say Larkin, Heaney, and Hughes. In theater, the brutalism which seemed so energetic thirty years ago, now appears repetitive and stale. Thatcherite education dies on the vine; the brain drain continues massive. There is a triteness about the life of the polity, a sense of sleaze and corruption similar to our own.

Here, in Berlin, the issues are closer to the ground and dramatized no doubt even more than they are East of here. The Wall comes down bit by bit, and a

---

4 See my answer to the enquiry "Is There, Currently, an American Poetry?" in "Is There, Currently, an American Poetry? A Symposium," *American Poetry* 4, no 2 (Winter 1987): 31–34. It may be worth pointing out that my view of a poet's role implies a mature development of both mind and heart. I have sometimes wondered if the fact that "writing" is now taught so abundantly in universities (i.e., to very young people, with intellectual processes often more developed than emotional ones) might not facilitate a *playful* attitude toward words whose links might then just as easily be disjunctive as junctive. The surrealists' fondness for children, the "primitive," and the "insane" was not co-incidental, although, in their case, other serious concerns have to be factored in.

fascinating future archaeology unrolls. Huge sections have been carted away to presidential libraries in the U.S. or the History Museum of Berlin City. Smaller pieces have been chiseled for sale to souvenir-hunters. The first layer is nearly gone; kids apply graffiti paint to the second layer and chisel that for sale. The pieces with a white surface are choice: they come from the Eastern side. The militaria of the DDR and Russia are also on sale. Are these real Russian Army caps, or were they made in East Berlin in the first place, or have some cunning buggers in West Berlin started a factory? The uniforms, insignias, badges, passports, etc., etc., of the DDR are real, of course: they are too recent to be anything else.

In East Berlin, people try to buy their buildings or apartments before Western speculation comes in. The compact little East German Trabant cars go down in value dramatically almost day by day, while groups of people stand gawping in the streets wherever a "Western" Mercedes or BMW is parked. Weightier matters: how is all the material culture in those divided museums, galleries, libraries, going to come together again and what is going to be "disappeared" in the process? A minuscule example: already, DDR philately has changed gear: a number of Socialist commemorative stamps are replaced by stamps of bees and flowers.

The Wall a shadow and the ground beneath it. A ground, previously marginalized, now to become the center of a re-united city. Values shoot up astronomically. Daimler Benz and the great Department Superstore Ka-De-We have, it is said, already bought Potsdamer Platz. Now West Berlin, at least, has had, in the last forty years, a respectable tradition of inviting world-class architects each year to design new buildings in the city. Question: will the new center area be planned? Or will it all ruin into McDonaldry because everything is going too fast?

The thought occurs in these surroundings that everything that has been said to date about Postmodernism is academic and sterile: *this* is Postmodernism. Why? Because the radical politics which had allowed certain societies to dream of a future better fitted to the dignity of man than capitalism had provided were a vital part of at least one branch of Modernism and because now no hope is seen on that side and these radical politics appear to be irredeemably dead except among the academy's armchair theorists. In one sense, the fate of Berlin and Germany signify, at least to the Germans, a great enrichment: the paralyzing disunity of the last forty years gives way to an impetus which, coming at the same moment as the unification of Europe, may leave us Americans feeling old, worn out, and done for as the energetic country of the twentieth century. On the other hand, there will be those everywhere who do not find this disappearance an unqualified triumph and who wonder how the disadvantaged among all people are going to be represented from now on.

I confess in a belief that poetry represents, more than ever now, the ground and constitution of a perpetual *opposition* which is ill served by the depths of social isolationism into which we have allowed our vocation to sink. I have been thinking lately that there is perhaps a more coherent model for this isolationism than I have found to date. Noting the distaste, on the part of most of my fellow poets when the matter is raised, I wonder whether we have not come to the view that there is absolutely no need for discussions about readerships or publics since our incest is entirely satisfactory to us, being a self-sufficient nation of producer-consumers among ourselves, an independent country into whose bourns no extrinsic traveler need ever come, or out of which s/he need ever return. A nation, a world—in Spanish a *mundillo*—numerous enough to allow us to forget about externals completely.

This would certainly explain why we can generate avant-garde after avant-garde with a guaranteed built-in public and completely avoid, even among those who claim to foreground them, the problems of accommodation and commodity. This too, leaving aside a number of surface enmities, would explain why we need mechanisms such as the writing schools to provide teaching jobs for poets, to produce more cannon fodder for our little internecine wars and to keep up the population levels necessary to the continued health of the *mundillo*. And insofar as the educational policies of our State continue to make sure that a truly viable higher education is the prerogative of an elite, the anchoring of the *mundillo* to the elite academies guarantees the symposium-like quality of all ongoing discussion: pro or con, apparently radical or apparently conservative, we are all part of one machine.

The question of Germany raises the question of nationalism at work now in a hundred contexts across Europe as if we were all back to 1939, 1918, 1870, or before. The cultural energies behind nationalism appear to be so renewed that one can hardly wish the nations ill: only, perhaps (and, of course, in vain regarding some), that they keep, or be kept, so small that they can never again physically be harmful. *Mundillos*, yes, as far as might and right are concerned. May the European Union hear this! As far as the spirit is concerned, one must say no. It is in the international movements that Modernism found its strength; one doubts, in a de facto situation of one-world media, that any difference is possible for Postmodernism. While poetry is nation/culture-bound by virtue of language, that is enough: there is no need of further binding in isolationism. The survival of the species "poet" is at stake and only the refusal of boundaries can save it.

Walls will have fallen too soon for poetry unless such questions are addressed and a great Highway rises on the ruins of them.

1990

On Refining a Model of Poetic Production

I

The origin of poetry? A question kin to the origin of language? Much was said about the breath at one time but as non-scientists we know little, nothing about how thoughts reach the mind, voice the throat. Probably together, inseparable. From inside, or outside? In the former, usually from great depth? In the latter, dictated from out there, above, below, a given side?[1]

Depth analogy: voice sources out of silence. Most dialectics offer that: voice/silence; silence/voice. For most academic critics: voice aspires to, say, light or music and falls back into silence. No word on the *nature* of silence. *De profundis:* under one ground, always another. Now, under unfathomable silence, posit a third realm.

I have proposed a model of poetic *making* with three operative levels. (a) the *Vocal:* that of the single poetic voice, idiolect of self (perhaps "*parole*"), representing

---

1 The refining process in the title of this piece refers to the various versions of the model contained in earlier essays published here. A topic so vast, of course, that it must be addressed at another time. For one formulation, see the *original* version, "Regarding the Issue of 'New Forms,'" in Nathaniel Tarn, *Views from the Weaving Mountain* (Albuquerque: University of New Mexico Press, 1991), 345–46.

self or ego in competition or even conflict with all others in a Babel of voices; (b) the *Silence*, often perceived as underlying the *Vocal* from which the latter seems to arise; (c) again "below" that, the *Choral*—being a co-operative, *non*-competitive, "my-voice-in-all-and-all-in-my-voice" level representing the ideal peace of non-self with all of creation. Models do not require fixed *loci* of elements: the *Choral* can be imagined as positioned "inside," or even "outside," provided it is initially in radical opposition to the *Vocal*.

I argue that *Vocal* and *Choral* are unimaginable from the point of view of the other—they are reciprocal illusions: they only exist in relation to, even though invisible to, each other and not individually. The reality in the effective *making* of poetry, poetic *action* if you will—i.e., the only place where the *Vocal* and the *Choral* can be synchronized as *praxis*—is in the *Silence*.

Anthropologically speaking: in the *Vocal*, self acts in reciprocity with other; in the *Silence,* with self; and, in the *Choral,* without reciprocity—since where there is no-self, there can be no other. The *Vocal* involves competition more than co-operation. Self, voicing its idiolect, can, must in fact to whatever degree, feel menaced by the idiolect of other: menace of influence from whatever quarter (mainly from the self's own generation, not from the previous generation or generations as has been "famously" claimed) and sheer rivalry. Idiolects are rivals in a very small, narrow world, for the same few places in the sun. The "Symposium of the Whole" here is an ideal more than a reality. In the *Vocal*, a self needing to perceive itself as original is constitutively mocked since all others think of themselves too as original.

The question of originality informs *making*. While the poem is ongoing, there is the illusion of the ongoing never being interrupted: Eluard's *poésie ininterrompue* which, for me, carries the sense of *ininterrompable*. Process in flight cannot be imagined to be falling back. The going-on is in the newly-said, essence of life, of immanence. The greatest peak of immanence, as in the Buddhist sage Tilopa, is the "Immanence without expectations" which nevertheless continue to survive: Benjamin's *Fortleben*. But expectations lead to contradictions. Here, all is believed to be "originality": however many voices are voicing together, each one inherently claims that it is unique. It has to make this claim or to make itself unacceptable in a system which is defined by progression. That is the myth of the *Vocal*.

By definition, the *Choral* would appear to be concerned with Utopia. Utopia can involve looking back as well as forward: there have been golden ages / there may be again. Utopia is the exasperation of human *expectation* to its ultimate limits: optimistic (the golden age to come) or pessimistic (either: the past golden age was *too* good ever to be repeated . . . or, [optimistic again: Survival required!] there is enough strength in this iron age for the golden age to be rebuilt). A view arising out of Asian Studies (together with a suggestion from Scholem, probably following Bloch) suggests that expectation is linked with *desire* attempting to en-globe all time, all space. All remembering, all foreseeing—the totality of history—are the constituents and manifestations of *desire*. *Desire* breeds *desire*. Any *desire* leads to another *desire* at the same time as it compulsively returns to an original *desire* again propelling it forward. What the self fails to see is that the inex-haustible circularity of *desire* mocks and renders expectation absurd.

I shall return to this later. To link up with another concern of these essays, let me stress again that the self's subjective desire for originality in the *Vocal* re-quires that the collective be an illusion. As illusion, it is displaced. Backward/downward—in which case, it reads as the myth of origin/presence/*logos*/*archē*. Or forward/upward—in which case it is the future classless society/the end of his-tory/*telos*. At the level of the individual poem, call these elegy (the backward look toward the at-the-time existing *opus*) and lyric (the forward thrust of the new poem toward its eventual life in *opus*). Elegy/lyric are the twin movement which determines any poem, reaching its apex through process, inevitably falling back into structure. In its turn, *Opus* will enter the realm of *Page/Text/Sound*, all possi-bilities of poetry past, present, future.

In this light, the *Choral* might be called structure (or even *langue?*)—that from which process/*parole* rises in optimistic flight, only to fall back at each inevitable landing or end of poem. We might also call it the already-said; tradition; tran-scendence; the realm of the *(living)-dead*; Baudelaire's *"N'importe où pourvu que ce soit hors de ce monde."* All is objective here, note: the subjectivity of the *Vocal* is an illusion. This is the myth of the *Choral.* The *Choral* can be said to enwomb *Page.* The poet often experiences the sense that s/he is in no way bound by time and that s/he is capable of knowing at any given moment the point at which poetry will climax, or cease, either for the time being or entirely. This is part of the "prophetic" power of the poet and it arises from the *Choral.*

The dead should be given some credit, in this model, for some realitude (*stet*): in almost all human groups, except for those of our "West," they are as much alive as those who, temporarily, occupy the seats of the "living." Postulate, then, under what I have called the *Silence*, a not-here, there, elsewhere. You could not call this a *place* which one would normally associate with a self but would now have to see as a non-self—you might have to speak of something like a uni-verse. This not-here would be characterized, not by the *Vocal's* reciprocity of *self-other*, but by the *Choral's* absolute non-reciprocity.

A parenthesis on the *"living-dead."* In so many tribal/archaic situations, the living-dead are distinguished from the dead-dead. The former are those who have had a deep, enduring effect on their society; whose memory is, in effect, ineradicable; whose poetry is uninterruptible: who have had social function. These are the *ancestors,* "returners," "twice-born," prophets risen alive into heaven; never-dead sleeping in caves; once-and-future kings; treasures of the living lineages—not your average dead. It takes time to distinguish the former from the latter and it is certain that society, initially, will almost always confuse the two; showering nonentities with the goods of their world, failing to reward the genuine until it is too late in their initial existence. In the *Choral,* we speak with the dead: those voices out there are the dead: we call them up to talk to us here in the unity of the *Choral* in which fraternity and justice rule for the time being.

Now, what about the *Silence?* Apparently untalkative, it closes everything off but itself, everything that is noise, allows only itself. It is the apparently "real" true present or "*now*" in which the interplay of *Vocal* and *Choral* is decided and acted upon at any moment of the poet's life or *Opus.* That *action* is the pivot of the whole system and nowhere else does any action take place. In this realm of questioning, the poet converses, but *initially* silently, with her/himself and asks her/himself questions. About what? About the status and destination of the poem at hand. This is *self–self* reciprocity.

Here alone *Vocal* and *Choral* can be thought to co-inhere; here the fact that they are reciprocal illusions of each-other can be fully understood, experienced, resolved. If the *Silence* is a reality—and from this viewpoint it is the only reality—it is perhaps the realm where we are brought to investigate "originality," you and I, and assign each one of us, in final reckoning, his or her due. Where we admit, in truth, what is already-said, what is newly-said—if we can ever truly tell them apart. Perhaps it is the realm where we ask why that rush to the new in the *Vocal* is so fierce and unforgiving, why that fall back to the old has to be so crushing. Or come to terms both with the birthing of lyric effervescence and the dying of slow-settling elegy, seeing the one perpetually turning into the other as the cycle of *Opus* thrives. There is a complex process at play: the poem inscribing itself while the poet looks back simultaneously at *Opus* elegiacally and forward lyrically, with the lyrical dominating after the poem reaches apex.

Opus: between individual poem and collective *Page:* all the poems that the poet has written / is writing / will write in a lifetime. The "prophetic" power (shamanism): mining backward-looking (nostalgic) elegiac archeology; predicting and projecting forward lyric architecture. Is the *Silence* an illusion or not? What do you say?

Or is the *Silence* the sense we have that our poems are not, after all, given to us by our own pitiable, small-minded, restricted, egos; that they are not virgin-born out of incest but truly engendered out of the marital air; that they come into being with a task in the world, a mission here, a function, a purpose: i.e., that we have something to do, produce, overcome, stabilize, so that *meaning* might come into being word-in-word with our life?[2]

So that the Sun might be perpetually re-born and held up in the sky day after day by our meanings?

II

I return to the matter of expectation and distinguish between expectation and *attention*. By the former, I imply assurance in a state of awaiting the coming about of a circumstance, favorable or not, out of a moment or *now*. Attention, absolutely and completely open to the moment as it arises (i.e., defines itself) and to the quiddity/*haceitas* of whatever then *is*, has *no* such assurance and does not desire it. It cannot know expectation or desire. In this sense it is Tilopa's definition and what Blake, realizing that the absurd "eternity" of orthodoxies arose out of the inexhaustible circularity of desire, called the true *Eternity*. It is Blake's Eternity that all true poets discover for themselves as the very condition of their existence.

The *Silence* as the only locus of the real has also to be Blake's Eternity. There is no distinction here between the orthodoxies' "sacred" and "secular": the likelihood is that *everything* is either/both depending on viewpoints and circumstances. There is no waiting here, no *deferment* (to refer to Scholem's "worm" in Messianic expectation). On the contrary, the discipline is one which may retain an implication for the future (*hope*, perhaps, instead of expectation) but in which future qua future, as well as past qua past, are studiously disregarded: here is no looking forward, no looking back. The possibility of utopia coming about thus continues to hold—though it is balanced on a virtually agnostic wire for all practical purposes.

We are getting closer, it seems, to the need for a more precise definition of the expression "the *now*." This *now* is often claimed to be the core of concern in the poetics of the New Americans and their successors down to our contemporaries. However, despite interminable reiteration, it never seems to be made clear just how this *now* is perceived by individual poets or, indeed, whether all poets of the same school perceive it identically.

I try to distinguish between (a) an "unguided *now*"—the *now* in a state of expectancy that other "*nows*" will follow but without influencing these; (b) a

---

2 See Nathaniel Tarn, *The Beautiful Contradictions* (New York: Random House, 1970); reprinted in Nathaniel Tarn, *Atitlán/Alashka* (Boulder, CO: Brillig Works, 1979); and partly reprinted in Nathaniel Tarn, *Selected Poems: 1950–2000* (Middletown, CT: Wesleyan University Press, 2002), 41.

"guided "*now*" that gets close to "expectation" again and in which the will does attempt to influence and impose order on the subsequent "*now(s)*"; and (c) a "presential *now*." In the latter, the constantly present attention primes over any sequence of successive "*nows*" to such an extent that it neutralizes these into a single vision: i.e., it gives all "*nows*" what might be called "a single flavor." Another way of putting this might be to say that there can be no plural form of the presential *now*: there can be no presential *nows*. At this time, (a) usually leads to the poetry of post-surrealist disjunctivitis, (b) leads to Creative Writing Schools' poems, while (c) leads to "visionary" poetry in the *praxis*—"visionary" in the Blakean sense.

Yet another way of saying this is to argue that, in the "presential *now*," the point has been reached in which all *nows* are perceived as simultaneously so. Any locus in the future or the past of any *now* can be apprehended not as an extension but as a constituent part of that *now* and discussed as such: there is not, nor can there ever be, any other *now* than this *now*. Such is the source of many phenomena known to poets that I group under the term "prophetic"—from substantial ones in which poets seem to know "instinctively" a great deal about how an *Opus* is born, lives, and dies, to small serendipitous ones related to the ways in which fraternalities or collegialities do or do not occur in poems. There is also the realization that nothing in poetry is ever lost: however apparently discarded, forgotten, or buried, it will resurface, often years later, provided it is important to the *Opus*.

I would like to add to this discussion a social content which I studied once in a paper called "Voice Politic / Body Politic." If we call *Idyll* the centerpiece of the *Silence*, the apex of perfect synchronous conjugation of backward and forward motion (circumventing that motion long enough to achieve perfection), we can perhaps take *Idyll* as the only point of exit, from top or center, out of the system's wheel into a Blakean "*eternity*." From this true, or shall we say *appropriate*, decision, action giving birth to the new poem is taken—action which indeed *is* the new poem. And "appropriateness" here is wisdom *achieved*. What then is this action, this passage from Voice Politic to Body Politic? I am very close to thinking that the poet's *sole crucial* or *vital* function is to be the carrier of a link between the dead and the living, speaking with the living as orators of the dead and addressing the dead on the part of all life in return. The time-bound voices of any given set of the living and their effect on their contemporaries would be but the very briefest of flashes in the cosmic pan. It follows that true poetry cannot speak at all except literally *sub specie aeternitatis*, in the context of an Eternity/All-Time/No-Time. Let me point out, however, to avoid misunderstanding, that such a view categorically does *not* lift poetry out of daily life into some woolly or smoky empyrean: on the contrary, it affords poetry the very best vantage point from which to survey all politics from the cosmic to the regional and local, no subject in any time or space whatsoever being alien to it.

In this sense the *Silence* or seed of the Voice Politic is the only possible source, as *praxis*, of the image of the Body Politic. The community of live and dead is closed to whatever or whoever favors the mere accumulation of "*nows*" in the ever-anxious flux of the *Vocal*. The formation of the image (a version of which might be Robin Blaser's *Image-Nation*) is the sole *praxis* allowed the true poet, more and more so in our very late time since the dead never do less than accumulate. "Hopeless" as it must often seem in the presence of ever-increasing "future shock"—and perhaps *because* of that very "hopelessness," poetry remains, even without expectations, the only *hope*.

III

A while back I wrote a poem, "Self & Other," which ended with these lines:

> *Now, simultaneously,*
> *a burning interest in the next facet*
> *of this life also the absolute*
> *desire to put an end to it.*

This moment in which it was simultaneously possible to think of ending one's life in the moment *and* of wishing to continue living forever seemed extremely relevant to the *Silence* and in fact could be taken as the main aspect of the process which emerges in the *Silence*. Many books back, in *The Beautiful Contradictions*, the concern with a wish to live forever was voiced in the seventeenth stanza of the last section as

> *All of a sudden life is very beautiful*
> *There is an everbloom in the center of my existence*
> *I want life to go on forever*[3]

a statement signifying to me that the enthusiasm and joy arising out of the act of making a poem generate that desire to continue indefinitely. In this essay, I have mentioned a high point in composition where the poet feels that poetry could gush forth forever as a *poésie ininterrompue* (a high point that I call, with a twinge

---

3   See note 2.

of irony as well as following Baudelaire, the *Rapture*). It is the point where the on-going process of the poem being made topples over into the recognition that the poem has to end and the bid is made to achieve Blakean "Eternity."

The *Silence*, in this reading, would be the time in which the poet communes with her/his self as, say, a windowless "monad." Let us now add that this moment is that in which, in my experience, it is most frequently possible, consciously or prob-ably unconsciously in the main, to simultaneously wish for immediate death and eternal life. To me this is a very strange moment. What could be its components?

At its most banal—banal but with the lasting importance of root experiences—the major component is related to the primal question: to be or not to be. While making a poem, however, it is unlikely that this question relates to anything else than the being or not being of the poem at hand, or, more precisely, the question of whether this particular poem is working or not and whether it is worth bring-ing into existence—or not. In an as yet unpublished *Autoanthropology*, I raise the question of what I call the *Throw* (like the throw of a pot in ceramics but there are other analogies) as being of cardinal importance to my concept of this giving birth. I mention there the idiosyncratic sense I had for many years that I could not write a poem before everything else I had to do that day was done; the sense that if I defied this, the poem would burn the paper like fire, leaving nothing behind it; the sense also that, if the first throw was unsuccessful, it would be best to abort the writing and wait, perhaps until the poem had further ripened inside or had re-vealed itself as being incapable of ripening. If all of this is not an aspect of the question whether to die or to live, I hardly know what it is.

A few weeks after defining the apex of the *Idyll* as the *Rapture*, I happened to be reading a book on the neurobiology of emotions and feelings as a result of hav-ing been studying Spinoza and Leibnitz just before that.[4] If I have been reading this book correctly, I believe that the author, starting from Spinoza's "the human mind is the idea of the human body," gives evidence for taking emotions and feel-ings as generated by the interpretation that a human being makes of maps of the state-of-his/her-body at a given moment, the report of that state being fed to the brain by an astoundingly complex system of humoral and neural pathways which are physical-mental components in his/her makeup. Of course, in the average hu-man, the moments continue remorselessly. The conclusion is principally reached by thorough examination of parts of the human brain and the ways in which, if lesions occur in any given part, certain normally exhibited behaviors are correspondingly

---

4   Antonio Damasio, *Looking for Spinoza: Joy, Sorrow and the Feeling Brain* (New York: Harcourt, 2003). The notes to the book (which would benefit by a bibliography as well as notes) give guid-ance to the vast literature of neuroscience. On the *Idyll/Rapture* matter, see note 7.

modified, inhibited, or accelerated. These modifications can range from the completely unconscious to the completely conscious. I am not qualified to link such science with my main concern here. However, the complexity of the ways in which a satisfying homeostatic normalcy is achieved, in which the "feeling mind" strives for "survival with well-being" or we could say a "good, largely satisfying life," is most interesting. It is as if it was following seventeenth-century philosophical preferences for seeking out the best possible solutions to the situations and problems of existence, and it suggests to me that the fate of an art work could be linked to the decision-making processes involved in such neurobiological operations.

How would one begin to list the series of concerns that occur in the cardinal moments of the *Silence*? High up on the list is whether the state of initial emotion, set off, in Damasio's terminology, by an "emotionally competent stimulus" (which a poet might agree to call a "trigger"), is going to carry a sufficient lyric energy to be in play while the force of the poem itself is in question. The wager: can this poem get born or not? To what extent is the poem going to issue from the real-time push of the initial trigger, or to what extent is it going to require buttressing from any one of a large number of, say, symbolic systems? To what extent is previous experience (success/failure // pleasure/pain) with this kind of trigger going to play a role in the making of this poem? Or is this particular trigger going to prove itself radically new, requiring a probably blind lunge into something felt (correctly or not) never to have been experienced before?

Turning to more specific questions of poetics as such, there is concern with the relation of the poet's "breath," the way in which the line sounds to him/her orally, sounded at each moment, to the evolving figure of the poem as it appears to write itself down. Questions of linguistic matter or stuff all the way from letter to syllable, to word, to sentence, to stanza, etc., as well as the uses ranging from colloquial and dialectal to elite verbalization or lexicography and whatever mix of these may or may not be required by the poem. Leading questions in these times of junction and disjunction between elements in the line (assuming verse in the first place: i.e., mainly, not a prose poem), elements between the lines and in the whole poem. Questions of how far the poem can go or will resolve, or not, problems inherent in its ongoing birthing/flowering/flying. One only has to try to think analytically of oneself starting a poem to realize just how many unconscious or conscious mental acrobatics are required by the act.

At the level of *Opus*, there are larger considerations. I have always found it impossible to deal with matters of aesthetic production—be it, *inter alia,* poem, painting composition, etc.—without declaring as a matter of poetic *fiat* (i.e., the poet as a radical free being has decided, said, done this, and there's the end of it) the absolute, unconditioned, unrelated to any other mode of being or action-production, relevance of any given World view to the being and production in question. I am now treating poets as a species apart—a status the world never grants us so that we might as well grant it to ourselves.

A poet (was it Auden?) once said that a striking aspect of the poet's existence—and s/he could have said any artist's—was that s/he never knew, on finishing a poem, whether or not there would be another. This regards each poem as a unique unit, thus it would be begging all questions relating to serial composition, also questioning my model of the roles of lyric/elegy as well as the relation of the latter to the positioning of a given poem in an *Opus*. However, it does point to one major concern of any member of the species poet, which is the question of poetic *survival:* i.e., that of his/her poem, his/her *Opus* (mainly in the realm of the *Vocal*), and the survival of poetry as a whole, home of the *Opus* (mainly in the realm of the *Choral*). At one point, Damasio writes, "In individuals who also have an autobiographical self"—the sense of personal past and anticipated future also known as extended consciousness—"the state of feeling prompts the brain to process emotion-related objects and situations *saliently.*"[5] He is discussing notions of a core-self and an extended, or autobiographical, self discussed in a previous book, *The Feeling of What Happens: Body, Emotion and the Making of Consciousness*[6] I cannot go into this in detail but the mention of "extended consciousness" strikes me here as extremely descriptive, albeit less "mysterious," of what I have called "prophecy" in relation to poetic production. Add that, to a member of the species poet, the survival of poetry is ultimately related to the survival of humankind. Another way of saying this, and of course one is not abrogating anyone else's right to such an act, is that a strong sense of poetry failing in the poet or in his/her community can and does bring about suicide. Kenneth Rexroth once pointed out that almost all the major poets of a named dark time in American history had committed suicide. And for us, in our moment, the extraordinarily complex matter of the Rimbaldian "suicide" still has a haunting power.

Back to "prophecy." In my experience, the mystery of how a certain line comes to a poet remains, in many cases, impossible to pin down. For centuries, this was usually dealt with under the heading of "inspiration." In terms of inspiration, the

5   Damasio, *Looking for Spinoza,* 177, 322.
6   Antonio Damasio, *The Feeling of What Happens: Body, Emotion and the Making of Consciousness* (New York: Harcourt, 1999). This is Damasio's reference: I am not yet fully acquainted with this book.

poem's creation would raise many of the questions I have already outlined, and perhaps primarily the one dealing with the relation of "inspired" lines to lines which are not felt by the poet to be "inspired."

My own preference has been to refer "prophecy"/"inspiration" to the timelessness of the *Silence* especially when the *Choral* is in the ascendant. Prophetic elements may, it seems, come out of the past (out of other poems already secured in the *Opus*) but they may also appear to come out of the future, as, let us say, a temptation, appeal, request, or call, thus directing the poet toward a creation, basically serial, of which s/he had absolutely no conscious pre-cognition. (This does not contradict a "known" serial intent.) That all of this belongs to the unconscious rather than the conscious aspect of the relevant decisions seems clear enough. What may not be so clear is the survival value of this "prophetic" experience. It is essential if everything from the poem to poetry itself is to survive, that poets, in spite of evidence provided by the social situations in which Western civilization increasingly places them (to deal with our own situation for the time being), continue to believe in the *possibility* of survival.

Social scientists have long dealt with major aspects of group interaction, a leading one being *co-operation* versus *conflict.* Damasio, incidentally, never strays far from this pair. Co-operation, unsurprisingly, seems mostly to be more successful in ensuring bio-social survival than its twin, conflict. When the *Vocal,* which is mainly conflictual, and the *Choral,* which is mainly co-operative, find it necessary to come to terms in the *Silence,* considerations of survival probably dictate that, most of the time, allegiance to the *Choral* eventually primes over allegiance to the *Vocal.* It is in that oceanically extensive realm that reciprocity/non-reciprocity die out as a social phenomenon because the realm itself, in its every atom, *is* the totality and therefore the question of reciprocity cannot arise. Because prevailing social conditions among us are so inimical to the existence of poetry and to its power for social action, it is in that predominance of the *Choral* that most poets will acknowledge that they are eventually obliged to *under-stand.* That *Prinzip Hoffnung* too must be the reason why such a large number of young people persist in attempting, adapting Keats, to "be among the poets when they are alive" despite all the facts of the production and reception of contemporary poetry which should absolutely, totally, and permanently discourage them.

There is another way of looking at this. I take the aim of art to be the creation of an order so surprising that it cannot fail to be perceived by receivers as new and different from what went before. This is very much still the case in, say, surrealist procedures or the currently popular disjunctive ones where the main ambition (at the cost of much attrition of the signified) is to reverse standing orders in the realm of the form-giving and formatting imagination and in that of socio-political fact. It is also true, of course, of the procedures I persist in which, by contrast, I have to call "junctive." A requirement of all creation is *selection:* a process of leaving out / leaving in. While there may be an urge to be all-inclusive, or as all-inclusive as possible (few creators immediately attain the desirable level of selectivity), the new order is little by little forced to give up on totality. Personally, my whole life has been haunted by the urge to totality, to the incorporation of what the Chinese call the Ten Thousand Things, on the one hand, and the radical pain of the obligation to select on the other.

If there is a certain kinship between the *Vocal* and selection and one between the *Choral* and totality (the refusal or lack of perceived need for selection), I would argue that a processual *haunting* is the ghost or specter, or perhaps image, of the *Choral* showing through the selecting activity of the *Vocal.* The *Vocal* is obliged to select since the poem must, for survival, have a more original order in any one of a thousand ways than the next one. What would be this *Choral* ghost of the selecting-for-order taking place in the *Vocal*? Doubtless the sempiternal drag of the desire to get rid of the desire to shine and be "original," to lose the reminiscence of ego or *self* on the road to the *no-self.* The feeling of "die now / never die" arises also out of the extreme difficulty of any form of abdication of the *self.*

If the *Rapture* is the apex of the process of poem-making—the moment in which the poem lyrically rising from structure achieves a moment of stasis (the true moment of the *Silence*) just before elegiacally falling back into structure as an achieved order—then, during this timelessness, the melding into each other of the *Vocal* and the *Choral,* the resolution of their conflict or the recognition of the loss inherent in their ignorance of each other, shows itself as totality, as *never lost / never gained: always there ab initio.* For that brief moment, all reciprocity is abolished, all self is merged into an entity which can be seen as a collective *self* but which I prefer to call the *no-self.* At that brief moment, the successful poem emerges as "*wisdom,*" the mind and roar of the Lion. For the poet there is no other "religion."[7]

It is in this moment, when I or another claims to be desperate, that the question of life or death is decided. I always end up by saying that there are two solutions and two only: you jump out the window or you do not. The intuition, or

---

7   In "Archaeology, Elegy, Architecture," the *Rapture* is referred to as the *Idyll.* I confirm that the model needs an environment, "*Idyll,*" of which the "*Rapture*" would be the climax or apex.

even illusion, arising in a poem, informing the poet that there is a moment in which one can simultaneously wish for immediate death and for eternal life, may be indicating that, ultimately speaking in the realm of *no-self,* there is no difference. After having climbed *that* mountain, the process of fighting for survival can continue.

Ombligo de Tesuque, 12.21–26.04 to 10.20–31.05

Section Four
Critical Study and Interview
by Shamoon Zamir

On Anthropology & Poetry

An Interview with Nathaniel Tarn

by Shamoon Zamir

Losing the Way in a Common World: An Introduction

Throughout the twentieth century there has been a sustained dialogue between American poetry and anthropology—from Pound's readings in Chinese culture and the works of Leo Frobenius, to the contemporary translation and reconsideration of primitive poetries by Jerome Rothenberg and others participating in the Ethnopoetics project. The crossing of cultural and disciplinary boundaries is not exclusive to the poetry of our time, but the ambition of this particular poetry must be understood, as Nathaniel Tarn himself points out below, in the specifically modern context of "the planet getting smaller and smaller"—a process Robert Duncan has referred to as "the drama of our time . . . the coming of all men into one fate, 'the dream of everyone, everywhere.'"[1] In an age in which contacts between cultures have been shaped by complex and often violent histories and by unprecedented rates of acceleration in communication, the meanings and consequences of such a common human horizon are diverse to say the least. The turn to anthropology has been part of the poets'

Dr. Shamoon Zamir is Reader in American studies, King's College, University of London. Slight alterations in the original have covered changes after publication.
1 Robert Duncan, "Rites of Participation," pt. 1, *Caterpillar* 1 (1967): 6.

attempt to be true to the range and contradictions of this diversity—this notwith-standing the often treacherous nature of twentieth-century literary politics, nor the fact that anthropology has had to work within imperial histories, though by no means always for an imperial project. At its best, anthropology has promised the rev-elation of a common world whose commonality is guaranteed paradoxically by its very plurality. But as a science its way of knowing this world has been very different to poetry's and, therefore, in its dialogue with anthropology, poetry has had also to consider the nature of its own way of knowing and imagining this world.

Tarn's work offers sustained investigations of all aspects of this confluence of "disciplines." His contribution to the particular poetic and disciplinary history sketched here can be characterized, quite objectively, as unique. The claim for such distinctiveness does not rest on the fact that Tarn has been both an anthropologist and a poet (Eliot's academic studies included anthropology, Gary Snyder was a stu-dent of anthropology, and the Native American poet Wendy Rose is an anthropolo-gist, to name a few); it is based rather on the *extent* to which he has been both an anthropologist and a poet (he has produced substantial bodies of work as both), and *also* on the fact that he has explored at great length the relationship of the two disci-plines not only in his poetry but also in numerous essays. In addition, unlike the other poets mentioned above, Tarn is American by choice, having immigrated to the United States at the close of the 1960s. In terms of his place in American poetry, this inevitably makes him an insider-outsider; as far as the dialogue between poetry and anthropology is concerned, it means that he brings to it a rich knowledge of a Euro-pean tradition of interaction between literature, social science, and speculative thought quite distinct from the American one. Tarn was first trained in anthropol-ogy by the likes of Lévi-Strauss and Griaule in Paris in the early 1950s, and was at that time also involved in a literary scene that included Breton and other surrealists. It is not surprising then that he can draw with confidence on both French literary experiments which have used and transmuted anthropological sources and experi-ence (he has written on Michel Leiris and Artaud, and translated Victor Segalen),[2] and a social scientific tradition which (in the works of theorists like Durkheim, Mauss, and Lévi-Strauss himself) has not severed its links with philosophy.[3]

2   Nathaniel Tarn, "Michel Leiris, Timor Mortis, and the Peopled Self: A Reading of *L'Afrique Fan-tôme* as Auto-Anthropology," in this volume; Nathaniel Tarn, "The Search for the 'Primitive' Out-side and Inside," in this volume; and Victor Segalen, *Stelae,* trans. Nathaniel Tarn (Santa Barbara, CA: Unicorn Press, 1969).

3   For comments on the philosophical aspects of this social scientific tradition, see E. Michael Mendelson, "Some Present Trends of Social Anthropology in France," *The British Journal of Soci-ology* 9, no. 3 (1958): 251–70. (N.B.: most of Tarn's work as anthropologist has been published un-der the heteronym E. Michael Mendelson.)

Born in Paris in 1928, Tarn spent some of his childhood in Belgium and then, at the age of eleven, was evacuated to England just before the start of the war.[4] After completing an undergraduate degree in history and English at Cambridge, Tarn returned to Paris and studied anthropology. Attention to the intricate symbolic system of Dogon cosmology and ritual offered by Griaule, Germaine Dieterlen, and others prepared the way for Lévi-Strauss's structuralist analyses of primitive classification and myth. These studies, along with Paul Lévy's courses on the relationship of folk and Buddhist traditions, were to have a lasting impact on Tarn's thinking.[5] They reinforced a childhood fascination with classification and system (a dream of order formed, at least in part, in the midst of geographical displacement and the chaos of war) and also provided a point of contact with Surrealism's interests in initiation and esoteric traditions.[6] Tarn's later experience as both poet and ethnographer would deepen the understanding of symbolic systems by opening it up to a sense of historical process and contradiction.

In 1951 Tarn was awarded a Smith-Mundt-Fulbright Scholarship and continued his anthropological training with graduate work at the University of Chicago, in the company of such notable American scholars as Robert Redfield, Milton Singer, Fred Eggan, and Sol Tax (he also attended Melville Herskovits's classes at Northwestern and met frequently with Paul Radin). Redfield, Tarn's doctoral supervisor, was a pioneer in studies of world view and social change, particularly the modernization of folk and primitive communities. Tarn's Ph.D., which was based on fieldwork in a village on the shores of Lake Atitlán in Guatemala, combined these concerns with his own interests in religious symbolism. Much of Tarn's published Latin American ethnography is centered on the figure of Maximón, an icon in whom Christian and indigenous Mayan beliefs meet and whose hybrid iconography reveals a complex history of cultural contact and violence.[7] With the

4 All biographical information presented in this introduction is drawn from several sources: a long recorded dialogue with Tarn, of which the interview presented here is a part; several essays in Nathaniel Tarn, *Views from the Weaving Mountain* (Albuquerque: University of New Mexico Press, 1991), and in this volume; the chronology in Lee Bartlett, *Nathaniel Tarn: A Descriptive Bibliography* (Jefferson, NC: McFarland, 1987), 1–4; and Tarn's own autobiographical essay in *Gale's Contemporary Authors Autobiography Series*, vol. 26, ed. Shelly Andrews (Detroit, MI: Gale, 1997), 271–89.

5 Nathaniel Tarn, "The Choral Voice: A Diptych re Anthropology and Poetry" (1986), in this volume; Nathaniel Tarn, "Reflections on the Work of Claude Lévi-Strauss" (1967), in Tarn, *Views from the Weaving Mountain*, 161–68; and E. Michael Mendelson, " 'The Uninvited Guest': Ancilla to Lévi-Strauss on Totemism and Primitive Thought," in *The Structural Study of Myth and Totemism*, ed. Edmund Leach (London: Tavistock Publications, 1967), 119–39.

6 Nathaniel Tarn, "André Breton, Anthropology, and the Limits of Culture" (1967), in this volume.

7 Tarn's fieldwork at Santiago Atitlán resulted in a massive 600-page text, "Religion and World View in a Guatemalan Village" (1957). This was never published but was preserved as Microfilm no. 52 of the Microfilm Collection of Manuscripts on Middle American Cultural Anthropology at the

doctorate still to be completed, Tarn returned to London in 1953 and continued work as a postgraduate student at the London School of Economics with Raymond Firth, Isaac Schapera, S. F. Nadel, and Maurice Freedman. Once the Ph.D. was out of the way (1957), Tarn undertook eighteen months of research on religion, politics, and esoteric Buddhism in Burma. The published work on Burma deals with two main areas: the modern relationship of *Sangha* (the Buddhist order of monks) and state politics, understood in the light of earlier periods, and the blending of Buddhist and folk elements in what Tarn refers to as "messianic" Buddhism, cults focused on the future Buddha Maitreya. It is a long way from Guatemala and Mayan-Christian hybrids to Burmese Buddhism, but there are clear continuities. In the work on messianic Buddhism, Tarn is again dealing with a complex symbolic order and its historical meanings, this time as an ambivalent vision of redemptive kingship and national independence—a response to colonial and post-colonial conditions. In the study of *Sangha* and state, the relationship of worldly affairs and a religion assumed to be detached from such is given within a meticulous account of a more pragmatic and institutional political history.[8]

Back from Burma, Tarn was appointed lecturer in Southeast Asian anthropology at the School of Oriental and African Studies in London and had the prospect of a productive career in the field. But in 1967 he resigned his post and turned his

---

University of Chicago Libraries. The Ph.D. was a drastically shortened version of this text demanded by Redfield and was later revised and published in Spanish; E. Michael Mendelson, *Los Escándalos de Maximón: Un estudio sobre la religión y la visión del mundo en Santiago Atitlán* (Guatemala City, Guatemala: Tipographía Nacional, 1965). See also Nathaniel Tarn, "The King, the Traitor and the Cross: An Interpretation of a Highland Maya Religious Conflict" (1958), in Tarn, *Views from the Weaving Mountain*, 91–101; E. Michael Mendelson, "A Guatemalan Sacred Bundle," *Man* 57 (1958): 121–26; and E. Michael Mendelson, "Maximón: An Iconographical Introduction," *Man* 59 (1959): 56–60. For comments on Redfield, see Nathaniel Tarn, "The Literate and the Literary: The Anthropological Discourse of Robert Redfield" (1981), in Tarn, *Views from the Weaving Mountain*, 169–94; E. Michael Mendelson, "World View," in the *International Encyclopedia of the Social Sciences*, ed. David Sills, vol. 16 (New York: Macmillan & Free Press, 1968), 567–79; and E. Michael Mendelson, "Introduction," in his *Los Escándalos*.

8   For the work on Burma and Buddhism, see, *inter alia*, Nathaniel Tarn, "The Sage of the Weaving Mountain" and "Buddhism and the Burmese Establishment," in Tarn, *Views from the Weaving Mountain*, 102–15, 116–31; E. Michael Mendelson, "Buddhism and Politics in Burma," *New Society*, no. 38 (June 20, 1963): 8–10; E. Michael Mendelson, "The Uses of Religious Scepticism in Modern Burma," *Diogenes* 41 (1963): 94–116; E. Michael Mendelson, "A Messianic Buddhist Association in Upper Burma," *Bulletin of the School of Oriental and African Studies* 24 (1961): 560–80; E. Michael Mendelson, "Religion and Authority in Modern Burma," *The World Today* 16, no. 3 (1960): 110–18; E. Michael Mendelson, *Sangha and State in Burma: A Study of Monastic Sectarianism and Leadership*, ed. John P. Ferguson (Ithaca, NY: Cornell University Press, 1975); and John P. Ferguson with E. Michael Mendelson, "Masters of the Buddhist Occult: The Burmese Weikzas," Contributions to Asian Studies 16 (Leiden: Brill, 1981), 62–88.

back on academic anthropology (though he would publish some work in anthropology in the years to come). Since his return from Burma, Tarn had in fact led a double life as both anthropologist and poet, keeping the two strictly separate. He had published his first book of poems, *Old Savage/Young City* (Jonathan Cape, 1964); and translated Pablo Neruda's *The Heights of Macchu Picchu* (Jonathan Cape, 1966). Torn between what he has referred to as "the recording angel" of anthropology and "the creative angel" of poetry, Tarn confirmed a life-long wish in 1967 to make poetry his primary work. At this time he became founding general editor of Cape Editions and a founding director of Cape Goliard Press. These two were to be among the most innovative publishing ventures in Britain in the 1960s, the former a remarkable international series of short multi-disciplinary texts and the latter a bold attempt to combine the distributive power of a large commercial press like Jonathan Cape with the flexibility and imagination of a small press like Goliard.[9]

Drawn to America since his childhood and more and more engaged in his own writing with the innovations of the "New American" poetry (between them, Cape, Cape Editions, and Cape Goliard published many American poets, including Zukofsky, Olson, and Duncan), Tarn immigrated to the States in 1970. Since then he has held a professorship in the Department of Comparative Literature at Rutgers University, has taught at many other institutions, has done further fieldwork (though not with the aim of producing traditional ethnographies), and has continued to write poetry and to explore issues in Ethnopoetics. In 1984 Tarn took early retirement and moved to New Mexico, where he lives today.

Since the first book of poems in 1964, there have been about twenty others. It is, therefore, impossible to generalize either about Tarn's poetry or about its relationship to his anthropology. Tarn is at home in both the long, book-length poem where a complex range of cultural and intellectual materials are engaged with, and, in books such as *October* (Trigram, 1969), *The Microcosm* (Membrane, 1977), and *At the Western Gates* (Tooth of Time, 1985), with simpler lyric modes. It is in the longer poems perhaps that the use of anthropological materials is most immediately visible. *Lyrics for the Bride of God* (New Directions, 1975) is an extended meditation on the *Shekhinah*, the bride of God in Jewish mysticism, in all her manifestations and so a mining of world mythologies in which poet and anthropologist

---

9   For more on Tarn's work for Cape Editions and Cape Goliard, see Shamoon Zamir, "Bringing the World to Little England: Cape Editions, Cape Goliard and Poetry in the Sixties. An Interview with Nathaniel Tarn. With an Afterword by Tom Raworth," in *Literary Devolution: Writing in Scotland, Ireland, Wales and England*, ed. E. S. Shaffer, vol. 19 of *Comparative Criticism* (Cambridge: Cambridge University Press, 1997), 263–86; and Bartlett, *Nathaniel Tarn*, 103–5.

inform each other. *The House of Leaves* (Black Sparrow, 1976) is a book of arrival, an attempt to make the newly adopted country a home through an exploration of the Americas that draws on early ethnographic experience and the life in Europe as counterpoints. That concern with the idea and experience of America continues in the more recent *Seeing America First* (Coffee House, 1989). *Alashka* (Brillig Works, 1979) is a collaborative work. Co-written with Janet Rodney and based on various extended working visits to Alaska, it draws on a variety of modes—ethnography, travelogue, cultural commentary, naturalist description, love poem.[10] However, it is in *The Beautiful Contradictions* (Cape Goliard, 1969), Tarn's third book of poetry, that the connections between the poetry and both his anthropological work and his anthropologically informed reflections on poetics are apparent in the most systematic way. This is not because Tarn set out in the book to *illustrate* his theories—the essays in which these theories are formulated were all written *after,* mostly well after, the book was published; it is rather that the essays and the other long poems that follow continue and transform the work that was begun in *The Beautiful Contradictions* (which may be why Tarn now thinks of the book as in some ways the proper point of departure for an understanding of his oeuvre).[11]

At the close of its eighth section the poem proposes that "There is no worthier subject for poetry in our times / than the fear that the races should rise and rend each other." In the face of this fear the poet concludes that "we have no alternative to taking the whole world as our mother" (section 1). And the poem *does* draw on cultural, political, and historical materials from all corners of the globe (Latin American religions and politics; Buddhism, Jewish, and Central European history from midcentury; Australian aboriginal culture; classical and medieval lore about winds and animals; the Oedipus mythology; Wagner's *Ring* cycle . . .). We are given fragments and collages seen through the eyes of many masks, not the singular

10 Other important books by Nathaniel Tarn include *Where Babylon Ends* (London: Cape Goliard, 1968); *A Nowhere for Vallejo* (New York: Random House, 1971); *The Persephones* (Santa Barbara, CA: Christopher's Books, 1974); *Birdscapes, with Seaside* (Santa Rosa, CA: Black Sparrow, 1978); *The Desert Mothers* (Grenada, MS: Salt-Works Press, 1984); *Flying the Body* (Los Angeles: Arundel Press, 1993); *The Architextures* (Tucson, AZ: Chax Press, 2000); *Three Letters from the City: The St. Petersburg Poems, 1968–98* (Santa Fe, NM, and St. Petersburg, Russia: Weaselsleeves Press and Borey Art Center, 2001); *Selected Poems: 1950–2000* (Middletown, CT: Wesleyan University Press, 2002); and *Recollections of Being* (Cambridge, UK, and Sydney, Australia: Salt Publishing, 2004).

11 *Atitlán/Alashka*, a collection of all of Tarn's major books up to 1979 (excluding *Lyrics for the Bride of God* and *House of Leaves*), begins with brief extracts from the first two books of poems by way of introduction, but *The Beautiful Contradiction* and *October* are the earliest complete books to be included. See Nathaniel Tarn and Janet Rodney, *Atitlán/Alashka* (Boulder, CO: Brillig Works, 1979).

coherence of panorama. The drive to excessive plenitude is a self-conscious "search for the ultimate simplicity through an attempt to grasp the unity of the 'ten thousand things,'" the Buddhist notion of detachment being one informing idea behind what Tarn means here by "simplicity."[12] Two organizing "models" help structure the materials: initiation and the medieval *mappa mundi* kept in Hereford Cathedral. "Structure" and "process" are presented as dynamic relation in the interplay of these two models. The interest in maps relates to Tarn's fascination with topographical organization in myth and ritual.[13] The poem, however, does not imitate the forms and content of a particular initiatic rite drawn from anthropological sources or fieldwork experience. Rather, Tarn uses anthropological theorizations of initiation to give form to his poetic persona's willed transformations of himself through a negotiation of a complex symbolic system (or map) of Tarn's own making. Tarn understands initiation as a "revelation of the true names of things" through a symbolic system which, for all its complexity, is always a limited model of the world and which uses this very limit to acknowledge that the total phenomenal world is not knowable.[14] The process of transformation proves, then, to be a paradoxical one because it leads to the realization that the moment of detached simplicity may be the very moment in which one is returned to the immeasurable plurality of the world.

The nature of this paradoxical process can be elaborated by taking a brief look at an early Tarn essay on initiation theory and by then tracing the impact of its conclusions on the later poetic thinking. In "Initiation and the Paradox of Power" (1965), published only a few years before *The Beautiful Contradictions*, Tarn rejects those interpretations of initiation which see it only in terms of the acquisition of a fixed body of knowledge or as a rite of passage which is part of an equally fixed socializing process. Instead, he argues that in its most complex forms initiation can be a continuous educative process, one in which the ceaseless drama of self-improvement and growth into self-reliance is valued as "social recognition" and "social conformity and integration" (*Views from the Weaving Mountain*, 132; and in this volume, 126). In anthropological terms, initiation not only binds the initiate into a nexus of reciprocity but also takes him toward a state of non-reciprocity. Tarn illustrates the point by drawing on his own work in Burma, work in which he has "attempted to see the whole complex continuum of Burmese religion . . . in the

12 From author's statement in the Cape Goliard section of the Jonathan Cape catalogue for Spring–Summer 1969, 38.
13 See especially Nathaniel Tarn, "Metaphors of Relative Elevation, Position and Ranking in Popol Vuh," *Estudios de Cultura Maya* 13 (1981): 105–23.
14 See Mendelson, "World View," 267–79.

light of initiatic theory." For Tarn meditation, "the primary instrument of Buddhist self-enhancement," is "a process of looking at the world and concluding, after examining all its aspects, that it is not worth the having. One after the other various forms of attachment are sloughed off together with the reciprocal action which they imply." In some schools, Tarn continues, "the meditator may discover eventually that all these attachments are the mere shadow-play of mind, thus drawing into 'himself' all the different aspects of the world and leaving only the task of putting an end to 'himself.' We thus have three stages: the first, while still in society, we may call self–other reciprocity; the second, after entrance into meditation, self–self reciprocity; the third wipes out reciprocity altogether, and can be termed non-reciprocity" (this volume, 129). In several later essays, Tarn transforms this three-stage process into "a model of poetic *making* with three operative levels: the *Vocal,* the *Silence,* and the *Choral.*"[15] Elsewhere Tarn describes the *Choral* level as perhaps the point at which "the *other* will be met and . . . the poet will come into his/her own society":

> The original, unimpeded, uninterrupted voice is many, not one, for the more itself it is, the deeper it reaches into its own inner nature, the more, beautiful paradox, does it come upon the truth of all being while also becoming the not-itself. The voice is not reached by going to others; it is met by going to one's own deepest self and discovering how un-self-ish it can be. To "become an informant," in the final sense, is to let a voice speak which is not the property of any one person—or only such in the liberality of allowing all voice to speak within it. To be an anthropologist in the final sense is no longer a bringing of many voices, the surface of other voices, to the collective singing place and exhibiting these voices in an ordered and governed fashion. It is a letting be of voice, in the confidence that the deeper it can go and the more free it is to express itself, the more *collective* it will be heard to be. (In this volume, 184)

Tarn is quick to follow this up with the recognition that "it is a far cry from where we are to such a *Chorus*" (in this volume, 186). But he is also right to point out that such a utopian vision marks out the outer limit or ultimate horizon for a writing attempting to bring together anthropology and literature because "the genre so long looked for which would assure a complete union of the poetic and anthropological enterprises (should such be desirable) lies *not* in the keeping of the anthropologist who cannot, for all his/her efforts, get beyond *belles lettres,* but with the

---

15 Nathaniel Tarn, "Voice Politic/Body Politic," *Talus* 10 (1997): 43–47. All further quotations from this text are simply identified as "Voice" (much of "Voice" has been included in "On Refining a Model of Poetic Production," in this volume). On *Vocal, Silence,* and *Choral,* see all essays in this book's section three.

poet who, in theory, still can. This is the question of a language which, without turning away from scientific veracity, abdicates not one jot of its literary potential. Undoubtedly utopian, the search is at home in poetry, incurably utopian, and probably nowhere else" (in this volume, 88).[16]

The notion that the singularity of voice may be the necessary condition for the emergence of a collective voice (an idea that may have affinities with the stress on the particular as the point of access to the universal in William Carlos Williams, Charles Olson, and other American poets) is radically different as a response to the contemporary dilemmas of anthropology than the turn to the dialogic in postmodern anthropology. This is so at least in relation to those cases where a theatrical display of multiple voices ruffles the surface of the postmodern ethnography without extending to deeper re-assessments of the nature of writing, authority, and scientific epistemology. At the same time, in order to adequately assess the nature of Tarn's response to the contemporary condition of anthropology, the deeply Romantic nature of his theorization of voice would have to be critically interrogated from the perspectives of contemporary social science and poetry alike.

Such a critical examination must await another occasion, but here it may be helpful to elaborate the description of Tarn's work a little further. The nature of Tarn's model of poetic production can be more fully suggested by putting his notions of the *Choral* and the *Silence* alongside each other and by looking at the way in which he conceptualizes the *Silence* as the place where poetic praxis or action takes place.

If in Tarn's "model of poetic *making*" the *Choral* is a necessary utopia, the *Vocal* is also unreal. In "Regarding the Issue of 'New Forms,'" Tarn takes the *Vocal* and the *Choral* as "two 'mythical' or 'illusory' poles of a continuum giving depth to the roles of 'self'/'non-self' in poetic production, the only 'real' level being that of the *Silence* out of which and into which such production periodically falls back." In so far as the *Choral* is utopian it is tied to expectation because "utopia is the exasperation of human expectation to its ultimate limits" ("Voice," 44). Following on his studies in Buddhism and Jewish mysticism, Tarn links expectation to "*desire* as the motor of all unenlightened human existence," noting that "what we fail to see is that the vast and inexhaustible circularity of desire mocks and renders expectation absurd" ("Voice," 44). If the *Choral* is tied to expectation (and one could argue the same for the *Vocal*, albeit in different terms, though Tarn does

---

16   An experiment, frustrated by market conditions, in finding such a language is Nathaniel Tarn, *Scandals in the House of Birds: Shamans & Priests on Lake Atitlán* (New York: Marsilio Publishing, 1997). See note 29.

not extend his argument in this direction), then the *Silence* is defined by "atten-tion." Tarn's distinguishing of attention from expectation brings out the character of the *Silence* as visionary perception:

> By expectation, I imply assurance in a state of awaiting the coming about of a favourable or unfavourable circumstance arising out of a moment or "now." Attention, absolutely and completely open to the moment as it arises (i.e. defines itself) and to the quiddity or *haceitas* of whatever then is, has *no* such assurance and does not desire it. In fact, it cannot know any desire or expectation. In these senses, it is what the great Tibetan scholar Tilopa defined as "Immanence without expectation" and what Blake, realizing that the absurd "eternity" of orthodoxies arose out of the inexhaustible circularity of desire attempting to englobe all time and all space, called the true *Eternity* found only in attention to the moment or *Now*. It is Blake's *Eternity* that all true poets discover for themselves as the very condition of their existence as poets. ("Voice," 44; also, in this volume, 209)

The "synchronous conjugation" of past and future in the present is what makes the *Silence* "the locus of true, or shall we say 'appropriate' action which gives birth to the new poem" ("Voice," 46).

It is likely that for some readers Tarn's deployment of the hermetic languages of initiation, Buddhism, and prophetic Romanticism constitutes a barrier to en-gagement with his work either in terms of contemporary poetry or as a critical di-alogue with social science. I cannot here offer a proper critical examination of the use of such languages and traditions by Tarn or by other American poets, such as Robert Duncan, Rothenberg, and Robert Kelly, with whose work Tarn's can be aligned. However, by means of a brief comparison of Tarn's essays with Hannah Arendt's meditations on speech, detachment, and plurality in her *The Human Condition* (1958), it may be possible to follow a different tack and to step back a lit-tle from Tarn's work and to re-situate it in the context of a broader post–World War II concern with planetary diversity and unity.[17]

Arendt begins her extraordinary exploration of what has been referred to above as a common human horizon with a meditation on the meanings of the first im-ages of the earth seen from outer space. She speaks of her fear that for some, these images invite a flight from the earth itself and so an abandoning of what she calls the human condition. Arendt approaches the human condition through an analysis of the *via activa* in which she distinguishes between labor, work, and action. Labor "is the activity which corresponds to the biological process of the human body" be-cause it is concerned with "the vital necessities" which must be "produced and fed

---

17   Hannah Arendt, *The Human Condition* (Chicago: University of Chicago Press, 1958), 1–6. Here-after cited as *HC*.

into the life process." Work corresponds to the idea of fabrication and "provides an artificial world of things." "The human condition of work is worldliness" and its logic is the logic of means and ends, the transformation of the world by violence. By contrast to labor and work, the condition of action is freedom from necessity and it is precisely this "un-worldliness" which makes it the supreme sphere for political activity (and which also makes the consequences of action unpredictable) (*HC,* 7, 243–47). Un-worldly because mere necessity and utility cannot be included in the political realm. The activities that constitute this realm are action and speech, and Arendt's commentary on speech as a form of action can help link back her argument to Tarn's. Discussing the Greek city-state, she writes that there "speech and action were considered to be coeval and coequal, of the same rank and the same kind; and this originally meant not only that most political action, in so far as it remains outside the sphere of violence, is indeed transacted in words, but more fundamentally that finding the right words at the right moment, quite apart from the information or communication they may convey, is action" (*HC,* 26). It follows from this idea of speech as political activity among free citizens that "action, the only activity that goes on directly between men without the intermediary of things or matter, corresponds to the human condition of plurality, to the fact that men, and not Man, live on the earth and inhabit the world" (*HC,* 7). In plurality human unity exists in absolute separateness: "Plurality is the condition of human action because we are all the same, that is, human, in such a way that nobody is ever the same as anyone else who ever lived, lives, or will live" (*HC,* 8). This condition of plurality Arendt also refers to as "the condition of the common world" (*HC,* 57).

Both Arendt and Tarn define "true and 'appropriate' action" as a form of detachment from the world (a detachment from necessity and the logic of utility in Arendt, and from expectation and desire in Tarn), as related to a plurality that is a commonality in the midst of individuality (Tarn's "my-voice-in-all-and-all-in-my-voice"), through speech (Arendt's activity of "right words" among free citizens and Tarn's "original, unimpeded, and uninterrupted voice"), and also through its unpredictability (Tarn's sense that there can be no "assurance" of outcome in the state of the *Silence*). And Tarn, like Arendt, is working from the awareness that there is no "real alternative to universalism, not once the planet has been SEEN from the outside" (in this volume, 44).

At the start of one of his essays which deals in most detail with the coming together of anthropology and poetry in his own work, Tarn places a quotation from Hawthorne as an epigraph. It reads, "Amid the seeming confusion of our mysterious world, individuals are so nicely adjusted to a system, and systems to one another, and to a whole, that, by stepping aside for a moment, a man exposes himself to a fearful risk of losing his place forever" (in this volume, 179). It is clear from Tarn's extraordinary and wide-ranging body of work that he has never feared loss but has in fact actively sought it out. A brief and largely descriptive introduction such as this one cannot hope to do justice to the full achievement of that risk taking. The dialogue that follows begins to probe some of the critical issues only touched upon in the introduction.

Interview

(The interview presented here is part of a longer conversation that took place at Nathaniel Tarn's home in New Mexico over a two-day period on September 4 and 5, 1996. It was edited and revised by both participants, and a small amount of new material was added during this process.)

Lévi-Strauss's work has clearly been very important to you and you've used structuralist analyses in some of your readings of literary texts (of Blake, for example, in "The Heraldic Vision" essay or the commentary on the Popol Vuh*),*[18] *but Structuralism doesn't play a very central role in your ethnographic work. Why is that?*

First of all I *was* working in an Anglo-American context where one could not yet adopt Structuralism wholeheartedly with impunity. (Edmund Leach, Mary Douglas, and so on came later.) Secondly, I was fascinated by Structuralism as a mental game—I've always said these are all games of the mind and Lévi-Strauss happens to have a fantastic mind. But I did not see myself as called upon to be structuralist in situations where I did not necessarily see the need of it. Certainly, in what I was doing in Burma there wasn't all that much. I suppose I could have angled the Guatemalan material to a certain extent in that direction, except that working for Robert Redfield I had to come up with something different. With "The King, the Traitor and the Cross" [1958; in *Views,* 91–101] you get a certain amount of that kind of schematic, oppositional way of going about things but that's as far as it gets.

I'm interested in Structuralism because it clearly plays an important part in your thinking about modern American poetry, particularly your critique of what you see as an over-emphasis on process—*from Olson down. For you process seems, in part at least, to arise out of structure and must also inevitably return to it. In your commentary on Blake, for example, you say that the movement is always integration–disintegration–reintegration or, in your terms from the essay,* ecclesia–sparagmos–ecclesia

18   See Tarn, "The Heraldic Vision" in this volume, and Tarn,"Metaphors of Relative Elevation."

(nova): *I'm just wondering whether from another perspective it isn't possible to argue that the representation of that process in Blake is a necessary fiction about a process that is actually* sparagmos–ecclesia–sparagamos. *In other words, that structure arises out of contradiction and then returns to contradiction. I guess one could argue that this is just a chicken-and-egg argument. On the other hand there may be more at stake here than a mental game. That would bring us back to Lévi-Strauss's well-known critique of Sartre at the end of* The Savage Mind. *I can't now recall the debate in detail but I guess Sartre's argument would be that structure is the result of contradiction and returns to contradiction.*

That's interesting. I guess it's very much a matter of temperamental orientation ultimately. I do indicate something of a chicken-and-egg dilemma in "The Heraldic Vision" essay, but Blake's and all other poems move in one direction only. I suppose I am more sympathetic to, and comfortable with, order than to disorder. And therefore ultimately I have considered order as the normal state. That is probably not very good Buddhism!—if I were to apply Buddhist theory to it, since for Buddhism everything is in flux and impermanent. In a sense disorder is the status quo over which one establishes some kind of control but that can never possibly be lasting. Poets obviously work with their deepest instincts and my deepest instincts have been for order, though I may be in the process of becoming more Hegelian now. I also think that the esoteric tradition (which, after all, is a reality—look at the work of Frances Yates) would, on the whole, tend to favor order–disorder–back to order rather than the other way around in the sense that religion (to which esotericism is, after all, reasonably kin) does have a tendency to favor order against disorder. Of course, the archetypal notion of creation is of something coming out of formlessness into form. Now, the way I kind of beat that into the shape of something which is endless, which has eternal return built into it and which satisfies both structure and process, is by positing that there was an original order from which one fell (which as I see it is the Blakean pattern) and to which one returns. You might recall "*Opus*" as pre *and* post "*Poem.*" I really do think that is the interpretation of most initiatic systems. I would argue probably that even in the non-spiritual forms of initiation (which probably kicked off the whole process anyway) you would take a child out of the structure of its birth kin and pass it through extreme disorder (fear, pain, disorientation, and so on) into a new orientation: that of the kin of affiliation. So by and large, while I can see the chicken-and-egg dimension of your question, I think that both in my work, and in the tradition which it to a certain extent fits into, there is a priority given to an initial structural state. One of the things that happens in the "Heraldic Vision" essay is trying to decide that this is actually the case. But in many ways the essay remains open—I'm sure that, given *x* twist or *y* twist, it can suddenly go off into the other direction. But I've never thought a poet (or anybody in fact) should be caught in a particular position from which s/he can't retreat or move—and that's the benefit of the whole *process* notion. And don't forget there's another matter that governed all of this, I'm sure you saw it, that here I was landing as a structuralist among all these Whitheadian processualists. Everybody from Kelly to Quasha. Process, process, process. As that statement from Olson puts it, "The only thing that doesn't change is the will to change." So I had to make sense of myself in that respect too.

I'm deliberately playing Devil's advocate to some extent. The "Heraldic Vision" essay was first published in Jerome Rothenberg and Dennis Tedlock's Ethnopoetics journal Alcheringa *in 1976 and it was a paper that you had delivered at the first Ethnopoetics Symposium. How was the essay received at the symposium, or after?*

My feeling is that it was probably ignored. Obviously those guys figured that I had caught on to something that they were not all that friendly to. But I also remember feeling that structure and process are two things which belong indissolubly together and anybody who tries to pretend to the contrary is bullshitting. All these guys, to that extent, no matter how marvelous the products (because in the end, who gives a shit about the theory—when it comes down to it, it's the poem— if the poem survives, fine), are kidding themselves. And I think at one point I used the comparison of the perpetual revolution idea, always one of the left-wing options but nonsense. I always come back to very, very simple things. The fact that a table is a table, a cup a cup, etc. I don't care how many atomic physicists, or even Buddhists, tell me that this cup will eventually go the way of all impermanence. As far as I'm concerned, for a poet the cup is there and the table is there— unless you are leading to a dissolution of meaning, what I've recently called a "crisis of the signified" (I think I used that in the "Voice Politic/Body Politic" talk at Robin Blaser's big Vancouver birthday bash).

It's a pity the Blaser talk is not in Views *because it is a very good distillation and further elaboration. A lot of material that develops over several essays just comes together there. I've referred to it above as "Voice."*

Well, much of it has been incorporated into the last essay of this volume.

Some of the things you've been saying lead onto some other areas I want to talk with you about. I'm interested in your theoretic and poetic uses of what you refer to variously as hermeticism, initiation, or occultation. In your essay on Breton you write, "Had the notion of occultation, announced with such mastery in Arcane 17, *been truly understood and postulated with the rigor as well as the freshness characteristic of the first surrealist revolution, the movement would have given to the second half of the twentieth century, but with still more nobility and depth than the first had done, a springboard, an enthusiasm, a responsibility, a path."*[19] *At that point you've been talking about the relationship of anthropology and poetry and I am interested in knowing what you meant by that statement.*

There *was*, in the fifties when I was involved with, and thrown out of, the surrealist group in Paris, this great discussion (a transform of discussions that had gone on throughout their history): would the flirtation with Marxism continue forever, or would they accept once and for all to limit their sphere of action—in other words, to give up the overt socio-political, which was far too complicated for them, particularly during the Cold War, and to follow the poet's initiatic pattern which had always been there, and which reached as great a depth as Breton ever reached in *Arcane 17*. However, do not forget that Surrealism *ab initio* saw itself as a revolution of life not just of art.

What was your involvement with the surrealists?

When I was in "public school" in England, evacuated to Cornwall, I would read the surrealist books that I had in French (this was part of my longing for [occupied] France) and I would think that all these people were dead. It was a great myth. When I arrived in Paris after Cambridge I *still* thought they were dead! I wasn't reading them at that point. One day I run into Henri and Nō Seigle, painters who have been friends most of my life. They were part of the movement. I found out that the group was still meeting; they took me there and introduced me. I sat there for about a year, going virtually every Sunday. Breton and I said hello, but I was never part of the "movement." The main friendship was with Octavio Paz. The Seigles were very much on the initiation side and in fact taught me a lot of what I know.

Why did you get thrown out of the surrealist group?

In collaboration with a photographer and Marcel Jacno (a major French typographer—he designed the Gauloise packet and the magnificent Théâtre National Populaire posters, and created several fonts) I did a book called *The Legend of Saint Germain des Prés*. SGP was a really nice place to hang out and, particularly in my first year at the Sorbonne next door, I would spend a lot of time in the cafes . . . which, of course by that time, Sartre and co. had deserted. But not *everybody:* you could still see Prévert, Tzara, others. . . . In the night clubs you had the

19 See the "André Breton" essay in this volume.

famous *chansonniers:* Juliette Greco at the Rose Rouge, Les Frères Jacques, Léo Ferré, all these guys who were part of that *SGP* scene and I just enjoyed it. I wasn't thinking, "This is existentialist and conflicts with the surrealists." It was a place . . . like Greenwich Village. All the tourists were there. So the book was a purely monetary thing but was also amusing, part of my young life. In the end the publisher totally re-wrote my introduction so I was no longer in it though my name was on the front, and he totally failed to pay us. In my naïveté I must have shown it to one of the young surrealists, Jean-Louis Bédouin, who wrote a book on Breton (he never came to anything but was also a friend of the Seigles, who were holding initiatic mini-seminars I joined with him and his lady). He denounced me to Breton. In the meantime, the Seigles had quarreled with the group over the socio-political issue and one day they just got up and left. Whereupon I got up and said, *"Monsieur!"* and left. Nobody's ever gotten over my saying "Monsieur!" to Breton. But it was all pretty naïve youthful stuff.

So there was obviously a social scene that you went to but were you reading the existentialists at the time? Were you reading Sartre and Camus?

Oh yeah. I read them but again not systematically. There was too much work to do in anthropology. I know I read *Le Mur, La Nausée,* and whatever early Sartre was around. I went to see his plays (*Huis Clos, Caligula* . . . all those). And I remember thinking, "You may be interesting as a philosopher but you're a bore as a playwright." And Camus, definitely. I was reading what any typical young person would read at that time.

From a more theoretical point of view this interests me because the Sartre–Lévi-Strauss debate at the end of The Savage Mind *turns up two or three times in your work. It relates to the broader issue of what you just referred to as the dead end of Surrealism's flirting with Marxism and its failure to pursue the initiatic path. Could you expand on that?*

If in all the years where Surrealism was trying to come to terms with Marxism, it hadn't happened and they hadn't agreed, then it meant there was something basically irreconcilable. And that, beyond the liberty of the artist from any party line, was probably the very notion of any kind of "spiritual dimension" to existence. Since I felt that poetry was in many ways related to that dimension, I thought it would serve Breton better to go that path (sanctioned after all by many of his heroes: Blake, Lautréamont, Nerval . . . many of them) and just follow it through thoroughly into this century. Pay more attention to people like Raymond Abellio for instance, or even the *Matin des Magiciens* folks. There was a *lot* of stuff on the horizon which Breton could have pronounced on authoritatively after all those years. Whereas anything he might say about Marxism had probably been said already and was not very profitable. I don't know to what extent in *theory* I would now continue to be as inclined toward the "spiritual dimension" as I was. I can't help feeling that over the years, faced with planetary annihilation, one begins to have more serious doubts.

It's never been a matter of faith, except perhaps in a fundamental gut reaction sense, saying "yes" rather than "no" to the universe. I told a poet in Ohio recently who was asking me questions of this kind: "I've always had the feeling that my poems are going to reach the promised land but I may not." And what mystifies me a little bit about this is that I *am* a depressive: I'm on anti-depression medication all the time. A lot of that is chemical, a lot comes out of physical pain from childhood on and is part of the life story. It may be related to the creative process: many people think so, particularly the bi-polar dimension of it. It may also be related to my not having had much luck in publishing or in reception. So, life is a constant battle between letting go of the rope and holding on to it. There *is* this fundamental yes/no aspect. I think it's extraordinarily difficult for poets, particularly for anyone whose work is often based on instinct and primal feelings . . . much of this is forgotten, in all this massive amount of "theory" we're saddled with. It's almost as if there was an insistence that it is *only* the mind, the intellect, the head. Almost everything that's written today seems to me to be head stuff and it's what I'm calling "writing" as opposed to "poetry." It's *production,* it's the "*piece.*" "I've done a *piece* on . . ." It doesn't matter whether it's art, painting, whatever, a poem eventually becomes a *piece* as well. In a consumer culture, you consume pieces.

In asking you the question about Breton and occultation, my main interest wasn't so much in Breton himself as in broader issues that may arise out of opposing initiation/hermeticism to, let's say, the Marxist model. I remember reading an interview with Jerome Rothenberg in which he says that, as far as he can see, many of the poets he is close to and he himself would conceivably be attracted to a Marxist type of thought were there anything like a genuine Marxist tradition in America. From a European perspective, where such a tradition has been more readily available and where many poets have been involved with it, I am curious about the turn to hermetic materials in poets like yourself or Rothenberg (who uses materials from Jewish mysticism). From this perspective, and going back to the notion that structure and process are indissoluble, one could, for instance, argue that Marxist thought, in its idea of the dialectic and (within it) of contradiction and negativity (going back to Hegel and so on), provides something like what you are describing—except it's "plus" the politics, so to speak. And one could argue that hermeticism, in certain forms anyway, can be seen as a with-drawal from that. So, for one thing, I'm just trying to see where one would draw the line between what you've referred to as those "masters of successive generations like H.D., Robert Duncan, Kenneth Irby, and Robert Kelly, in whom esoteric interests are constitutive, the very breath of life" and "the guru-hunters of all persuasions who adopt jargons from their latest enthusiasms and do little but muddy the flow of common discourse"?

I think it may be very *precisely* in the question of the latters' refusal of politics. One of the reasons why I try to keep my work in movement and in a state of contradiction, to the extent that nobody ever knows quite where I am, is that I see enormous merit in the fundamental Marxist argument and the messianic hope of the revolution and I would agree with Jerry about a convincing American Marxism. The problem *is* that I'm massively aware of what Eliot Weinberger discusses in his last book of essays[20] which is that there has not yet been such a revolution. Not even Cuba, which was the great hope (which is why we went there and did our *Con Cuba*[21] and all the rest of it): not even there have they managed really to give the artist the kind of freedom s/he needs. In fact, for instance, they've persecuted and imprisoned gay artists. It is true, that when you get down to the facts on the ground, the revolutionary position does not seem to *do* what it *says* it's going to do, particularly for the artist. In a recent poem, which is ostensibly about Blok (and part of a series of poems that I wrote for Tsvetaeva, Mandelstam, et al., now published as *Three Letters from the City: The St. Petersburg Poems, 1968–98*),[22] there is something about a confusion between "the Girl" and "the Revolution." But after all, the Girl and the Revolution: he's never been able to tell the difference. So there is a kind of erotic attitude to the revolution, an erotic hope which is indestructible.

I have no disagreement at all as far as the status of any kind of interesting art within state Communism goes—and indeed even within the European left wing (in Britain, for example, the left's interest in matters cultural is pretty negligible). But that's not quite what I meant. I would still want to distinguish a Marxist (or marxist) intellectual tradition from (a) state Communism and (b) from the messianic element, as important as that is. What I was trying to get at was that the whole process of

20 See Eliot Weinberger, *Written Reaction: Poetics, Politics, Polemics* (New York: Marsilio, 1996), 216–27.
21 See Nathaniel Tarn, ed., *Con Cuba: An Anthology of Cuban Poetry of the Last Sixty Years* (London: Cape Goliard, 1969).
22 Tarn, *Three Letters from the City.*

ecclesia–sparagmos–ecclesia *etc., which is a kind of dialectical process, would seem to find very strong analogies in ideas of the dialectic, contradiction, negativity, and so on—forgetting for the time being where this dialectic may end up.*

I have to confess to a weakness which is that I just haven't had sufficient training in that line of thinking. I am a romantic Marxist in the sense that I believe in the ends but perhaps not the means. Despite the feeling of total exhaustion I get from the present academic "theory" context, if I had another life, another dozen lives, one of them would be as a Marxist, pure and simple. There are profound and apparently interminable *injustices* in the world, ecological and sociological, which *demand* a political approach irrevocably.

That kind of answers what I was trying to probe toward. I wasn't sure whether the absence of that kind of material was a conscious rejection.

Absolutely not.

The other thing that I guess I am driving toward by proposing a possible analogy, however rudimentary, between the hermetic process and the dialectic (I think there is actually a book by David Punter on Blake and Hegel!), is the very notion of analogy. The idea of contradiction in your work can illustrate the point. It is clear from what you've said here and from what you've written that the Romantic tradition of thought and poetry is very important to you. So, for instance, in thinking about the very central role of contradiction in your work (from The Beautiful Contradictions *[1969] onward), I inevitably think of Blake's "without contraries there is no progression." At the same time you also seem to get much of your notion of contradiction from the Buddhist tradition.*

Yes.

There is, in fact, a footnote on Buddhism in your essay on Lévi-Strauss where you speak of "the 'self's' painful discovery of its original condition through the mind's more and more exasperated efforts to break down all possible contradictions."[23] *So the poetry and the writings bring together ideas of contradiction from two very different traditions of thought (in fact more than two). Do you see that as a fairly easy analogy to make or are there in fact fundamental differences in the notions of contradiction in those two traditions?*

Like many people I tend to try to think something out when there is an essay to write. We all live in a state of total syncretism with twenty different ideas in conflict with each other in one's mind at the same time: so then you have to clarify a

---

23 Mendelson, "The 'Uninvited Guest,'" 138 n5.

model. I haven't necessarily thought out the Buddhist contradiction elements in relation to the other contradictions but there is *undoubtedly* a link—and it's one which is a kind of an existential problem you work your way to solving. But one thing Buddhism contributes is that once you find that its argument is the one that makes most sense to you, and I've always operated on that (again it's not a question of faith from which I seem to be divorced, except in the most visceral sense, simply because all the "religion" I was taught as a child, and then with anthropology, has never made any sense qua religion, so Buddhism as the best of a lot of indifferents in a way), once you adopt that view as a hypothetical guideline, then you *do* realize that a huge amount of what we take as given in almost any sense is *not* given at all. The great thing about Buddhism is that it is, in its philosophical core, the *least* "spiritual" and the *least* "religious" of all the systems. It is the most relentlessly questioning. I was talking about the table and the cup. Well, the nature of the reality of the table and the cup is questioned in Buddhism as it is in sub-atomic physics. Something that is playing all the time in my background is that, whatever I will say on the level of everyday action (which includes, of course, the production of poems), it can be shuffled, changed, and radically altered, almost put into derision by a deep Buddhist interpretation.

I can't help feeling that one of the reasons for Blake's power is that he went most deeply into experiences of the kind of impermanence which throws everything into question. There were others also, obviously (Hölderlin, for example). I was teaching Blake for several years, particularly the Prophecies—it's mind-boggling where that guy got all that. And it's more and more mind-boggling the deeper you go into it until you almost retreat in fear because there is a sense in which Blake was impossible to his time, as the record shows, and maybe still be to ours. It took the combined efforts of Kathleen Raine, Northrop Frye, David Erdman, Damon Foster, all of them, and it continues, to unveil this unbelievable character. Now, whether that actually makes the Prophecies more readable today I honestly don't know.

Going back to the issues of analogies, one of the related issues there is the one of universals or archetypes. To what extent is the series of analogies or the dialogues that build up in the poetry through structures of analogies meant to imply some kind of acceptance of archetypal structures?

Lévi-Strauss's attitude, of course, was always that the Jungian archetypes were not necessary because if you're going to be structuralist about the human mind and its possibilities, then structural constraints on the mind's operations will rapidly be revealed. And, to a certain extent, I felt that way. But I think you'd have to point to some specific examples because I'm not sure that I'm getting it in the abstract.

I'm really thinking of the whole ability to move between cultures, between mythologies, and to find in them analogical structures.

For instance, the fact that Persephone and Eurydice and the going down and the coming up and what is meant there recur in my work? I think I have a reasonably good crack at that in the "Archaeology, Elegy, Architecture" essay in this book. Again a piece I can't get anybody to talk to me about. I don't think anybody who's talked to me has looked at this thing and said, "Hey, this is interesting because . . ."

Along with the "Heraldic Vision" essay, that seems to me to be the key essay.

Absolutely! Those two are absolutely key. Those are the places in which I originally forced myself most to think the model out and try to get it to work. Anyway, when I taught the Mayan *Popol Vuh* for instance, it immediately became clear to me that we were again faced with the descent of the living into Hades and the going back up: the primordial initiatic journey. Now, one of the problems with that is it's been very much cheapened by a number of projects. I was tempted one time by a friend into attending a Joseph Campbell weekend in New York. I had a sense from him of a great deal of scholarship, of thought and certainly of passion—I'm not trying to lower the man in any way—but there was a certain rounding off of corners which I found undesirable, from a fairly elitist point of view I admit. You go down from Joseph Campbell to the kind of infantile "newage" that happens in the Santa Fe area time and time again, over and over and over, and you realize the extent to which this stuff is being impoverished by the way it's being exploited.

Campbell (along with Jung) is, in fact, one of the people I was thinking about when I asked the question about archetypes. I agree that there is a good deal in Campbell which may be admirable. But one of the problems I have with analogical structures, with the idea there that these world mythologies have a core underlying structure, is that there is never any consideration in Campbell as far as I can remember that what appears as an almost identical or similar structure in two different cultures at two different times may have its meaning radically shifted by that difference in culture and time. Admittedly, humans have more or less identical bodies, we have two arms, two legs, and so on. So we also perform fairly uniform acts like walking back and forth, going up and down. But that going up and down may mean very different things. So, having spotted the similarity of structure, the question is where does history then pop into it? Obviously that is very hard as far as poetry is concerned.

Well, yes. It's almost as if the poet were a scuba diver at the bottom of the sea, looking at the stuff going up, and the critic, or whatever questioner, is swimming on the surface looking down and is aware of all the contradictions on the surface around him. This issue is still open, to be honest. It really depends on the level of interpretation and we are *not* the masters of all the levels. I would tend to be more interested perhaps, if pushed, in a psychological level where I would ask, Well, what is it that causes in *me* this endless repetition of Persephone; why is she always coming back in the poems? She's even in the new sequence of seventy poems, *the Architextures*.[24] Each of the *ARCs* is in three sections and the third section is her. Right from the start there she is. Why? All right, the surface explanation: is one lazy? But there is something more to it. The hypnotic effects of particular myths. Do they have the rank of archetypes? I have not studied Jung in depth. Granted that every poet might have a different obsession, why is it that the Persephone comes up so many times? I do say that the Persephone/Eurydice model is very much in my view *the* guiding myth of lyric and, therefore, it manifests in *many* bodies of work. If I were purely a theoretician, or were given more experience in life and more thinking in that direction in order to produce another volume of essays, well, who knows? The perpetual business of what lies under the *Silence*, what lies under those voices (the whole business of the *Vocal*, the *Choral*, and so on). I have not gotten beyond that yet and I don't know whether I will.

Another area which emerges for me when I read the essays in Views *alongside your poetry (and also alongside other contemporary work in Ethnopoetics) is that it reveals new and complex areas of engagement and crossover between the work in anthropology and the poetry. So, for example, one of my earliest reactions to a book like* The Beautiful Contradictions *on first reading it was a sense of excitement at the enormous range of cross-cultural material that is there as content and of thinking that this was the role the anthropology played in the poetry. But going back to it after reading* Views, *I have a much clearer sense than before of other and different levels of engagement—particularly the ways in which you are, in fact, using the anthropological material to probe the very nature of the poetic imagination. So that, instead of a cultural anthropology, a kind of philosophical anthropology begins to emerge, not, of course, a "science of man" in this case but something like a comparative poetics.*

Yes, which may be where the link with Buddhism comes: that, ultimately, you've got this strange relativism which questions everything. There is no way that you can finally say anything about a culture because everything is relative in the cultural domain. If it happens in this culture, it's this; if it happens in that culture, it's that. Same with Buddhism to a certain extent. And yet, behind all of *that*, there are felt to be universal laws, whatever form those take. So what you're saying

24 Tarn, *The Architextures*.

may be very true, but there is a limit to self-observation. Sooner or later somebody like you comes along and says, "What I'm seeing is x, y and z." And you say, "Absolutely! I hadn't thought of that." That seems to me the function of the real critic. Let's face it: nine-tenths of criticism is for the birds. It's also a "piece." It's turning round and round; doing its own thing to the glory of the critic rather than to that of the work which the critic is supposed to be studying. The point at which the critic "becomes" the poet—you can *see* it, for Blake, in Kathleen Raine, in Frye, in Erdman. The fact that the reader is part of the process, *that* applies in real criticism also. Let's also remember the preface to *Views* where I state specifically that formal procedural rules out of anthropology, not just content, can play a role in the poetry.

In "The Heraldic Vision" there is a point at which you differentiate your own work from what you see as the more performative interests of someone like Rothenberg. . . .

Yes, Jerry is most interested in the oral, in performance, in ritual, and so forth. I believe that his major influence has been in the jacking up of primitive and archaic poetries from, say, "Georgian" English into twentieth-century American. He has also been hugely important in bringing such materials into the world of poetic discourse by an ever-expanding set of anthologies: from *Technicians of the Sacred* to *Poems for the Millenium*. This assimilates his view of Duncan's "symposium of the whole" to the universe at large. Following many major twentieth-century artistic movements, he has also stressed various relationships between primitive/archaic and modern avant-garde poetries: the whole question of the poet as shaman, with its attendant problems as we discuss elsewhere. All of this amounts to a major achievement. But how much deeper the *theory* in Jerry's work goes, I am not quite sure.

The issue of the differences between that kind of Ethnopoetics and the more speculative and theoretical approach to the poetic imagination which seems to characterize your work (though I don't really want to suggest a hard-and-fast distinction here) links back to the point I was trying to raise about philosophical anthropology. It seems to me that in the current critique of anthropology, that original object thought of as a "science of man" has almost been let fall by the wayside. I know that there are elements of the grand imperialist project in that but I'm not sure that we should be in a hurry to totally abandon it for that reason. The idea of the local has come to dominate so much that putting one local together with another one and another has almost disappeared. But buried within the diversity of the essays in Views, *there seems to me to be an attempt to think about that kind of big picture. Including questions of how the mind works, and so on.*

I suppose I should say that I integrated into the Ethnopoetic adventure because Jerry was extremely welcoming and because it seemed to be the most interesting direction. But there has always been a certain courtesy element too—the feeling that, when the chips were down, what I was doing was not necessarily the same, and indeed in many ways was quite far from what the other guys were doing, even Dennis Tedlock for instance. It's not that I'm now trying to pull out of the enterprise, definitely not. But I think that may be one of the main reasons why nobody took "The Heraldic Vision" or "Archaeology, Elegy, Architecture" really seriously. I was never granted *discussion* about it in the way that you, for instance, have pushed various buttons.

Well, one thing that strikes me reading the essays in England is that they appear to me to be, in some ways, very European, particularly in the way you think and speculate. And I can see why, in certain American contexts (especially where the processual out-look may dominate), they may pose certain kinds of problems for some people.

The issue of Nathaniel Tarn remaining a European, becoming the outsider watching the American scene but at the same time insisting on being American, *has* been raised (by Doris Sommer especially).[25] Eliot Weinberger has picked up on that. He knows my sensitivity to the question so he'll never radically say it. But if you look at the preface to his anthology, "this weirdest of American birds": it's essentially what he's saying.[26] So, there is still a mystery for me as to the extent to which anyone here really accepts me. I've also written about being an "Atlantean."

In relation to these comments, I'm curious about your relation to Duncan because if there is one poet that I would have thought would find your work sympathetic, it would have been Duncan. Was there ever a correspondence or dialogue?

Yes, and indeed it is in "Child as Father to the Man" here where I quote Duncan's acceptance. Remember? In essence he wasn't saying, "Tarn, you're a good poet." He was saying, "You're a good poet because some of your ideas are so close to Duncan." But nevertheless, it was a very important acceptance. After that particular statement, I gather that he cooled somewhat—which was very typical of him, all through with almost everybody, except perhaps with his ultimate favorite, Michael Palmer, who helped him in his illness? But the only evidence of any kind that I have is that some-one told me that he had told somebody else, in Colorado or someplace, in the course of a walk or something, that both Kelly and Tarn had disappointed him or had somehow "sinned" by being too explicit about sex—too explicit about the physical nature of the muse, that might be a better way to put it. In some ways it makes

25   In a special anthro-poetry issue of *Dialectical Anthropology*, ed. Stanley Diamond (Dordrecht: Martinus Nijhoff, 1986).

26   Eliot Weinberger, ed., *American Poetry since 1950* (New York: Marsilio Publishing, 1995).

sense. I don't think that Robert turned against me or anything; he continued to manifest signs of friendship. But it wasn't quite the same thing as that first letter.

I assume that the structuralist emphasis also does not go down very well here. I was thinking of a comment by Rothenberg (I can't remember where he says it) where he criticizes the structuralist reading of myth because such readings don't seem to be interested in the poetic aspect of myth.

And of course Tedlock was in on this as well. He is one of the major processualists.

I see the kind of problems Rothenberg is pointing to but I also thought that Lévi-Strauss in fact distinguished between poetry and myth.

Yes, I think he did.

So the so-called structuralist reduction of myth into its basic components which do not alter need not conflict with the poetic approach to myth?

Well, here there's a mystery and the mystery is inherent particularly in the discussion of music in the introduction to the four-volume *Mythologiques*. And that's where I found it almost impossibly difficult and just couldn't keep up with him. Much to my chagrin because I *did* feel that there was a fundamental understanding on his part of the arts. You've only got to read the *Conversations*.

Or Tristes Tropiques.

Or *Tristes Tropiques*. Nevertheless, there *was* this ambivalence on his part. When I gave him a copy of my first book of poetry, *Old Savage/Young City* [1965], I wrote in it, "To the greatest French poet of the twentieth century." And there is every reason to believe that he was absolutely furious!

You never had a direct response?

No. It was after I was a student. I was already teaching at the School of Oriental and African Studies in London. There was a kind of "Humpf. Thank you very much!" But the whole business of the reference letters he wrote speaks strongly to that. I always asked him for a reference, but I eventually discovered that he was sending two-line references, along the lines of "This man is all right as an anthropologist but as for poetry, I know nothing about it." That, of course, was professionally fatal. I wish that someone had pushed him about this question of the arts. Of course, there are recent writings of his I have not yet read.

Part of the problem, as you yourself have said somewhere, was that before he'd really had a chance to complete his project, a lot of it was killed off by the amount of adverse criticism he received.

I think he was buried. One of the things that makes me furious, particularly in this culture where there are five generations per lifetime, is the ease with which people bury somebody. I've often protested against this. You don't bury someone like Lévi-Strauss just because a fashion has changed! I think people who've been through the mill do recognize that, however much you may disagree with someone, there is a question of the *quality* of mind.

I'd like to talk more about the confluence of anthropology and poetry and perhaps to focus a bit more on the poetry and poetics. Obviously, as far as your own work goes, the confluence of anthropology and poetry needs little explanation. But there is also a long tradition of such a confluence among poets who are not anthropologists as such, even if some have anthropological training (in America Pound, Eliot, Olson, Duncan, Rothenberg for example). Do you have any thoughts as to why that has been such an important aspect of the poetry?

I think I've come to a sense of that. To put it bluntly, it may be that poets having a kind of prophetic function, albeit frequently unconscious, sensed, before the time, the coming of multiculturalism. I don't mean that just in the sense used in this country (i.e., "You've damned well got to get used to the fact that Americans come in all colors, and that's the way it should be, and they should be equal"). I mean it in the sense of the planet getting smaller and smaller; communications getting closer; the fact that we're all nose to nose, that the visibility of our destruction of tribal peoples particularly is becoming more and more obvious. All these things play into that. There *is* a very interesting contradiction which needs bringing out here (and I have brought it out in places but perhaps not all that explicitly). In Modernism many poets, as we know, went to the right politically because they felt that "nation," "*ethnos*," the "folk," the "traditions" were all giving way. Across the board: Yeats, Pound, Eliot, Lawrence, Rilke . . . so many of them! At the same time, these were the very people who were getting interested in anthropology which, daughter of imperialism though it may have been, was part of what you just described as a progressive attempt to understand the human race *as a whole* as opposed to bits of the human race, the British "race," the French "race," and all that blather! A lot of the contradictions in Modernism in that regard may well have come from the fact that this *worlding* of the world was inevitable and exciting, but that it was also scary. The fundamental truth of it is, perhaps, that those old right-leaning poets are in a *transitional* stage between a culture of folk or *ethnos* or nation (it's difficult using these terms) and Wendell Wilkie's "one world." On the one hand, by an extraordinarily negative and deeply embittering process of eliminating a lot of differences (i.e., as I said somewhere, whether we're right or left politically, we *will* have the land and we will *kill* the people on it), we are a disappearing species, through pollution, greed, stupidity, and so on. On the other hand, there is another contradiction within this: that by reducing diversity, you are allowing a *certain kind* of multiplicity to come into play. I've thrown a large cat among the pigeons here because I think that there are a large number of points to finesse out. (A paper I gave in Antwerp, published in German and in Flemish but never in English, reviews the question of *ethnos* and small groups. I felt that it was pretty controversial in many ways and that maybe I should roll it around in my mouth a few more times before spitting it out.[27])

This relates to a proposition that you and also others have made, that if one is looking toward the future transformation of poetry, then part of that transformation will come when the former "informants" as it were cease to be informants and become poets in their own rights. Apart from a few exceptions, that remains, as far as I can see, a kind of utopian horizon which, every time one tries to reach it at present, turns into a kind of debased multiculturalism.

Because multiculturalism is, to a large extent, being burrocrasstically imposed. I remain uncertain as to how deeply it is accepted in *practice*.

Statistically, almost demographically imposed rather than qualitatively. But as far as the poets I've mentioned are concerned (Pound, Olson, Duncan, Rothenberg), are there any other names you would include in that list?

To a certain extent somebody like McGrath, relatively unknown, but very interesting in many ways. His stress, of course, was almost always political though I think there was a lot of stuff behind it. Reznikoff perhaps. With his Holocaust and Jewish poems, he preceded Jerry's *Poland/1931* (one of his best books, along with *Seneca Journal*). Ed Dorn has written brilliantly on anthropology, and Lévi-Strauss figures in *Slinger.* Jonathan Williams's work on Southern folklore. A *lot* of people have been tangentially touched by this, even if it wasn't the center of their concerns. And one would probably find them even in the ranks of the mainstream conservatives, those I call the "MFAs." Someone like Merwin: his interests are very multicultural. At this point he's an ecologist working in Hawaii. I don't know the work of the conservatives all that well but there must be others. In other languages: imaginary ethnographies by Segalen, Michaux, Cortazar, and a long list.

27   Nathaniel Tarn, "Small Where Space Is Not," in *Vertoog en Literatuur. Cahier 3: Provincialismen/ Ontworteling*, ed. Bart Vershaffel and Mark Verminck (Antwerp and Cologne: Meulendorf and Verlag J. Dinter, 1993), 37–48 (in Flemish and German). |

I think it's very hard to imagine poets with any kind of serious range who haven't been at least touched by the anthropological. But I guess one would have to distinguish between those who have seriously immersed themselves in it and those who haven't.

Right. And Rexroth, of course, who's always forgotten, who worked with Chinese, with Japanese, who had a very wide World view. He wasn't all that much of a theoretician necessarily but, by God, his essays on the masterpieces and so on kept an enormous amount of historical material alive! Historical and to a certain extent ethnographical, certainly multicultural stuff—where most people haven't read Shakespeare since high school days! His *Classics Revisited*, his mixture of Catholicism and Buddhism, all of those things. He's *in* there! I guess to some extent you'd have to look at Ginsberg's contribution. There is the whole involvement with Buddhism which has been fairly long-lasting and substantial. Some of the poets close to Ginsberg: Anne Waldman, for instance, should be included.

Ginsberg is a good case in point here because, as Eric Mottram points out in one of his pamphlets on Ginsberg, in something like the "Angkor Wat" poem there is just no mention of the fact that the thing is built with slave labor.[28] That side of this whole poetic area seems cause for concern.

Well, there are terrible weaknesses in Ginsberg after the genial first period. I think he's become almost a daddy longlegs although nobody wants to admit it yet.

By contrast Neruda in Macchu Picchu, *which provides a good point of comparison, raises the issues of politics more directly.*

He certainly does. No, I'm very familiar with the feeling a politically conscious person might have that this whole initiatic or esoteric tradition finds it much too easy to glide off from the basic social issues. I've been very conscious of this and have tried to do the best within my fundamental orientation to say so. If, for instance, you look at "Towards a New Realism," the preface to *A Nowhere for Vallejo*, it's there! And I rhyme "newage" with sewage.

We've been talking about the influence of the anthropology on the poetry. I'd like to reverse the direction now and talk a little about the influence of the poetry on the anthropology. Understandably, this is an area that is more tentatively treated in Views. *In one of the essays there you say that, in your opinion, the current flirting with literature in anthropology has resulted only in* belles lettres *and you argue that only if one works from a genuinely literary stance is a real transformation of the disciplines and genres possible. You also point at some of your own as yet largely unpublished work as*

---

28   Eric Mottram, *Allen Ginsberg in the Sixties* (Brighton, UK: Unicorn Bookshop, 1972), 7.

an illustration of the type of writing that may be moving toward this kind of transformation. Is one of the implications then that you are proposing or desiring the end of anthropology?

The end of anthropology *and* the end of the academy in its present form. Although, for many guessable reasons, I'm ambivalent or multivalent about this. Partly because it is all very well to call for the destruction of something but it is also irresponsible before you know what you're going to put in its place. There is also the fact that I have, to a certain extent, been defeated by the market. The fact that *Scandals in the House of Birds*, the Guatemalan book which is looking for a new language for experimental ethnography, has been fifteen to seventeen years in the making (much longer if you count the fact that it is a prolongation of *Los Escándalos de Maximón* from the fifties, so we're actually talking about *forty* years or so!) because in all that time it has not been possible to write what I had in mind.[29] I have to look at the battlefield and say, "Well, maybe I haven't been either Napoleon or Wellington on this one!" There are various things involved here. Bluntly, there may well be a question of individual talent, that I simply did not have the *nous* to do it. I cannot discuss that. The more interesting thing is the question of whether it would be possible for *anyone* to do it. My answer to that has been getting more negative simply because, to put it in a very elementary way, if you think beyond the stage of *belles lettres* even at its finest, then you start going toward Joyce, Gertrude Stein, and the like. So, first of all: is it possible for anyone to have the talent to be a Joyce or Stein again? And here you come up against the problem I discuss in the essay on "New Forms" here of whether the avant-garde *can* continue for*ever* or whether, in the end, it simply doesn't disappear up its own ass. There is a very serious question here of viability and possibility within a given cultural situation, viz., *this* one. So there you get something fairly crucial and have to say, "All right, I've been defeated fairly because my idea was probably ill conceived." And then you start going back to the poetry as the fine and wonderful battleground—but one to which nobody pays any attention. So you're constantly to and fro.

The argument for such a new kind of writing, to some extent, is clearly intended as a utopian argument in so far as the necessary precondition for the full emergence of such a writing may well be what we referred to earlier as revolution. The world will have to have been transformed by that first. This is not to say that the whole argument is ill conceived. One thing that it does do is perhaps to suggest that much of the debate about the relationship of literature and ethnography coming from anthropological and

---

29 Tarn, *Scandals in the House of Birds;* eventually published by Marsilio Publishing (New York, 1997). The firm died soon after. See note 16.

academic circles may be what is in fact ill conceived. They do seem to me, as you your-self have pointed out, only to be flirting with literature for the most part. And they cer-tainly haven't produced any new ethnographies that would come any way near the theoretical propositions for a new kind of writing. So while as a theoretical proposition I am attracted to the idea of the future abolition of anthropology, I also begin to feel that in the given, present world, it may still be worth defending certain aspects of the anthropological project.

Yes. But one of the other parts of this is whether there is going to be anyone to anthropologize anymore.

In "The Choral Voice," you speak of the de jure if not de facto end of anthropology and you also say that there are no more informants left in the traditional sense of the word. It's a little bit like "there are no more servants"—the cry of the elite?

But I feel that that is a slight over-statement because, in the world at present, even the voices of emerging nations and cultures are not free of a fairly heavy mediation by colonial or post-colonial power. So, within that it seems to me that some kind of west-ern intervention on their behalf as a positive thing is still a possibility.

Yes, we are short-cutting at the expense of those people. But I think the point might be that we haven't come to the end but we've seen it. And if you see it, from the point of view of a theoretician, prophet, poet, or whatever, then you already begin to argue what has to happen.

The same goes for planetary ecology.

That's why, in our conversation yesterday, I was going back to Reinventing Anthro-pology, *the volume edited by Dell Hymes in the seventies, because there is a very dif-ferent political and methodological orientation there than the one that is available among the contributors to the* Writing Culture *volume in the eighties.[30] I'm not very sure or clear about the relationship between modifying or revising our models of ethno-graphic writing and the possibilities for the transformation of the lives of the infor-mants. So, for instance, various claims are made for "post-modern" ethnographies such as Vincent Crapanzano's* Moroccan Dialogues, *where the informant has played a more active part in the shaping of the dialogue than is usual. But even there, as far as I am aware, there is still the question of the editing, shaping, and production process taking place over here and under the control of the anthropologist, the academy, and the university press.*

30 Dell Hymes, ed., *Reinventing Anthropology* (New York: Pantheon, 1972); and James Clifford and George E. Marcus, eds., *Writing Culture: The Poetics & Politics of Ethnography* (Berkeley: Univer-sity of California Press, 1986).

I don't think we should leave this tack, because there are tough nuts to crack here.

Well, let me pursue a related issue then. In imagining the confluence of anthropology and poetry toward a new writing you also say that one characteristic of such a writing would or should be its fully literary status but without the sacrifice of scientific verac-ity. While I don't see science and literature as being totally separate domains, it could be argued that the notions of truth embodied in the two may be very different. So could you say more about what that idea of veracity or truth could be?

Oh boy! It suddenly occurs to me that the very materialistic kind of writing which you find in the *nouveau roman* and its heritage could in some ways be in-voked as one of the forms of writing that might have come out of my proposi-tion, notwithstanding the fact that it only appears anthropological in some writers like Marguerite Duras rather than others who stick to their French roots. The *nouveau roman* is the only thing that comes to my mind immediately but what one has to do, to a certain extent, is to look at the productions of the con-temporary avant-garde with that particular searchlight on them, and not neces-sarily just in literature. For instance: "installations." To me these are shop windows; the equivalents of the window at Bloomingdale's or your local supermarket. That's why this word "piece" has this super-materialistic sound to me. These are, in essence, reflections of consumerism where the major pursuit of anybody is not food gathering, wisdom gathering, or the "techniques of the sacred," but simply *collecting.* Adding to the contents of a house, and God knows I should know about that because I'm the squirrel of all squirrels! Incidentally, a lot of "Lan-guage Poetry" seems to me to be of that nature. In so far as it comes out of France, I am pretty sure there is a goodly component of *nouveau roman* in there, for instance in writers like Hejinian. That's only just occurred to me. So it may be that this famous writing of the future is actually there now but we're not see-ing it as such. Since this is relatively new I'd probably have to think about it and see what I come up with.

In broaching the subject I don't think I expected an "answer." I was just probing be-cause the relationship of science and literature is something that interests me a lot.

There is also the archaeology issue. It's not just going across the spectrum of actu-ally existing societies but the spectrum of all of human history. I mean, what has been done by this relatively late-appearing animal man, in geological terms, only a speck in time. So, however much the richness of cultural variety may overwhelm us (the Assyrians, the Babylonians, all the details of the Silk Road . . . !), it is still limited. It's not infinite; it's not stretching out into the millennia either way. It's *there;* it can be encompassed. So archaeology comes into the picture (and there, people like Foucault are very important).

The conceptualization of the poetic voice as a multiple or "choral voice," which occurs in several of your essays, is one site in your work where anthropology and poetry meet most clearly and where literature seems to offer the possibilities of a real synthesis with or transformation of anthropology. One of the most radical propositions in this volume is that a genuinely choral voice is only possible as a truly individual voice. Your "Choral Voice" essay came out the same year as the Writing Culture *volume (1986). In the essays in that volume there is also a concern with dialogics and polyvocality but in the opposite direction. So there the difference between thinking from a poet's point of view and an anthropologist's seems very evident. To what extent do you feel that that idea of the choral voice has been present in your work from an early stage or do you think that it is something that has been emerging slowly over the years?*

It may have been there unconsciously but, for getting explicitly into the essays or the poetry, it's been emerging gradually. For a long time I started from George Steiner's version of a bottom level of silence and everything coming out of that. Then I began questioning.

It occurs to me first of all that the choral voice is utopian—and incidentally, the choral concept is wider than just equaling a "truly individual voice." I should stress that my use of "model" is not just a fancy contemporary chat term for me; I really was very turned on by the whole Lévi-Straussian notion of the reduced model and what you can do with it as a tool of understanding. It is more natural for me to write a poem than to write one of these essays: one trains a whole lifetime to write essays as one goes through the academic mill. But I find that if I think in terms of models, it clarifies my thinking. It liberates me also in the sense of always standing back and being the observer, even of your own inner motive. My impulse toward triadic models is always fairly fertile for me. It is quite possible that I was not very happy with the silence–speech binary because it seemed to me that something was missing. After all, if you start with absolute silence, *where* is the seed in the silence that leads to something else? I don't know exactly what started this choral business, but I had always had the idea (this goes very, very far back) that the more individual your voice is, the more it will actually tap into the . . . call it "collective unconscious" if you like, substratum of truth, universal experience, or whatever. That idea is very old with me though it predates me. So all of these things churning around together led to the question of whether it was conceivable that there was something "*under*" the silence. And when I started thinking about that, it immediately had the feeling of being something generative. Incidentally, it is noticeable that Clifford talks virtually never about contemporary poets.

On the level of voice this seems very similar to Williams's idea that you only get to the general through the particular.

Well, induction, yes. One should add a footnote to this. The notion of voice is very unpopular at this point, all the "death of the author" stuff, everything that the "Language" poets are doing is against that. But I remain stubbornly pro the voice idea on the same basis as the ego notion we were discussing yesterday. If the poet doesn't have an interesting ego, then what actually *is* the hope s/he can offer to the human psyche? So I'm not at all worried that all of this is couched in terms of voice. I think those people are going to come back from the desert one of these days because they will discover that it really *is* a desert.

One of the aspects of the contemporary criticism of poetry which seems to me to be irritating is that there is very often a confusion between certain statements on poetics by poets intended to be heuristic aids and the actual practice of the poetry. Some of the critics seem to take the statements and apply them to the poetry with a damaging sense of rigidity. Am I right in thinking that the relationship between the playfulness of the models in your work and your poetry should be seen as an open one?

Absolutely. I very much doubt that there are any poets who, when seized with the desire to write poetry, sit down and try and fit the writing into a model they may have previously described. I've always had the feeling that poems happened naturally, and that you then went and mined them. So, particularly if there is such a thing as a prophetic function in art, the artist does his or her thing and then goes and looks at what's there. If it were a question of searching for various aspects of a model in the poem, it would be *post hoc* and not the reverse. That can work out extremely well, particularly if there is a major theme that comes up all the time with variations, like the Persephone thing (which is also always triadic: she is on the surface, she goes down, she comes up again).

There is a comment you make in an earlier interview which may lead us further into the idea of the choral. There, speaking of the experience of being homeless or without roots and about your choice of living in America, you say that "The attachment to the whole world, of The Beautiful Contradictions, *simply did not work out. It was too big. . . . God knows, the American continent is big enough."*[31]

I remember now—there was a particular question being discussed there. One of the things early on in *The Beautiful Contradictions* is the statement to the effect that I have no alternative to taking the whole world as my mother because I've never had a particular place of my own. And I think what the interviewers were

31   Jed Rasula and Mike Erwin, "An Interview with Nathaniel Tarn," *Boundary 2* (Fall 1975): 6–7.

getting at, particularly in view of my relatively recent arrival in the States, was what was my relationship to the continent and the American scene going to be? They had, actually, been working on the British scene. So coming to see me was in fact part of that. I can't remember whether the rectangle poems had started at that point, but *Seeing America First,* a lot of *At the Western Gates,* and *The Desert Mothers* are a continuation of the Americanicity of *Lyrics for the Bride of God* (because *Lyrics* is very much part of the American entity). So that statement was a bending back onto this continent as part of the whole enterprise of entering American poetry. It was in that context. But where do you see the link with the choral?

I guess I'm trying to bring up various issues to do with range of materials and voice. In relation to The Beautiful Contradictions, *one of the things that interests me is that, in terms of range of material, it is one of your grandest projects. It isn't that the range then disappears from later work, but it is for the most part very differently handled— more quietly perhaps, and more grounded in an American localism too.*

Well, *Lyrics* is equally wide. But localism is once again breaking apart with a current interest in Russia.

In the earlier interview you also talk about the Pound, Williams, Olson tradition and the ways in which these poets all tend to have and work from a cosmic or world model. To what extent do you see the work from The Beautiful Contradictions *as being in that tradition or in any way altering it?*

The world model is always there with the idea of models generally. In *The Beautiful Contradictions* the guiding world model is the Hereford *mappa mundi*. In *Lyrics* there are some diagrams which were intended as a particular guide to a lot of different things. One of them is that you have a quadri-directional and central system there, four parts and a center part, the latter being the Invisible Bride's. Even in the early books there is the idea of the directions: *Old Savage/Young City* is dedicated "To my East"; and *Where Babylon Ends,* "To my West." In the new *Architextures* I also make use of the Mayan solar model. Reference the "tradition," what I find seems to happen in the mechanics of publication is that my books tend to alternate between collections and full (single long poem) books. Ideally, I would like to have only full books. The cosmic model has a tendency to come back into the full books but not necessarily into the collections. The length of poems is also interesting. With the *Cantos, Paterson, Maximus,* and Duncan's *Passages* in my head, I guess I've always been attracted to the idea of a poem without end, a poem as long as life. But it doesn't seem to happen that way with me. I *start out* with the idea that it's going to go on and on and then I'm just too damned interested in something else and a closure occurs. I obviously *do* have long works

(*Contradictions, Lyrics,* etc.) but on a more restricted scale than these life-long po-ems. Also remember Poe. Do the life-longs work? Pound's conclusions are heavy food for thought.

On the other hand I suppose there are very obvious and strong connections between the individual books over the years. When Rothenberg brought out his New and Selected Poems *he wrote in the "Pre-Face" that he was becoming aware of the emergence of a single long poem from all the individual books published over the many years and that he was trying to isolate that poem in some way.*

Of course, some people may respond to the fact that the long-as-life poem is the dominant mode by feeling slightly dismayed that they haven't done such a thing. This is silly. Oppen, for instance, is a very great poet but did not do that. Even in Duncan, the *Passages* are interspersed among all the books. So perhaps that Jerry statement is to some extent partly strategic.

I think the at least apparent dominance of the long poem has in some ways been detri-mental. It may, for one thing, have contributed to the obscuring of the achievement of poets like Oppen or O'Hara.

The other thing that may be worth bearing in mind theoretically is that the whole initiatic tradition works on the macrocosm and microcosm as reflections of each other. So if one sees the cosmic model in small poems, it may well be because it is there. The moment, for instance, that you speak about head, belly, feet, hands, you're already talking about a cosmic model, as the East's cultures well knew, in all their Yogic, Tantric, and Taoist charts.

Since Pound said that he, unlike Dante, had "no Aquinas map," it seems to have be-come embarrassing for poets to actually have a map. Yet, in some ways, the project of a mappa mundi (though not in any rigidly ideological or systemic sense) may well be worth having a look at again.

There *is* the Lévi-Straussian notion of the reduced model. The value of the re-duced model is practical: seeing certain things at work which don't spring to sight in the macro reality on the ground. In a sense that is what *science* is about. You take certain things out of this vast continuum which are manageable and you op-erate on *them.*

In relation to Olson I'm also interested in your comment in one essay about how sur-prised you were to discover how much of Maximus *is collaged out of borrowed bits and pieces (and Duncan's indignation at that comment). How would you see your own very catholic use of mythological and cultural materials in* Contradictions *or the use of Vallejo's texts in* A Nowhere for Vallejo *in relation to that?*

Frankly, I've had reason to be embarrassed after making that statement and to re-
tract from it to a certain extent, seeing my own usages. What I was reacting to
there in particular was, again, this "death of the author," end of "inspiration"
business. My general sense now is that poetry and myth are universal, cosmic
models from which you can borrow. Also Picasso's "I do not search, I find." The
criterion there is that, if you use somebody else's lines to enhance your own because your own are not strong enough, then that should be a signal to you to forget it? If, on the other hand, you're at a pitch of excitement where you honestly
feel that your words do have the strength to marry and match with the other person's, then I think it's reasonably legitimate. Also, if you're not hiding it, if you
put it in quotation marks or whatever.

In Views *you speak of the dangers for contemporary poetry of a kind of rarefied obscurantism which may make the poetry the concern of only a very elite and incestuous
group. But given the general level of cultural illiteracy on both sides of the Atlantic, one
could argue that there is only the smallest difference in terms of general difficulty and
accessibility between the kind of referentiality some of your work involves and, say, the
kind of "Language" work you are uneasy about.*

True. Generally a huge question: how much, how, at what level, and to whom do
and should bodies of knowledge (science, poetry) *communicate?*

Maybe, for poetry, the separating criterion is that, in my kind of "obscurantism," if you do the work you can usually trace the source. In a book like *Contradictions* there *are* references. You've also got to look at the amount of internal
explanation. You say something obscure and then you imply "i.e." and you translate it. Not so in much "Language" and "Language"-influenced poetry: you can
search as much you like but you're not going to get it. You shouldn't confuse, as
people sometimes do, personal idiosyncrasy and public idiosyncrasy—stuff that
you can in fact trace in the *public* domain and stuff that you cannot.

The question of "obscurity" has always worried me. I keep on going back to it.
It links up to the whole business of amateur versus masterly hermeticism—which
I'm not very comfortable with either. That in turn links up to my not being happy
with only poets reading other poets, even if, since there are now *thousands* of people acting as "poets," the audience is of the same, if not greater, size than it would
have been previously! I continue being impelled to talk about a producer on the
one hand and a receiver on the other, and the business of the producers being simultaneously the receivers at both ends of that pair I find embarrassing—to the
extent of going back to anthropology and using the incest–marriage model: endogamy–exogamy and so on. But then getting personal about it, rather than theo-

retical, where does that leave me? I know that I'm erudite and have been fortunate to have a very wide education and to be interested in a zillion subjects: I can't exactly keep this out of the work and if it constitutes a kind of obscurity that keeps readers away, so be it. I add that I've always tended to write alternatively complex and simple poetry: maybe the "full" book versus the "collection." But often, for some reason, people fail to *see* the simple stuff.

Given the range of cross-cultural material in poetry such as yours, there is also the question of appropriation. I realize that a great deal of nonsense is spoken about this, but there is nevertheless a genuine political problem here. Native American writers, like Leslie Silko for instance, have attacked writers like Snyder and Rothenberg for their use of Native American materials. To what extent do you feel that this is a real issue, and how do you yourself deal with it?

In the days when Jerry and I were in great proximity, that issue did get raised and I remember talking with Jerry about it. I recall Jerry's not so much anger as just pained puzzlement. He was shocked. In his view he was enlarging our vision of the world and our consciousness. Suddenly he gets brought up short by accusations of "stealing." There are all sorts of answers to that. One is "Well: why don't you 'steal' *my* stuff?" which of course they do. I've been very torn about this. There was a period when I was reacting positively to people like Wendy Rose, who were at the second Ethnopoetics conference at LA, invited by Jerry. With a growing discomfort about the sense of the anthropologist as a transitional figure who looks after a certain body of tradition and knowledge *only until* the owners can truly *act* with it, I began to feel that much of the criticism was true. Then I started swinging back. I say, "Here I am, I'm interested in all these different things, for better or for worse, so it's very difficult for me to think of all them in terms of *ownership*." I've always been Wordsworthian in the sense of the Preface to *Lyrical Ballads:* the poet is the most available human who takes the availability of everybody else for granted. Again, I think this is one of the contradictions we are living with: there are those two sides to it. Jerry may have sat down and theoretically worked through all the pros and cons but I am not aware of this. *I* sure haven't done it. I *could* sit down and write about all the ambivalences, what their implications seem to be, what their *insolubles* seem to be, because, God knows, we can't solve all things! On the other hand, tons of "theory" does it for you today!

One of the problems for me is the lumping together of figures like Snyder and Rothenberg because it seems to me that they do very different kinds of things. More importantly, in these critiques the only model of cultural dialogue or interaction that seems to be imagined is appropriation. There seems to be the assumption in them that, because we live in a world in which there are very real issues of power, exploitation, and so on, then any use of another culture's materials must be tied to that abusive use of power. It also seems to me to be setting up one criterion for people like Rothenberg and another for people like Silko. For one thing, Native American writers like Silko usually publish with fairly major, mainstream publishers, which means that Anglos form a major, if not the major, part of her readership. This raises issues of why the material is put out there, what it is for, how it is to be used. In all the debates about multiculturalism today the actual and ancient fact of multiculturalism throughout human history seems in fact to have been forgotten. The culture of the Silk Road for instance!

On the one hand the "owners" are, *de facto,* laying claim to the universality of their own tradition. They're compelled to do it—because if they stick only to the argument where tribe *X's* tradition is good for only tribe *X,* then it becomes a question of "You come to the market and grab my tomatoes from my basket and you run." So they have to say no, this is general humanity. So they themselves are caught in that particular ambivalence. I don't see any way out of it. Not to mention the other ocean of copyright problems.

You've obviously developed your tripartite model of the vocal–silence–choral over many essays and have tried to refine and modify it in each. One of the earlier statements of the model occurs in the Choral Voice *which is one of your more pessimistic essays, as far as your thoughts on the future of anthropology and the relation of anthropology and poetry are concerned. There you write, "Perhaps we must give ourselves up to the evidence that the only collective we will ever meet is 'among the dead.'" To contextualize that statement a little, you are there speaking about the near impossibility of meeting the Other in any creative way in this fratricidal world of ours. As put, the statement seems problematic to me. Are you really saying that the only dialogue possible is with the dead?*

No. I'm saying that, according to the ratio of pessimism and optimism inside yourself at any given moment, you do lean lifeward or deathward. However depressed I am, the fundamental principle is one of *hope,* the *only* indispensable prerequisite of poetry. But the question of the dead is not just an expression of pessimism. It goes deeper than that. First, in all cosmic models which are to a certain extent circular, you go from birth to death to re-birth on a three-point path. On the other hand you've also got the feeling, which has always been strongly mine, about the prophetic function of poetry, and one of the aspects of the prophetic function is that time is eliminated. The reason why you can see into the past and into the future is that everything is *here.* So my ultimate view of life is simultaneity. I feel and experience *deeply* the fact that I am here at this moment talking to you, but I'm also *already* over there in my grave in the South of town lying in my box. So the notion of talking with the dead which a poet might have out of her/his own experiences and which an anthropologist–poet might have having lived with such people as we've been discussing may make a lot of sense. (Both Maya and Burmese have such a cyclical view.) The more I go, the more I discover that I'm not the only poet to feel this way. There *is* in this the contradictory element of despair at the fact that nobody is listening to us or reading us, and therefore it may sound very pessimistic, but I don't think it's only that. It's not apolitical. There's no reason why talking to the dead should preclude talking with the living and paying close attention to what's happening to them. There is also the new hypothesis (since *Views*) in this book's last piece about *Idyll* being concerned with a simultaneous desire to die immediately and to live forever.

It's the last part of what you've just said that I was trying to get at. I have no problems with the idea of the poet talking to the dead.

I guess it's not so much that the poet talks to the dead as that s/he is the *medium* between living and dead. The "new" *Idyll* is also involved in this.

I have one last question, and it is about the prophetic model you've just been speaking about. One of the aspects of Views *which interests me is the sense in the essays there (and also in some of your unpublished work) that the meditations on the choral model are leading toward some sort of re-imagining or re-invention of the visionary model. In some ways in* Views *you seem to me to provide a sustained re-consideration of the visionary model from Blake down to the present but through an anthropological lens. To what extent do you feel that in that confluence of anthropology and poetry, the visionary model is either revived or revised for the present moment?*

I think it is, and this links up with what I was saying earlier about the anthropologist–poet as the prophet of a future true multiculturalism. The utopian model has always been of some kind of universal brotherhood, right? If we take an optimistic view of the world and feel that, in spite of all the horrors, there will be more and more inter-marriage and merging (*with* great losses, because most tribals are going to be massacred or hopelessly marginalized in the process), there is some kind of genuine multiculturalism occurring, not just in the mind but in the body and will of the world—then, if the poet is the prophet of that (utopian or possibility), there is simultaneously a return to the visionary process of "one world," universal brotherhood, whatever you want to call it, Beethoven's *Freiheit!* The *revision* is that you are taking present-day facts which didn't exist before into consideration, namely that, despite the persistence of nationalism (so much a great *curse*) and the abject footling around with the concepts of "freedom" and "democracy," the world *is* growing more into one body—to the extent that one *can* begin to envisage some form of planetary government which will then send out colonies into the stars. In *The Beautiful Contradictions* there is already something about "we will have gone into the stars." In that poem, there's even an inter-species fantasy! Here *would* be my answer. That there really is a bringing forth of the visionary again, but it's a re-envisioned and re-formulated scenario in view of the atrocious menaces which face humanity and the planet.

INDEX

Index of Names and Places

By Nathaniel Tarn

POETRY

Old Savage/Young City (1964)
Selection: Penguin Modern Poets, 7 (1965)
Where Babylon Ends (1965)
The Beautiful Contradictions (1969)
October (1969)
The Silence (1969)
A Nowhere for Vallejo (1971)
Section: The Artemision (1973)
The Persephones (1974)
Lyrics for the Bride of God (1975)
The House of Leaves (1976)
The Microcosm (1977)
The Ground of Our Great Admiration of Nature
    (with Janet Rodney, 1977)
The Forest (with Janet Rodney, 1978)
Birdscapes, with Seaside (1978)
Atitlán-Alashka (*Alashka* with Janet Rodney, 1979)
The Land Songs (1981)
Weekends in Mexico (1982)

The Desert Mothers (1984)
At the Western Gates (1985)
The Mothers of Matagalpa (1989)
Seeing America First (1989)
Home One (1990)
The Army has Announced that Body Bags . . . (1992)
Caja del Río (1993)
Flying the Body (1993)
A Multitude of One (editor; poems by Natasha Tarn, 1994)
The Architextures 1–7 (1999)
The Architextures (2000)
Three Letters from the City: The St. Petersburg Poems (2001)
Selected Poems: 1950–2000 (2002)
Recollections of Being (2004)

TRANSLATIONS

The Heights of Macchu Picchu (Neruda) (1966)
Con Cuba (1969)
Stelae (Segalen) (1969)
Selected Poems (Neruda) (1970)
The Rabinal Achi, Act IV (1973)
The Penguin Neruda (1975)

PROSE

Views from the Weaving Mountain: Selected Essays in Poetics and Anthropology (1991)
Scandals in the House of Birds: Shamans & Priests on Lake Atitlán (1998)

The authorized representative in the EU for product safety and compliance is:
Mare Nostrum Group
B.V Doelen 72
4831 GR Breda
The Netherlands